UNDERSTANDING FACILITATION

THEORY & PRINCIPLES

CHRISTINE HOGAN

To my parents, Marjorie and Frank Hogan, who inspired and helped me to love learning and experimenting.
To my husband, Steve, who patiently mentored me through the trials of computing.
And to Katie, John and Gill, my wisdom friends who challenged my thinking and patiently gave me feedback.

First published in 2002
Reprinted 2009

Kogan Page Limited
120 Pentonville Road
London N1 9JN
UK
www.koganpage.com

British Library Cataloguing in Publication Data

A CIP record for this book is available from the British Library

ISBN 978 0 7494 3826 5

Typeset by JS Typesetting Ltd, Porthcawl, Mid Glamorgan
Printed and bound in the United Kingdom by Bell & Bain Ltd., Glasgow

Contents

The author *v*

Acknowledgements *vii*

Introduction 1

1 **Setting the scene: the emergence of the field of facilitation** 7
Introduction 7; Fields contributing to the development of facilitation 8; The concept of facilitation: sources and meaning 10; Reasons for the rise in facilitation 11; Conclusion 13

2 **Development of facilitation in management** 15
Introduction 15; Historical perspective of facilitation in management 15; Conclusion 24

3 **Development of facilitation in education and training** 25
Introduction 25; Key educational innovators 25; Training versus facilitating 31; Conclusion 34

4 **Development of facilitation in community development** 35
Introduction 35; The contribution of the Quaker movement to facilitation 36; The meaning of 'participation' 37; Facilitation in developing and developed countries 42; Conclusion 47

5 **Definitions and metaphors of facilitation** 49
Introduction 49; Definitions and metaphors used to define facilitation 49; Conclusion 57

6 **Models of facilitation** 59
Introduction 59; Models 59; Conclusion 84

7 Definitions of co-facilitation **85**
Introduction 85; Definitions of co-facilitation 85; Requirements for co-facilitation 86; Choosing co-facilitation 87; The outcomes of co-facilitation: easier or harder? 88; Choosing whether and how to co-facilitate 93; Models of co-facilitation 94; Stages of the co-facilitation relationship 99; Ways of working: with the group 101; Ways of working: together 102; Managing differences 105; Conclusion 112

8 Basic theories and concepts of group work **113**
Introduction 113; Contexts and systems 113; Diversity 117; Communication: dualistic thinking 120; Group theory: stages of group development 121; Individual behaviours and needs 134; Size of groups 139; Developing adult learning skills and knowledge 141; Experiential learning 143; How do we learn? 147; Unlearning 151; Self-development 151; Conclusion 152

9 Facilitating culturally diverse groups **153**
Introduction 153; What is culture? 155; Making culture visible 156; Cultural dimensions 157; Co-facilitation 162; Multicultural groups 164; Conclusion 169

10 Facilitation and technology **171**
Introduction 171; Technology to serve facilitators and groups model 171; E-moderating learning groups competencies model 183; Comparison of models 188; Conclusion 188

11 Professionalism and ethics **189**
Introduction 189; The facilitation movement 189; Two case studies 190; Professionalizing facilitation 198; Education of facilitators 203; Professional accreditation 210; What are the future developments for facilitation? 212; Conclusion 216

Appendix 1: Journals, e-mail discussion groups and Web sites *217*

Appendix 2: IAF Statement of Values and Code of Ethics *225*

References *229*

Index *242*

The author

Dr Christine Hogan is a professional facilitator and educator. She is committed to helping people learn how to facilitate and to enhance innovations in facilitation through reflective practice, networking and research.

Her extensive consultancy work in Australia and Asia focuses on personal, organizational and community development. She has worked in Nepal, Mongolia, Malaysia and has just returned to Australia after two years in the Lao Peoples' Democratic Republic.

She was a Senior Lecturer in Human Resource Development in the School of Management, Curtin University of Technology in Perth, Western Australia for 13 years. She co-ordinated Graduate Human Resource Development Programmes and taught in the areas of facilitation and group processes skills, conflict resolution and cross-cultural communication. She is now an Adjunct Senior Research Fellow and international consultant.

Christine is also the author of *Facilitating Empowerment* and *Practical Facilitation* (both published by Kogan Page) and *Facilitating Learning: Practical strategies for college and university* (published by Eruditions).

In her spare time Christine paints on silk under the name of 'Isadora' after Isadora Duncan, the famous educational innovator and dancer.

Christine would welcome feedback and dialogue about ideas in this book. You can find out more about her work and how to contact her by going to the following Web site: www.hogans.id.au

Acknowledgements

Many people have been involved in the development of this book. Nothing occurs in a vacuum; I am indebted to many friends, facilitators, and workshop participants, too many to mention here, who have in some way contributed ideas to this book.

I want especially to thank my wisdom friends, Kati and John Wilson, who not only mentored and supported me through my PhD, but also engaged in lively discussions, patiently read manuscripts and gave me feedback with love, hugs and humour.

Thanks to my adopted sisters, Gill Baxter and Carol Newton-Smith, for your support and laughs and especially to Gill for your expert counselling through the 'ups' and 'lows' of the writing process.

One of the most difficult jobs is keeping a computer under control and formatting a book. Thanks to my husband and best friend, Steve, for his computer mentoring and for the thousands of times he carefully listened to and answered my queries with patience and clarity.

Thanks to facilitation students over the years and to members of 'Facnet', the facilitation network in Perth, for all the lively discussion and support.

Research was made so much easier with the help of kind and considerate librarians at Curtin University of Technology, sleuths extraordinaire who also patiently helped me decipher the eccentricities of the Endnote referencing system.

I am indebted to Marie Martin, a long-term friend and colleague, for Chapter 7, which explores the issues of co-facilitation, the focus of her PhD research. Marie welcomes dialogue on this topic and may be contacted on marie@iinet.net.au.

I have, of course, utilized work from many sources which have been acknowledged in the references. There is now a wealth of information that has entered the 'common domain' of facilitation through Internet discussion groups. I have attempted to trace the sources of these ideas. If I have inadvertently missed or wrongly referenced works, please let me know and any error will be rectified in future editions of this work.

Thanks to Philip Mudd and Fiona Meiers at Kogan Page. Every time I have communicated with you I have learnt something!

Last, but not least, thanks to my Mum for all her cheers and support through the years and to my Dad who taught me so much. I wish they were both here to see the completion of this book, but I know they are with me in spirit always.

Christine Hogan

Introduction

The world needs more dialogue
Facilitators help people to engage in dialogue
Dialogue is a better way to solve disagreements than war
Facilitators therefore are involved in peace making and peace building.

I have a dream
One day facilitation skills will be part of mainstream curricula in schools and colleges
One day there will be free speech for all
We will learn to talk instead of kill and bomb
We have the brainpower to do this
One day there will be world peace.

Chris Hogan

Introduction

'Facilitation' is a term that has grown in use in the business, education, and development worlds in the second half of the 20th century. Many people talk eagerly about the new jobs that have evolved out of technological change in computing and programming. I think there is a new and important area of human endeavour which is more exciting, ie facilitation, a field that has developed in order to help us communicate better as human beings and make more sense out of our world; indeed I would argue that if everyone was taught some facilitation skills at an early age, the world would be a more peaceful place.

Facilitators are like midwives; they help families through many stages of the birthing process. However, they are not present at conception, nor do they have any long-term responsibilities for babies. This means that they do not participate in, nor do they enjoy, the ongoing lifelong iconic moments in the life of a child. Facilitators help groups of people by identifying and using a variety of processes that help participants to bring ideas to the surface, and enable them to reach their goals. Facilitators, like midwives, are rarely present (unless they work within an organization) to see the results of their labours.

The fascinating thing about the emergence of facilitation is that facilitators have come from so many different fields, cultures, disciplines and backgrounds. There appear to have been for these facilitators many different 'hero's or 'heroine's' journeys (Campbell, 1973); for some it has been a kind of trial by fire and experience that has led people to discover and/or invent new ways of 'doing' activities together.

As a result of these changes, facilitation has grown into both a profession and a rigorous discipline. For example, it is now possible to earn a living by planning, facilitating and evaluating meetings and workshops. It is also possible to undertake short as well as long, formal courses in this field.

Why has facilitation evolved? Facilitation has evolved from the necessity to make sense of life in many different contexts. It involves strategies to help us make sense of our increasingly complex and fast-changing global village. One such strategy is that progressive organizations are using facilitators and participatory processes to address those changes.

Why this book was written

Why did I write this book? It is the result of my PhD research into facilitation in which I interwove two stories: firstly, an autoethnography of my own development as a facilitator and secondly, that of the development of facilitation as a profession (which is the focus of this book). My story was explored as an autoethnographical study in which I examined my path as a facilitator and analysed not only what facilitation is, but also what has led me to become a facilitator. I endeavoured to describe how I have developed the concept of 'facilitation' and praxis in different cultural and organizational contexts through time. In doing so, I recounted and analysed critical incidents that have been included in this book as stories and case studies for teaching and additional research. I critiqued models of facilitation and developed two further models.

When I submitted my manuscript to Philip Mudd, the editor at Kogan Page, I had produced almost twice my quota of words. He suggested that I split the book into two: one focusing on the theory and history of facilitation and another on the practical side – hence the two titles of the companion volumes.

Facilitative theories, techniques and processes provide the framework, but other components also influence the outcome of facilitation practice. The output from groups is dependent on many variables:

- the breadth and depth of the skills and experiences of participants;
- the supportiveness of the work and/or community environment;
- the skills, style/s, adaptability and personality of the facilitator;
- the processes and procedures used;
- the amount of time allocated to achieve participatory tasks;
- the context;

and, last but not least, the magic! – the serendipities that emerge from people and groups working towards joint goals.

> Learn the theories as well as you can, but put them aside when you touch the miracle of the living soul.
>
> Carl Jung

Book 1: *Understanding Facilitation: theory and principles*

In Book 1 I shall focus on the development of facilitation through time; the practice of facilitation: definitions, models; issues that are emerging as facilitation embraces technology; and the steps towards becoming a profession.

Section 1: The development of facilitation

In Section 1, I explore how the concept of facilitation has evolved in the second half of the 20th century and, more specifically, why there have been concurrent movements towards facilitation in such fields as management, education, psychology and community development across the world. However, to the best of my knowledge, no books have actually addressed why this phenomenon has come about. There are many practitioners 'out there' doing facilitation who have indicated that they require an overview and background knowledge about how their 'craft' came about and how it is used in associated fields. The aim of this book is to meet this need. My aim is to demystify 'facilitation' and explore where this new profession is going.

I address the reasons for the rise of facilitation in the second half of the 20th century and the fields that have contributed to its development. Chapters 2, 3 and 4 are devoted to an overview of the development of facilitation in the fields of management, education and training, and community development.

Section 2: The practice of facilitation: definitions, models and issues

In Section 2 there is a discussion of how practitioners define facilitation and the models that have evolved to help us understand what the practice of facilitation means and involves.

Chapter 5 includes a discussion of definitions and metaphors used to define facilitation. Chapter 6 illustrates current models of facilitation and includes my description of how I came to develop two models: one of these is of my own practice. A second model appears in Chapter 10 under the uses of technology for facilitators.

I am indebted to Marie Martin, a long-term friend and colleague, for Chapter 7, which explores the issues of co-facilitation, the focus of her PhD research.

In Chapter 8, I discuss some of the basic theories pertinent to groups and learning. These theories are extended in Chapter 9 with a description of cross-cultural dimensions that are relevant to facilitators.

Technology is changing so fast. I include in Chapter 10 a model summarizing facilitator/group needs that can be met by using technology. Chapter 11 elaborates on current issues facing facilitators, including two real case studies and the ethical issues that arise from them. This is followed by a discussion of where facilitation is heading as a profession, including codes of conduct and accreditation issues.

Book 2: *Practical Facilitation: a toolkit of techniques*

Book 2 complements the theoretical approach of Book 1. As the title indicates, this book elaborates on the breadth, depth and diversity of a facilitator's toolkit. The book starts with the consulting and contracting with clients and ends with a discussion of evaluating and ongoing learning for facilitators.

Value stance

In a previous book entitled *Facilitating Empowerment*, I described my value stance, which is that empowerment (and participation) generally encourage discourse and that discourse is a valuable commodity when we are often presented with a *fait accompli* for increasingly fast social, cultural and technological change. However, participation is not necessarily 'good' in itself. It depends on what the issue is and what participation is used for and why. If there is a fire in a building I am not proposing a participatory approach to discuss and decide on various methods of escape. It must be remembered that participation is not a 'natural' concept in all cultures. Some ways of learning and situations do not foster participation as it generates many questions, and raises issues of power and control. Likewise, in some political contexts, participation may be actively frowned upon. Even where participation is encouraged, if and when things go wrong someone once said 'democracy is an orphan'. At extremes, facilitation can even foster negative outcomes when evaluated against a particular set of values. However, I value participation to prevent:

- unquestioning following of instructions (for example, in some organizational, political and military contexts);
- forced dualistic choices: 'You are either with us or against us';
- regrettable actions that could have been averted through more thorough deliberation regarding the context and long-term implications of 'action for action's sake'.

How to get the most out of the book

This book has been produced as a result of the need to place the burgeoning amount of literature on facilitation in its theoretical and historical context. It is not intended to be a definitive text, but more a foundation on which facilitation practice and styles are being built. As the theory on groups is immense and still developing, I have culled the resources available to present ideas that have been useful in my practice of facilitation.

Change

This book is a snapshot in time. New and exciting developments are going on in group work all over the world and I know that as soon as I submit this manuscript I will be trying to do some things in a new and different ways. You too are encouraged to be critically creative.

I have included some Web sites, but know there are hundreds more. Daily some die and new ones appear.

I welcome dialogue on any issues in this book or reminders of things I have omitted or should improve.

Happy facilitating!

Christine Hogan
Web site: www.hogans.id.au

1

Setting the scene: the emergence of the field of facilitation

Listen to everyone, learn from everyone
Nobody knows everything, but everyone knows something.

Charlie Hough

Introduction

In this chapter I explore how the concept of facilitation has evolved since the Second World War and, more specifically, why there have been concurrent movements towards facilitation in such fields as management, education, psychology and community development. Like establishing wide-angle shots at the beginning of a film before the introduction of characters, this chapter is intended to provide the reader with the background to the growth of facilitation. In Gestalt terms it is the 'ground' (or establishing shot of a movie) and the toolkit of facilitation is the 'figure' (characters in the movie).

The fascinating thing about the emergence of facilitation is that facilitators have come from so many different fields, cultures, disciplines and backgrounds. There appear to have been, for these facilitators, many different 'hero's or heroine's journeys' (Campbell, 1973), a kind of trial by fire and experience that has led people to discover and/or invent new ways of doing activities together.

Why has facilitation evolved? According to Hanson (in Burbidge, 1977: 237), 'Facilitation has evolved from the necessity to make sense of life in many different contexts.' It is one of the many interpretative strategies needed to make sense of our increasingly complex and fast-changing global village. According to Pierce, Cheesebrow and Braun (2000: 24), 'Organizations across all sectors of global life are confronted with a myriad operational, purpose, value and relational issues' combined with technological innovations and the speed of change. One such strategy is that progressive organizations are using participatory processes to address those changes.

As a result of these changes, facilitation has grown into both a 'profession and rigorous discipline' (Pierce, Cheesebrow and Braun, 2000: 24). (The current movement towards the professionalization of facilitation will be discussed further in Chapter 11.) For example, it is now possible to earn a living by planning, facilitating and evaluating meetings and workshops. It is also possible to undertake short courses and formal undergraduate and postgraduate courses, as well as undertake doctoral research in this field.

Fields contributing to the development of facilitation

In order for me to describe, understand and explain facilitation, I have found it useful to identify who uses facilitation techniques. So I have taken a multi-disiplinary approach. There are numerous concepts and trends that people have developed contiguously across the world: it seems that these creative efforts at times interact, overlap and interweave like strands in a rope; at others, for example in community development, in developing countries, they have evolved separately.

In looking at facilitation at the beginning of the 21st century, I contend there are many fields that have contributed to the development of this phenomenon. I will describe each briefly in turn:

1. In organizations there has been a growth in participatory approaches to management and facilitation of teams and quality circles (Deming, 1986), workshops and new and/or Interactive Meetings (Doyle and Straus, 1976) as opposed to Robert's Rules (Robert, 1979, 1989) which will be discussed later in this chapter.
2. In formal education there has been a swing from didactic teaching to experiential and group learning. This movement started with Dewey (1916, 1938) at the beginning of the 20th century and is still growing. There have been many successful models of informal learning, such as Neighbourhood Learning Centres and Internet Discussion Groups that have broken away from the formal school and college-based structures.
3. In therapeutic and social work there has been an increase in the use of groups as opposed to one-to-one counselling, throughout the 20th century, for example Alcoholics Anonymous and personal growth groups (Brody, 1987). Jackins (1994) led a movement of revolt in the USA against the power of therapists and established 'co-counselling' or 're-evaluation' processes, that is, ordinary people who are trained as facilitators to listen and support one another in pairs.

4. In community rural development in the 'South' (Third World), there has been a swing away from top-down development to facilitation of problem solving groups through the rise of participatory action research (PAR) and participatory rural appraisal methodologies (PRA) (Chambers, 1983, 1994). Likewise, adult literacy methods in the 'South' have been transformed by using facilitative 'reflect methods' (Phnuyal, 1998). In communities in rural and urban centres in the 'North' (developed world) there have been swings away from the pay-for-service economy to LETS groups who share and barter skills. Also, disillusionment with expensive legal systems has led to the development of alternative dispute resolution centres staffed by mediators. Skillshare and mediation practices have contributed to the fields of conflict resolution and decision making, both important aspects of facilitation.
5. The feminist movement and women's groups and peace movements (Eck and Jain, 1987) have contributed to new ways of thinking about how power is used and shared as opposed to hierarchical decision making.
6. Mediation practices have contributed to the fields of conflict resolution and decision making, both important aspects of facilitation.
7. Restorative justice participatory methods are now being researched as one way of lessening the rate of reoffending and also as a means of healing so that victims of crime can deal with their hurts and move on with their lives.
8. In the field of research, facilitative techniques are used for group-centred discussion, from the first experiments by Kurt Lewin in the 1930s with focus groups (Barbour and Kitzinger, 1999), to cooperative inquiry in the 1980s and 1990s (Reason, 1988; Heron, 1996) where the roles of 'researcher' and 'subject' become interlinked.
9. Government officials have learnt they have to trust and listen to people at grassroots levels in order to create and maintain environments that satisfy both individual and community needs and that are enjoyable to live and work in, through citizens juries for example.

In the many fields described above, facilitation skills and knowledge are becoming professionalized and institutionalized. Courses and qualifications in facilitation have proliferated. For the purposes of this book, I have chosen the three areas that have had the most impact on my role as a facilitator, that is, the fields of management; education and training; and community development.

I will make relevant connections between the three areas. I argue that the field of facilitation has grown in the areas listed above, at times with relatively little discourse between practitioners in these related areas, for example, community development in the 'North' and 'South'. However, my experience shows me that the Internet has already enhanced, and will continue to enhance, dialogue between the realms of management, education and training, and community development. I acknowledge that different disciplines have different languages and cultures, but an examination of the practical and philosophical bases that underlie the uses of facilitation may provide some insights into both the nature of facilitation, and its utilization.

The concept of facilitation: sources and meaning

In order to discuss the concept of facilitation, I contend it is necessary to identify its essential nature or ingredients, that is, what facilitation is and what it is not. I intend to look at the source of the word 'facilitation' and how and why it has taken on new meanings in the second half of the 20th century by examining the rise of facilitation in the fields of management, education, psychology and community development.

The word 'facilitation' comes from the middle French 'facile' and the Latin *facilis*: 'easy to do; of persons courteous; from facere to do or to perform, meaning to make easy' (Barnhart, 1988: 364). It sounds simple; at times it is straightforward, but at other times it may be very complex and may involve some of the highest levels of human interaction and communication skills. (These will be discussed in the next chapter on models of facilitation.)

Sometimes, there is confusion as the word 'facilitation' and its derivatives may be used in many different ways as shown in Table 1.1.

As with many evolving phenomena, there is no one agreed definition of facilitation. According to Zimmerman and Evans (1993), 'facilitation' is possibly one of the most misunderstood and abused terms used in management, partly because some trainers and managers think or say they are facilitating when they are not (ie they may stay in a predominantly 'presenting mode' or 'directive leadership mode'). Facilitation is concerned with encouraging open dialogue among individuals with different perspectives so that diverse assumptions and options may be explored. This is in contrast to the current dualistic, win–lose, competitive, debating styles of

Table 1.1 Facilitation and parts of speech

a noun	a facilitator and facilitation
a verb	to facilitate
an adverb	behaving facilitatively
an adjective	a facilitative individual or a facilitative group (one in which the majority of participants have facilitative mindsets and behaviours)

discourse in western societies. I will next address the reasons for the rise of facilitation in the 20th century and will return to definitions of facilitation in the next chapter.

Reasons for the rise in facilitation

Throughout history, and in all cultures, there have been wise people with outstanding communication, mediation and facilitation skills. The roots of facilitation have their origins in the helping professions: teaching, counselling, social work, development work, and religious people from shamans to rishis (sages) to clerics (Zimmerman and Evans, 1993; Egri and Frost, 1991). Socrates encouraged people to question ideas; shamans used talking sticks and talking stones to encourage people to speak the truth from the heart; rishis or sages like Gautama Buddha, Mahatma Gandhi, Rabindranath Tagore, Sri Aurobindo and Swami Vivekananda used, among other techniques, storytelling, metaphors and self-reflection to engage people in changing their mindsets and psychological states in order to enhance new ways of thinking about their lives (Chakraborty, 1998). Zen masters often asked their students paradoxical questions called 'koans', for example 'What is the sound of one hand clapping?' The student would then get involved in looking for various meanings through intense reflection. On presenting answers to the master, the student would be told the answers were wrong, leading to frustration and eventually to new and varied ways of viewing reality (Tashlik, 1995).

I will now turn to a discussion on the reasons for the increased focus on facilitation roles and skills across the world in the 20th century. Firstly, there has been a swing of the pendulum between participatory and autocratic ways of doing things. This pendulum appears to have changed direction many times throughout history and in different cultures (Tarnas, 1991). Before the 17th century, there were two main divisions in many societies, that is, the rulers and the ruled. Subjects were socialized to think of duty and non-questioning obedience to parents, teachers, officials and rulers. Indeed, in countries where there are few social support services, the issues of duty as opposed to rights are still paramount (Chakraborty, 1998).

Heron (1993), however, cites a major swing in the 17th century towards a doctrine of natural rights formulated by Locke (now called human rights). Locke proposes that people have a right to participate in decisions being made about them. The issue of people's 'rights' was raised by the revolutionaries in Europe and the USA. Heron relates this to the march for democracy, but also calls for a more widespread, shared meaning of 'rights'. He believes that children have a right to participate in parental decisions about their lives and welfare; students in higher education have rights to participate with staff in decisions that impact on their education; patients have rights to be included in decisions made about their treatments; workers have rights to participate in managerial decisions that affect them; subjects of research experiments have a right to participate in researcher decisions about what questions to ask and how to present findings. While these are laudable values, I am convinced it is not so simple. There are skills, duties and communication strategies on all sides that need to be learnt and managed.

The second reason for the upswing in professional facilitation in many domains is that there is a widespread need for making better use of 'knowledge workers' (Jago, in press) in complex decision making (Robson and Beary, 1995). Jago alleges that 'knowledge work' cannot be effectively managed in the old 'chain of command' paradigm. Knowledge workers (who are increasingly all workers) not only have the best overview of their jobs, but also have knowledge across departmental boundaries. Facilitation enables increasing integration of managers and knowledge workers in decision making and implementation.

Robert Reich (1987) also writes of the need to tap into the creativity and synergy of groups of workers. He postulates that 'collective entrepreneurship' is the next frontier if companies are going to stay competitive in a global economy. He challenges the dichotomy of 'entrepreneurial heroes' and 'industrial drones' and the suggestion that Lee Iacocca (CEO of Chrysler) and Henry Ford (founder of Ford Motor Company) were successful 'alone'. Goods and commodities will not have the usual product life cycle of a bell curve, but will evolve as technology changes. He claims that for this to happen 'collective entrepreneurship' characteristics are necessary, such as: integration of individual's skills into a group, giving a collective capacity to innovate; close working relationships between people at all stages of production and with customers; and different organizational structures, flatter hierarchies: 'Coordination and communication replace command and control' (Reich, 1987: 81). Many organizations now employ the use of cross-functional teams, self-directed teams, quality circles and natural work teams as mechanisms for collective problem solving and decision making (Niederman and Volkema, 1999; Wellins, 1994). In most cases these groups require the use of some form of facilitation. In some groups the facilitation is rotated amongst group members, whilst in complex situations, for example conflict resolution or strategic planning, they may employ the use of a facilitator who is external to the organization. Of course there is a great advantage to be had by having both an internal and an external facilitator working together as co-facilitators, provided that the two people can work together as a team. I will explore the differences between internal and external facilitation in Chapter 4.

Thirdly, there is a need to help large community groups formulate plans and resolve issues and conflicts where their constituents have remarkably different views of the world. Kaner (1996) cites an example of a meeting to reduce violence on a high school campus. The participants included students, parents, teachers, the school board, frustrated neighbours, social workers and the police:

> Despite a common goal, their frames of reference are very different. . . Most groups *do not know how* to solve tough problems on their own. They do not know how to build a shared framework of understanding – they seldom even recognize its significance. They dread conflict and discomfort and they try hard to avoid it. Yet, by avoiding struggle to integrate one another's perspectives, the members of such a group gently diminish their own potential to be effective. They *need* a facilitator.
>
> (Kaner, 1996: 32)

A government employee, for example a chemist or an engineer, who has to communicate with concerned public interest groups regarding pollution and its control, legislation and regulations, may choose to take more facilitative and consultative roles rather than the expert or bureaucratic information and speech-giving roles. Likewise in management, there has been a diversification of roles, which is the focus of the next section.

Fourthly, groups have to deal with increasing complexities of data and/or needing to adapt to change. As a result they require assistance, processes and technology to enable them to make effective decisions.

Lastly, developments in technology, for example audioconferencing, videoconferencing, group support systems (GSS), computer conferencing and e-mail discussion groups have led to the development of 'e-moderators': people who preside over electronic online meetings or conferences. E-moderating involves new ways of teaching and learning, particularly in higher education (Salmon, 2000). Indeed, educationalists and learners are experimenting with new and varied ways of 'networked learning'. In addition, in some forms of GSS meetings a 'chauffeur' manages the technology and works in conjunction with the facilitator (Whiteley and Garcia, 1996). Advances in technology have motivated many facilitators to learn new technical skills and communication strategies to enable themselves and their groups to be at ease and make the most effective use of technology. I will develop the issues of e-moderation further in Chapter 10 in Book 2.

Conclusion

In this chapter I have given an overview of the emergence of facilitation. The next three chapters focus on facilitation in management; education and training; and community development in turn.

2

Development of facilitation in management

Introduction

In this chapter I trace the development of facilitation in the management field. I utilize the 'Managerial Competency Framework' designed by Quinn *et al* (1990) as a background.

Historical perspective of facilitation in management

Quinn *et al* describe eight key roles of managers that have developed over time (see Figure 2.1). Each of these will be summarized in turn in order to give context to the emergence of the facilitation role for managers. They argue that models and definitions keep evolving and that even though 'new' models develop it does not mean that old models should be overlooked. Quinn *et al* chose four 25-year spans that illustrate major themes in the history of management thought. For convenience, I will use their model to illustrate the rise of facilitation in the management context. In this framework, the horizontal axis 'internal–external' shows the changing focus of managerial work inside and outside the organization. The vertical axis 'flexibility–control' shows the variations in command in managerial work.

1900–25 The emergence of the 'Rational Goal Model' and the 'Internal Process Model'

The drive for mass production and urban living at the turn of the 20th century led to rigid systems of management which became focused on goals and outputs which Quinn *et al* call the 'Rational Goal Model' (see bottom right-hand side of Figure 2.1).

According to the authors, the move from family-based agricultural communities to factory-based work in the cities in the 17th and 18th centuries led to new problems in human communication. In the industrial cities of Europe and North America, strangers worked together in closer proximity and in larger numbers than ever before. People lost autonomy over their work. The 'Rational Goal Model' focused on productivity and profit. There was emphasis on clear goals (given by management), rational analysis and the 'bottom line'. The manager's job was to be a rational, hard-nosed director and producer.

The beginning of the 20th century was a time of optimistic growth and progress for managers through invention and innovation in agriculture and industry. However, there was little unionism or government policy to protect workers. This was the time of Henry Ford and the assembly line. Also of Frederick Taylor, the so-called 'father of scientific management', and the

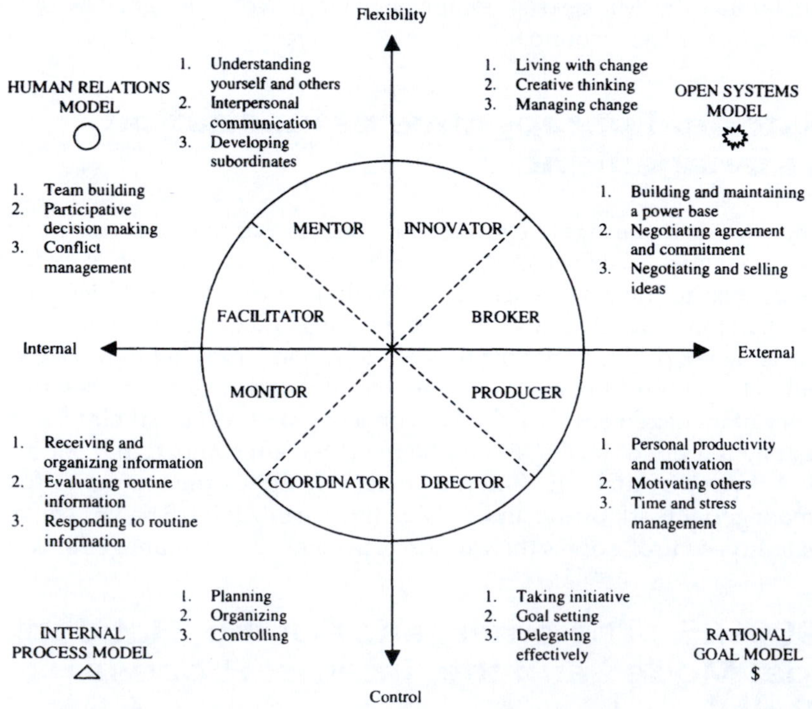

Figure 2.1 The Quinn competency framework of management development
Source: Quinn, R E (1988: 86) *Beyond Rational Management*, San Francisco

command paradigm with planning and control centralized under top management (Taylor, 1911). These approaches are now considered outdated. They de-skill and dehumanize employees by metaphorically making them leave their hearts and minds at the door of their organizations.

The 'Internal Process Model' focused on definition of responsibilities, measurement documentation, and record keeping in hierarchical organizations. The work of the German sociologist Max Weber (1864–1920) was translated and stimulated discussions on the concepts of bureaucracy and alienation (Weber, 1947). Rules, structures and traditions were of paramount importance. A manager was seen as a monitor and coordinator of workflow. The leaders in the Great War (1914–18) who viewed their troops as expendable 'cannon fodder' took this approach.

The interest in efficiency led to an increase in attention to the productivity of meetings (in the USA, Germany and the UK) and this movement made significant contributions to the development of facilitation, as will be illustrated below.

In 1876, Major Henry M Robert, a military engineer with a religious background, published his first *Robert's Rules of Order* in the USA. At that time there was an obsession with efficiency, so Robert researched British Parliamentary procedures and published his own manual:

> to assist an assembly to accomplish the work for which it was designed, in the best possible manner. To do this it is necessary to restrain the individual somewhat, as the right of an individual in any community, to do what he pleases, is incompatible with the interests of the whole.
>
> (Robert in Patnode, 1989: 14)

Robert's book was highly successful though he made many alterations in following editions. *Robert's Rules* became the bible for many businesses, clubs, unions, boards and societies. These meeting 'rules' are still widely used today in the western world. Following his guidelines, a 'chairperson' orchestrates formal meetings. There are many rules governing how people should address one another 'through the chair': rules for proposing 'motions' and 'amendments'. Debate is conducted about motions and decisions are made by voting (with the inherent problems of win–lose outcomes). Other formal roles include secretary and/or minute taker and treasurer. I will return to the topic of meetings later.

In contrast to the prevailing thinking of the era, Mary Parker Follett (1868–1933), a Quaker social scientist and social worker in the USA, recognized the significance of groups and argued that members are continually influenced by their groups and that group members have the capacity to control their own activities (similar to later semi-managed teams). She also advocated that managers should operate on a 'power with' rather than 'power over' basis. She argues that power should be cooperatively developed between managers and employees. She advocates conflict resolution through integration. Her ideas heralded modern methods of conflict resolution in Metcalfe and Urwick (1940). Despite the significant contributions of Follett (1918, 1989) to modern management and facilitation, it is interesting that references to her work are seldom seen in introductory management texts.

1926–50 The emergence of the 'Human Relations Model'

The second era was shattered by the stock market crash, the depression and the Second World War. The models of the previous era were still popular, but even then it became clear that the concept of management was becoming exceedingly complex. Unions were now a significant force in changing the balance of power between employers and workers. In Europe and the USA there was a rise in demand for consumer goods and labour-saving devices in homes. Managers started to recognize that the control and command paradigms alone were failing. There was less unthinking obedience by workers to authority. Managers learnt that they had to build informal relationships with workers, as indicated with the Hawthorne studies (Roethlisberger and Dickson, 1939); that is, workers are motivated when someone shows an interest in their work.

Kurt Lewin, a social psychologist who escaped from Nazi Germany to the USA in the late 1930s, undertook research into group productivity and leadership styles. He observed that most groups were 'task mesmerized'. However, during the war he tried to help the War Office who wanted to get people to use nutrition-rich cuts of offal. Lewin set up an experiment. A large group of housewives were given a talk on the nutritional value of previously underutilized cuts of beef, and given recipes and demonstrations. Then half the audience went home. The other half was invited to form small groups and discuss ways in which they could use the off-cuts. At the end they were asked to make a public commitment to try the recipes. Six months later the researchers found that the people who had stayed for the small group discussions made far more changes in cooking habits than those who only heard the lecture (Bunker and Alban, 1997; Lewin, 1943).

Lewin set up the Research Centre for Group Dynamics in 1945 at the Massachusetts Institute of Technology and made major contributions to the research and literature on groups. He invented the term 'group dynamics' to describe group interactions. Amongst many aspects of his work, he posed two important questions: 'What goes on in groups that produces these changes in behaviour?' and 'How do we understand the power of groups over individuals?' These questions are still being discussed today.

After workshops on race relations in 1946, Lewin, his colleagues and one of his students, Ronald Lippitt, started to meet informally to discuss the group's activities during the day. Gradually the group members also became involved. From this the National Training Laboratory in Group Development (NTL) was developed at Bethal in Maine and the concept of T Groups (Training Groups) was born. These unstructured training workshops in which participants commented on their own and others' styles of behaviour often led to frustration. Whilst popular in the USA and Europe up until the 1960s, their often destructive nature and perceived lack of transferability to the workplace led to their decline (Bunker and Alban, 1997).

Weisbord (1992) tells the story of Lewin using paper rather than blackboards so that he could carry around and show many people diagrams of complex human problems. In 1946, driving through Connecticut to a conference, Kurt Lewin and Ron Lippett realized they had forgotten the paper. As it was Sunday and the shops were closed they decided to stop at a newspaper office and were given some end-roll of newsprint. This was the beginning of the use of visual 'group memory' techniques.

Ron Lippitt noted that when he listened to tapes of groups undertaking problem solving, he frequently became de-energized. Since problem solving appeared to drain his energy, he decided to devise processes to invite people to think about their 'preferred future'. This formed the basis of Emery and Trist's work in the 1960s in the UK at the Tavistock Institute (Bunker and Alban, 1997).

Coch and French (1948) experimented with resistance to change in work methods in a pyjama factory. In one experiment a non-participation group was given no say in changes. A second group was allowed to give feedback on changes. A third, total participation group was allowed fully to redesign their work routine. The third group rapidly increased its efficiency rating. There were no resignations and there was little conflict for the two and a half months of the experiment. 'It is interesting to observe that in the meetings with these two (latter) groups suggestions were immediately made in such quantity that the stenographer had great difficulty recording them' (Coch and French, 1948: 530).

The 'Human Relations Model' valued commitment, cohesion and morale. The means–ends theory indicated that if workers were involved there would be commitment. Managers received conflicting messages. They were to be sensitive mentors and facilitators of teams as opposed to controlling leaders. Some managers tried to become benevolent autocrats. The Human Relations movement led to the emergence of the idea of facilitation in western management which Quinn *et al* some 50 years later defined as:

> The facilitator is expected to foster collective effort, build cohesion and teamwork, and manage interpersonal conflict. In this role the manager

> is process oriented. Expected behaviours include intervening into interpersonal disputes, using conflict reduction techniques, developing cohesion and morale, obtaining input and participation, and facilitating group problem solving.
>
> (Quinn *et al*, 1990: 17)

1951–75 The emergence of the open systems model

In the third era, the USA played a key role in the capitalist world. At the end of the era the Vietnam War proved that 'might' is frequently neither 'right' nor always 'successful'. Japan had made huge inroads into the manufacturing of cars and consumer goods partly by following the work of Deming (1986) and harnessing the power of workers in 'quality circles'. Graphic photographs and computer images from space projects changed our view of ourselves from the moon and societal values changed radically. The Vietnam War and the 1960s 'flower power' movements for self-fulfilment changed power balances and perspectives towards authority figures. Books abounded on topics such as group dynamics and participative management.

Henry Mintzberg (1975) tried to identify what managers actually did. He found that they were not systematic and that they had very little time to organize and plan as interruptions and requests for information and/or decisions constantly bombarded them. Rosemary Stewart (1982) continued this work and developed a model through which managers could identify the 'demands, choices and constraints' of their work.

The 'open systems model' of management developed in order to help mangers cope with a constantly changing 'turbulent environment'. Effectiveness was seen to be based on adaptability and an amoeba-like response to environment. Survival was possible by continual adaptation and innovation. The manager was expected to be a highly adaptable innovator and broker between the internal organization and the environment outside.

Fred Emery (an Australian researcher) and Eric Trist at the Tavistock Institute of Human Relations in London (1965) developed the 'Sociotechnical Approach' to management, that is, focus should be placed on the ways in which work can be socially organized as well as technically organized. Working with managers in the coal mines of Yorkshire, they showed that workers had many good ideas and strategies when faced with new mechanized forms of production. The sociotechnical approach led to major changes at General Motors in the USA, Volvo in Sweden and Philips in Australia. Managers placed semi-autonomous work groups at the centre of the change process and focused on quality of work life (QWL) with varying degrees of success.

Emery and Trist realized the need for workers of all levels to be involved with managers in planning for the future. They developed the Search Conference Process in 1959. The first workshop was called the Barford Conference (Trist and Emery, 1960) which they designed to bring together the Bristol and Siddeley Aero-engine companies. The managers of the two companies mutually disliked each other, but were about to merge. Although the process was to undergo further refinement (Emery and Purser, 1996), Trist and Emery (1960) found that certain formulae worked, for example, if the facilitator eliminated the roles of visiting outside experts; kept meeting notes in an open fashion, for example on flip chart paper; focused the group on contextual issues; and focused the group on areas of agreement regarding 'desirable futures' of the organization.

1976–the present The emergence of 'both/and' assumptions

By the last quarter of the 20th century it became evident that no single approach to managing people would work over time. The demise of mega-corporations in the USA, Europe and Japan indicated that size and huge profits did not go on indefinitely. The number of companies described by Peters and Waterman (1982) in *In Search of Excellence* as 'doing it right' declined. Unions lost power. Job security became a thing of the past as organizations developed a plethora of euphemisms for sacking people: 'downsizing', 'restructuring' and 're-engineering'. Charles Handy (1986) wrote of the 'shamrock organization' with three tiers of people: permanent staff, an increasing number of consultants, and less permanent technical support staff.

Rhetoric like 'your people are your most valuable asset' has become laughable in the light of widespread 'downsizing'. Reich (1987) queries the veneer of management strategies for excellence, 'preferably within one minute', a quip at Ken Blanchard (1981) and quick fix-it 'one minute' books in the management field.

Cynicism has increased in the 1990s as new buzz words increase daily, for example 'excellence', 'quality', 'mission statements', 'rightsizing', 're-engineering'. Burnout, stress and smart drugs have become major issues. Micklethwait and Wooldridge (1997) have criticized some of the management gurus or 'witch doctors' and fads from Taylor onwards. Frost and Robinson (1999) describe the casualties as a result of the 'toxicity' in part caused by continual restructuring and change. Many managers, as Micklethwait and Wooldridge (1997) point out, demanded 'quick-fix' solutions; but change is anything but instant. Unfortunately, facilitators have sometimes become 'lackeys' of managers. Both parties have sometimes failed to analyse critically the latest buzz concepts in the literature before attempting to implement them.

One outcome from all the free flow of ideas on managerial practice from the seventies onwards was changes in the ways in which meetings were organized. In the USA, 100 years after the first development of *Robert's Rules* in 1876, Doyle and Straus (1976) outlined strategies for 'Interactive Meetings'. They criticize *Robert's Rules* (described earlier) as being too formal. They argue that 'win–lose' debates often led to the loss of new ideas and the problems of hidden agendas. They quote Harold Reimer, a researcher in this field, who estimated that the cost of time lost after ineffective meetings was US$800,000 per year for every 1,000 employees (1976: 9). They called this loss the 'meeting recovery syndrome' which impacts negatively on teamwork, communication, morale and productivity.

Doyle and Straus identify the problems with having managers as chairpersons in meetings with their teams. They maintain that in meetings managers had too many roles. When acting as a chairperson, managers were both the main power holders in the group and guardians of group process. In a sports game we would not expect one individual to umpire, score, defend and attack yet in meetings the chairperson is expected to do all of these things. Doyle and Straus suggest dividing the labour, roles and responsibilities. They advocate that the role of facilitator should not be undertaken by management, but by a person who could solely concentrate on group dynamics. They maintain that managers should retain the role of chairperson, but with modified responsibilities. They should be participants (most managers want to be able to put in their ideas) but they should also remind group members of company rules and/or legislation. Where necessary, managers should call for a vote if the group cannot reach consensus.

> The facilitator is the meeting chauffeur, a servant of the group. Neutral and non-evaluating, the facilitator is responsible for making sure the participants are using the most effective methods for accomplishing their task in the shortest time.
>
> (Doyle and Straus, 1976: 35)

Doyle and Straus identify the need for a scribe to record ideas on flip chart paper and a timekeeper to give people warning when time is almost finished on each agenda item. Regarding the preparation for meetings, they criticize the often cryptic, one-word agenda items and suggest that an open-ended question would better invoke prior thought. They designed a different framework for planning participatory meetings and proposed that an agenda should be developed using the headings shown in Table 2.1.

As a result, participants can 'see' how the meeting will be run and contribute to group processes. This process lessens the possibility of 'hidden agendas' and manipulation.

Table 2.1 A sample meeting agenda (after Doyle and Straus, 1976)

Content	*Process*	*Time*
'What' the item is about	'How' the item would be dealt with	'How long' is designated to that particular item

Doyle and Straus also analysed the 'friction of distance' down the conventional, rectangular boardroom table from the chairperson to participants. They highlighted the problem of a 'Wimbledon-style' tennis match if two people become locked into a personalized debate. To militate against this they recommend that the board table should be removed and that participants should sit in a semicircle facing the wall minutes. As a result, issues may be addressed in a more depersonalized way. By 1976, Doyle and Straus had successfully used their Interactive Meeting methods with IBM, Xerox and the Bank of America as well as government departments and community groups.

At the same time in West Germany, the brothers Eberhard and Wolfgang Schnelle (1979) developed 'Metaplan Meeting Methods' in retaliation against their fascist upbringing under the Nazi regime, and wrote: 'When we were young we were so maltreated by hierarchies' (Derschka and Gottschall, 1984: 22). The brothers studied psychology, hierarchies and office 'landscapes'. 'Hierarchy is a procedure which not only makes criticism impossible, but completely immunizes the person in a higher position from criticism. . . we don't need separation of competencies, but overlapping of them' (Schnelle in Derschka and Gottschall, 1984: 24). They developed the role of 'moderator' (similar to a facilitator) whom they defined as 'the catalyst in the learning and decision-making process of a group' (Schnelle, 1979: 32). I think that the word 'catalyst' may be problematic. According to Sirolli (1995) and Jago (in press), it is not the role of the facilitator to motivate the group. Nobody can make participants learn, plan, and/or problem solve. However, I hold that a facilitator may act as a 'catalyst' at the beginning of a workshop to energize participants to tackle the task ahead or act as 'provocateur' to challenge participants to recognize their mindsets and/or perceive them in a different way.

The Metaplan Company and the Schnelle brothers revolutionized conferences and moderated/facilitated groups of 10–1,000 people in BMW, IBM, Philips, Siemens and Volkswagen using visualization strategies. They developed visualization techniques, including a variety of colours and sizes of coloured cards (ovals, rectangles and circles) and dots to enable participants to design 'problem maps' (ie coloured cards pinned to huge sheets of brown paper) showing critical interrelationships and dependencies.

These visualization tools have now been made more accessible through cheaper mass-produced Post-its (in varying sizes and colours), Easel Pads and Post-It glues and sprays developed by 3M.

Half a century of management commentary has consistently upheld the efficacy of participative methods. 'The notion that people will be more comfortable with and more committed to changes that they have decided for themselves, and not had forced upon them, is also consistent with western notions of freedom, individualism and the proactivity of human nature' (Buchanan and Boddy, 1992: 20). What also became clear to Buchanan and Boddy is that a facilitator's roles are multi-layered, multi-skilled and at times enormously time consuming.

Conclusion

As this chapter illustrates, facilitation has now become a key competency for managers. However, it is difficult for managers to stay out of the content of discussion, and also team members are often swayed by the opinions of managers, so frequently external facilitators are required who can work with groups whilst staying out of the content and politics of organizations (see also Chapter 5). In the next chapter I turn to the development of facilitation in education.

3

Development of facilitation in education and training

Introduction

This chapter focuses on the many educational and training reformers from different cultural backgrounds who embraced the philosophy and practice of facilitation in their work through the twentieth century.

Key educational innovators

John Dewey (1859–1952), an American philosopher and educationalist, was a principal of a progressive school and also a fervent believer in lifelong education involving learning from one's experiences. He advocates that teachers should be more like 'facilitators' and establish conditions for learning by guiding and helping rather than directing and imposing. He advocates a problem-solving approach and influenced the ideas of Bruner in the role of experience in education and Gagne in the problem-solving method. Dewey also advocates a cooperative rather than dictatorial use of power in learning situations (1938). He believes that the ability to participate effectively in society is a core skill required for living in a democracy (Webne-Behrman, 1998).

Another educational innovator whose ideas have stood the test of time was Maria Montessori (1870–1952). She was the first female in Italy to complete medical school. She turned to education and developed child-centred, experiential, multi-sensory learning and encouraged children to have self-discipline and responsibility for learning. She was amongst the first to introduce the 'science of observation' to teachers to monitor and develop her methods. Her contribution to education is manifest in the number of Montessori schools that exist today around the world (1974).

In contrast, Alexander Sutherland Neill (1883–1973) also advocated a libertarian approach to schooling and founded Summerhill in England in 1924. He accused Montessori of having an over-scientific and moralistic approach to education. At Summerhill, general assemblies were chaired by elected pupils. Children discussed and solved problems and made their own rules. Neill's vote had no greater weight than any of his pupils'. Although Neill had considerable success, and elements of his approach are utilized today, the freedom was too much for some children and the buildings were frequently vandalized (Neill, 1978).

Kurt Hahn, a German-Jewish educator, founded the 'Outward Bound' movement as an antithesis of the authoritarian schools in Germany in the inter-war period. After escaping a prison sentence, he fled to Scotland and founded Gordonstoun School in 1934. He involved students in outdoor learning through survival training and mountain and ocean rescue exercises. Today there are over 34 Outward Bound schools in over 17 different countries. These and other consulting companies offer short-term outdoor programmes to managers and teams (Bank, 1994). I will develop my experiences as an outdoor facilitator later in Book 2.

Meanwhile in the field of psychology, Carl Rogers (1902–87), a prominent American psychotherapist, developed the humanistic 'client-centred' approach to psychology in the 1940s (Rogers, 1951). His work had a profound impact on education. He reacted against what he saw as extreme behaviourists like B F Skinner. According to Rogers, Skinner underestimated the impact of the environment on learning and dismissed the power of free will either to motivate or to demotivate learners. Rogers, on the other hand, believed that the success of counselling sessions was based on the perceived ownership of the process by the client.

It was Rogers who did much to popularize the term 'facilitator' in the 1970s and 1980s through his work 'Freedom to learn: a view of what education might become' (Rogers, 1969). He proposes that education should maximize the freedom of the individual to learn by removing threats, boosting self-esteem, involving students in learning planning and decision making, and using self-evaluation techniques. As a result, he believes the learner would 'learn how to learn' and become autonomous (Rogers, 1967,1978). He believes that most people prefer to manage learning in their own ways and that the role of the teacher should be more of a facilitator.

It was Edgar Schein (1988) who extended the idea of 'client ownership' into the concept of 'process consultancy' where the client is expected to know the solution, as opposed to the doctor–patient model of 'expert consultancy' where the consultant diagnoses the problem and comes up with a solution. The facilitator, according to Schein, is clearly a 'process consultant'. 'Process' is an abstract term and the development of the term 'process consultant' was a major step in identifying the distinct role of facilitators.

The acknowledgement of adult learners and experiential learning

One of the most influential yet controversial writers on adult education was Malcolm Knowles. He believed that organizations and indeed society as a whole would improve by providing people with opportunities to learn and develop. Knowles invented the term 'andragogy' in 1970 and describes the characteristics of adult learners, many of whom flourish with a facilitative approach (as opposed to 'pedagogy': child learning). He describes three main assumptions that differentiate adult from child learners (Knowles, 1984).

Firstly, adults are less dependent than children and seek self-directed learning. Secondly, adults have greater stores of experience; indeed their self-concept is often closely linked to their experiences which they like to draw on during the learning process. Thirdly, children are more accepting of knowledge and skills that 'will be useful one day'. Adults want their learning to be useful now and related to current problems rather than subject-centred. From these assumptions Knowles implies that there should be a learning climate of mutual respect with minimal use of authority and formality. He believes that adults should be actively involved in experiential learning.

The differences between andragogy and pedagogy really relate to the philosophy of the New Education reformers of the 20th century, rather than a distinction based on the age of learners. Tennant (1986) criticized Knowles and asserted that all his assumptions cited above may also be applied to children in that they, like adults, delight in telling their experiences and being actively involved in problem solving. The work of Knowles was not based on research; it is more a humanistic theory of education based on the ideals of the humanistic psychologists. It is a philosophy of education that encourages educationalists to recognize the individuality of each learner and evaluate their approach to teaching and learning. In order to practise the dimensions cited by Knowles, educators of children or adults have to take on more facilitative rather than didactic, authoritarian roles.

In 1984, Knowles showed the relationships between the teaching models and researchers (see Figure 3.1). It is based on two dimensions: the complexity of the learning task on the vertical axis and the level of the individual's learning ability along the horizontal axis. This diagram shows the contrast between a training and/or directional teaching approach in the bottom left and in the top right area, a self-directed approach more akin to a facilitative approach.

Knowles developed his ideas further and advocated the use of learning contracts, which require a facilitative approach. He described a learning contract as a 'process plan' (Knowles, 1986). The focus is on the learners'

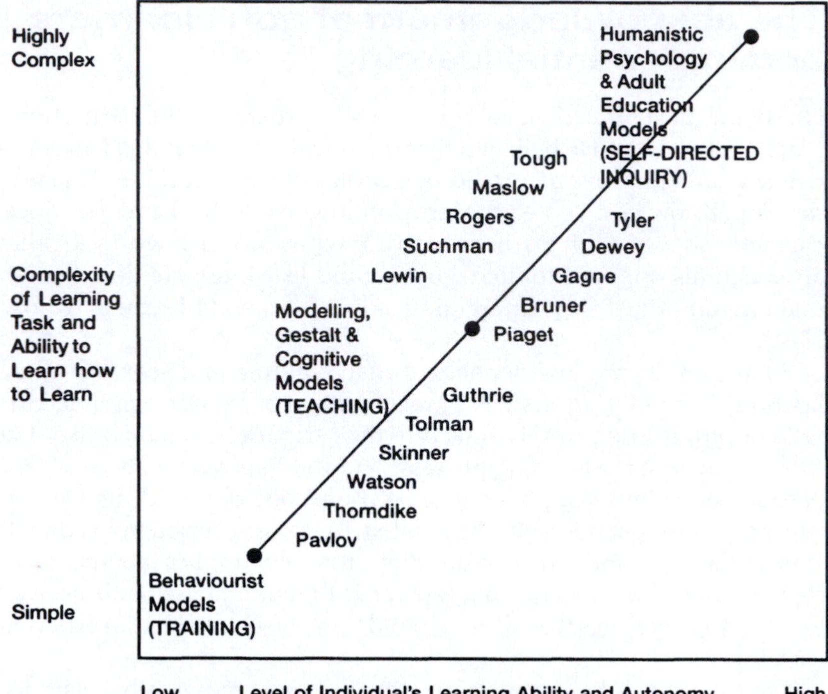

Figure 3.1 Relationship between teaching models and the learning situation
Adapted from Knowles, M (1984, 3rd edn)

needs and learning styles as opposed to the teacher or the subject. Learning contracts are similar to any plan at work. In many ways they are similar to performance appraisal systems whereby workers (in conjunction with a manager) set goals, devise strategies to achieve them, and at the end of a period of time assess progress and reasons for lack of progress.

At the same time, David Kolb (1984) was writing about the value of experiential learning based originally on the scientific experiment (ie conduct an experiment, observe, conclude, and set plans for the next experiment). He incorporated the value not only of past experiences, but new, active experiences in an experiential learning cycle comprising four stages (see Figure 3.2):

1. concrete experience, that is, being directly involved in an experience;
2. reflective observation in which the learner thinks about the experience;
3. abstract conceptualization in which the learner summarizes, generalizes or condenses new learning into a theory;

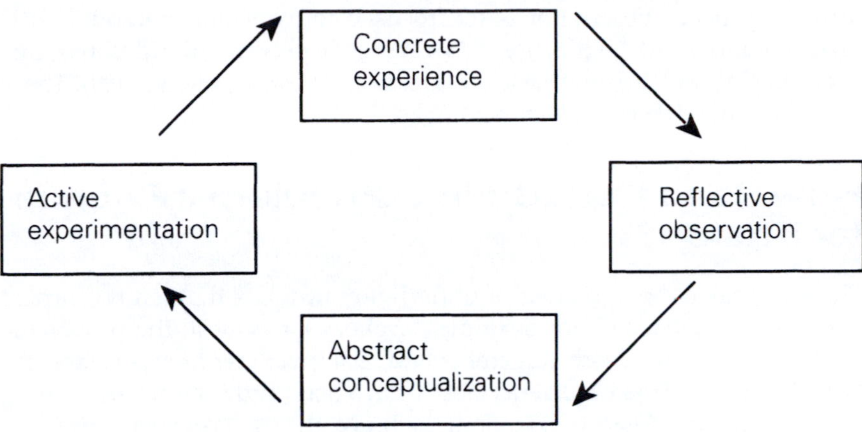

Figure 3.2 Kolb's experiential learning model
Source: Adapted from Kolb (1984)

4. active experimentation whereby the learner decides what new learning to put into practice.

The model is of course simplistic. Indeed experiential learning is not sequential. One student pointed out to me in her journal that as she stood at the front of the class facilitating, she was moving through the four stages of the Kolb model almost concurrently as she received cues from the reactions of her classmates.

Do people learn intuitively from experience? Of course the answer is 'yes', otherwise young children would never survive. However, often there is the intervention of a parent or guardian. Frequently, in order for groups to be able to process experience in a meaningful way there needs to be a 'process person' or facilitator to enable people to draw out learning from experience. This is how John Heron perceived the facilitator role:

> a facilitator is a person who has the role of helping participants to learn in an experiential group. The facilitator will normally be formally appointed to this role by whatever organization is sponsoring the group. And the group members will voluntarily accept the facilitator in this role.
>
> (Heron, 1989: 11)

David Boud (1985, 1995) in Sydney, Bob Dick in Queensland (1984) and Marilyn Spencer of the Institute of Cultural Affairs (1989) in the USA developed models and processes for reflecting on experiential learning further. Spencer's description of the 'focused conversation method' (ORID process) and the LENS process (a card sort process to aid consensus decision making) are now basic tools for facilitators (Spencer, 1989). These methods will be discussed later in Book 2.

How does the hidden curriculum influence facilitation?

There appear to be a number of underlying attitudes that many learners may have internalized: for example, teachers know best; the role of the student is to listen, absorb, remember and recall; a student's experience and knowledge are not as valuable as those from a book and/or teacher; learning is confined to the classroom; you must achieve, that is, 'task mesmerization' (Robson and Beary, 1995). These attitudes result in self-talk or driving language or 'scripts' in Transactional Analysis (TA) terms. (TA is a branch of psychology developed by Eric Berne (1961).)

The role of the facilitator, I think, is to help participants to unravel these scripts, and that is not easy. In the unravelling process, people are taken out of their 'comfort zones', that is, the ways of behaving to which individuals have become accustomed. It is the role of the facilitator to challenge assumptions and to create an environment that is conducive for people to move out of their comfort zones. People will not shift until they are ready, willing and able and facilitators should respect the 'choice' of the individual. Defences play an important part in an individual's strategies for survival in the world as they have experienced and therefore perceive it. Facilitators need to be very careful when deciding whether, when and how to confront resistance. Facilitators need to be able to build secure, trusting environments where participants can experiment and break out of or rewrite the scripts that inhibit their growth and learning.

Bottom-up approaches to educational reform

By the 1960s, changes in educational philosophies finally reached tertiary establishments because of student unrest. The counter-culture movement of the post-war baby boomers resulted in the student riots of the late 1960s and early 1970s. These upheavals seriously challenged the values of the established, tertiary educational bureaucracies in the UK, France and the USA. In that era there was a sense of idealism and hope for a better society. However, many of the activists lacked the political nous to make it happen. In my experience at the University of London, the responses of academics varied. Many members of the 'old school' were averse to power 'sharing';

others welcomed students and their ideas and inputs to committees. It is now the norm in western tertiary institutions to have student representation on many governing boards and committees. However, even when people are co-opted onto committees they are sometimes manipulated, since it is very difficult for one individual to go against the mainstream thinking, as Asch's (1952) experiments showed. However, even today, our education system does not teach people how to participate in, and/or facilitate work, home and community systems towards creating a civil society through either direct or indirect democracy (Honey, 2000).

Training versus facilitating

Robert Crapo, an Associate Professor of Management at New York University, stresses the need to let go of content to enact the philosophy of 'andragogy' as defined by Malcolm Knowles. Crapo believes it is difficult to change excellent trainers into group facilitators. He comments that 'there is an adult life crisis to go through in the process of becoming a group facilitator' (Crapo, 1986: 48). It is not just a crisis that needs to be resolved by the facilitator, but also by participants. For some facilitators, like myself, who started their careers as more autocratic trainers/teachers, some crises and/or training in facilitative skills may be necessary in order to change a person's style. However, I hold the art of human resource development is in interweaving the two: sometimes training and inputting content, at others, facilitating and focusing on process, but importantly making this changing of roles clear to the participants.

There is another reason why some trainers do not move into facilitative mode: because the latter requires managing and/or letting go of one's ego. Facilitators need to give away the need to be the fount of all learning or expertise. They have to learn how to adapt group processes according to the needs of the group and how to react if under attack. That does not mean facilitators should not have feelings (obviously that is impossible); it means that they need to be in control of themselves. If anger is used to counteract abusive and/or inappropriate behaviour, it must be controlled anger.

Crapo (1986) states that 'successful facilitators' have internalized several key experiences and/or assumptions. Firstly, they have already experienced being successful trainers, found training exciting, but have outgrown that stage. Secondly, that there is no such thing as a hostile group, merely people who are expressing their problems. Thirdly, they trust people and groups and believe in and practise adult learning techniques, that is, 'andragogy'. Fourthly, they expect their groups to possess knowledge rather than lack it, and treat them with that expectation. Fifthly, they use the Johari window (Luft, 1969) as a model to determine the degree of knowledge the group possesses about a particular topic at hand. (The Johari window is a model drawn like a window with four panes: arena: what is known by self and others; blind spot: what is known only by others; façade: what is only known by self; unknown: what is unknown by self and others.)

Facilitation skills are not superior to presentation and/or training skills. A skilled facilitator, that is, one who has presentation and training as well as facilitation skills, can interweave seamlessly between the three when necessary.

A facilitator also has to be comfortable with anger and conflict. When I contract with students at the beginning of my facilitation classes, a dominant issue of fear emerges from new facilitators in the class every semester (for the past six years). Many new facilitators understandably fear loss of control and/or how to handle verbal or even physical attack. They want to know how to deal with so called 'difficult people'. Unlike Crapo, they believe that there are such things as hostile groups, and some have deep concerns on their ability to facilitate in those circumstances.

Why do some people train rather than facilitate?

According to Crapo, there are many reasons why some people train rather than facilitate. Many fear losing control of the group. It is more difficult to prove to management that certain objectives have been met when facilitating. When under stress and/or perceived threat, individuals tend to go back to the approach they know best. For most of us, it is the directive approach, that is, the one we observed most in our formative years in school. Crapo believes that many trainers neither know nor value the precepts of andragogy.

I assert there are more reasons. Firstly, some trainers have a very limited range of approaches and processes, partly because they have limited comfort zones and do not value experimentation and improvisation. This is similar to a carpenter whose only tool is a hammer and all problems as a result are solved with nails. Secondly, facilitation superficially takes more time than training and 'quick fix-it' strategies. Some managers are scared of 'taking the lid' off simmering pots of worker discontent in case it shows them in a bad light. Many people in high places neither encourage nor listen to 360-degree feedback.

Facilitators do not just let so-called 'able' participants have the floor indiscriminately when they are running meetings or workshops. For example, some people who think they have been chairing good interview panels for new personnel for years, and who think they 'know it all', often are the very ones who need to update themselves on the new Equal Employment Opportunity legislation. Facilitators need to be thoroughly briefed and should be au fait with some of the social, political and economic contexts, that is, key content issues of the group. They need to know about tension points and issues that are likely to arise. They also need to know some process issues. For example: Who are the people most likely to dominate? And how can this energy be channelled? Who are the people who have suitable background knowledge of the issues under discussion? Who are the ones who think they know a lot and talk a lot about very little? This is why professional, full-time facilitators often specialize in particular fields, for example: agriculture; small town development; hospitals and health organizations; education; small business.

What are the advantages of facilitating rather than training?

There appear to be many advantages to facilitating. New ideas surface that may be suppressed during top-down training. Groups do not necessarily come up with 'right' answers or approaches to a problem when being trained, but with facilitation may come up with more creative responses. In my experience, workshops on facilitation and meetings have often produced recommendations to management for improvements and changes to the status quo. Facilitators are often better sales people for changing the perception of the training function than trainers (Crapo, 1986: 448).

Facilitation enables people to hear other people's viewpoints and perhaps shift from polarized paradigms. In the process it enables participants to identify and work through 'emotional baggage' which may have been blocking communication and productivity.

Peer support groups

There has been a movement away from structured courses to group learning focused on the immediate needs of participants on a 'need to know' basis. Ian Cunningham (1994) points out the increasing focus on learning as a collective activity in groups and now organizations as a whole. He describes the need for people in organizations to help learning in their learning sets, communities, and society and as a result the world. Peter Senge (1990) also focuses on this in *The Fifth Dimension: The Art and Practice of the Learning Organization*. (This aspect will be discussed again later under the section on future seekers in Chapter 14.)

Cunningham describes 'learning sets', that is, groups of managers who come together with a facilitator to learn about a common issue, through their collective experiences and action learning. He proposes that facilitators should focus on 'assisting' and not become over-obsessed with group process. He also warns against facilitators becoming focused on 'rescuing' and as a result developing dependency in learning set members.

Klinck (1992) uses the term 'collegial support groups' for mechanisms for groups within the same organization who may combine for an agreed period with an external facilitator. In Perth, she worked in government departments with women from different levels in the organizational hierarchy who met over a period of a year and then disbanded. Throughout the process, members were able to examine their own roles within their organization and examined ways in which they could more effectively contribute to the goals of the organization. As a result, members became more aware of their inner strengths and the value of mutual support.

Heron (1993) uses a broader term, 'peer support groups', to describe groups that deal with personal life, professional issues or the boundary between the two. These groups may choose to focus on a critical incident or issue of group members. He proposes that once started, a group may run indefinitely without any dominant facilitator, but with individual group members taking on facilitator roles when necessary.

Conclusion

In this chapter I described the contributions of various authors to participative learning and raised questions concerning the slow changes towards more involvement by learners in their education and workers in the workplace. Both children and adults like to be actively involved in the learning process, as this chapter has illustrated. The next chapter focuses on facilitation and community development.

4

Development of facilitation in community development

Introduction

At this point I will draw the reader's attention to wider contributions to the general literature on facilitation, that is, community development. Why? Firstly, because I believe community initiatives have so much to offer the management field. Secondly, because of the tremendous grassroots creativity and energy in numerous countries across the globe to solve problems at a local level. Thirdly, because my facilitation journey has led me in recent years to delve into and learn from and with people in the community development field.

Numerous people have found that working in groups produces different results from working alone. Firstly, I will briefly describe some of the contributions of Quakerism (a mystical/spiritual/religious movement) to facilitation and movements towards social change. Then, I will describe Sherry Arnstein's Ladder of Participation which aids the understanding of various levels of participation in development. I describe changes in approaches to development through facilitated 'Participatory Learning and Action' influenced by Paulo Freire and Ivan Illich in the 'South' (ie developing world). I outline two initiatives that have developed from the work of Paulo Freire: firstly, the successes of the 'Reflect' method and its impact on adult literacy and community development, and secondly, the facilitation of the 'Theatre of the Oppressed' and street theatre in raising consciousness and instigating action. Finally, I describe a small business development project in Western Australia which has drawn on learning from community development in the 'South' or developing world.

The contribution of the Quaker movement to facilitation

The use of groups to help individuals and committees develop has a 350-year-old history within the Religious Society of Friends (Quakers). This movement sprang from the social and religious upheavals in 17th century England. Early adherents included soldiers in Oliver Cromwell's army who, at the end of the English Civil War, were so disillusioned with warfare and its outcomes that they renounced all 'outward weapons', declaring their peace testimony to King Charles II in 1660, in a document entitled 'A Declaration from the harmless and innocent people of God, called Quakers'. They were clear that their use of inward weapons, or 'weapons of the spirit', was legitimate (Sharp, 1974). Since then they have tried to live by this moral code of pacifism, although how each generation has interpreted the code has varied. The witness of the Religious Society of Friends and theories of its founder, George Fox, spread to Pennsylvania in the USA and across the world. Quakers, through their active involvement in peace and justice issues, were involved in campaigns for the abolition of slavery; prison and education reform; and conscientious objection to war. They helped to establish schools to provide aid to native American Indians and worked for women's suffrage. British Quaker Peace and Service workers currently work in Sri Lanka, Bosnia, Lebanon, Israel, North Africa, Northern Ireland and Geneva.

All Quaker meetings are grounded in the use of periods of silence to open participants to the guidance from the 'spirit', and this principle applies to all meetings, including business meetings. In the 18th century, Quaker John Woolman in the USA led many 'clearness meetings' with Quaker slave owners. Through these meetings, many Quaker slave owners came to the realization that they could no longer own and/or work people as slaves. This movement contributed to the abolition of slavery and the growth of the human rights movement (Whiting, 1999).

In Quaker practice, a 'focus person', who needs help to become clear about a dilemma or problem, calls a 'clearness meeting'. In 'clearness' meetings the facilitator, or 'clerk', is often an elder. The clerk consults the focus person concerning personal preference for a structured or informal meeting. Quakers use silence and centring techniques. The group norms are simple, but adherence is sometimes difficult. Questions are asked to enable the focus person to think more broadly about the issue; members cannot provide answers. Hoffman, in Green, Woodrow and Peavey (1994: 129), states that in Quaker meetings 'Nothing is allowed except honest, probing, caring, challenging, open, unloaded questions!' Any written record of a Quaker meeting is read to the gathered group which is able to suggest amendments before accepting the minutes.

To this day these techniques have been used to trigger community action and to enhance the peace process through campaigns for disarmament, protection for the environment and against genetic engineering. In the UK there is a powerful programme called *Turning the Tide* which is based on the services of trained, volunteer facilitators. The aim of the programme is to advance the understanding of active non-violence for positive social change, building on the experience and insights of previous non-violence movements. The programme offers facilitated workshops for activists; training for non-violence facilitators; and consultancy help for activists in using the media, preparing for non-violent direct action and managing under stress. The facilitators offer a wide variety of interactive exercises aimed at stimulating awareness of the values and repercussions beneath any action for change.

To enhance their role as change agents, the Quakers established a publishing house, 'New Society Publishers', in the USA with a branch in Canada to promote societal change through Quaker and other facilitation techniques. They have successfully published widely in the fields of facilitation, conflict resolution, mediation and peace studies.

I will now move on to a discussion of the meaning of participation in development.

The meaning of 'participation'

> A citizen is one who participates in power.
>
> Aristotle

Community development and indeed all facilitation work relies on participation. However, in English the word 'participation' means different things to different people. One of the most useful models of the levels of participation I have found was developed by Sherry Arnstein (1969), a consultant in urban affairs in the USA. She worked with numerous government agencies and community groups. As a result of her experience, she identified eight levels of participation which she defined as degrees of citizen power and depicted as the rungs of a ladder (see Figure 4.1):

Levels 1–2 she calls 'Non-participation'.

Levels 3–5 she calls 'Degrees of tokenism'.

Levels 6–8 she calls 'Degrees of citizen power'.

A brief description of each level is necessary here. Although Arnstein writes about community use of power, I have added organizational examples here:

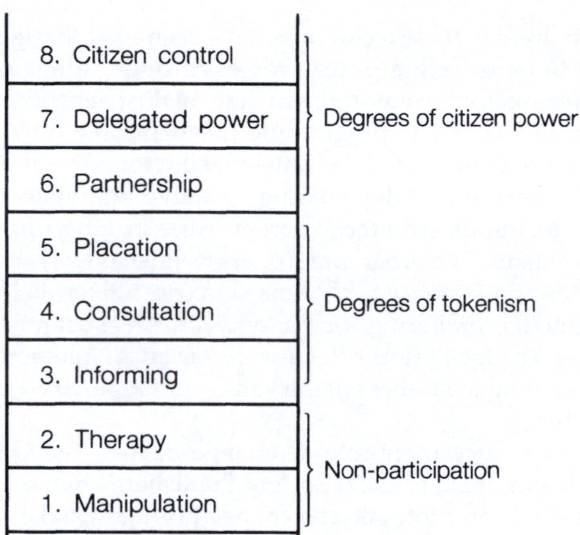

Figure 4.1 Arnstein's 'ladder of participation'

1. **Manipulation**. At the manipulation level, citizens or members of private organizations merely serve to 'rubber stamp' the desires of local government advisory committees who perceive their roles are to 'educate', 'cure', advise and persuade participants rather than the reverse. Power lies firmly in the hands of various forms of government and management.
2. **Therapy**. Managers allow workers to 'let off steam' under the masquerade of participation. Yet their anger or frustration is not heeded.
3. **Informing**. Arnstein maintains that information giving is the first step towards legitimate participation since citizens and workers at least become aware of some of their rights, responsibilities and options. As communication is only one way, there is no feedback and as a result there is scope for misunderstandings. This one-way communication may be achieved though such channels as pamphlets, faxes, e-mail, etc.
4. **Consultation**. If consultation takes place, the communication should be two-way in that ideas and opinions are solicited in a two-way discussion through neighbourhood meetings, public enquiries and attitude surveys. Preferably prior warning is given so that people have a chance to think about their stance before a meeting.
   Consultation is fine if this level of decision making is made clear from the outset, that is, it is 'transparent' and the officials have not already made their decision before the consultation process begins. However, Arnstein suggests that this is just window dressing.

Some officials go through the motions of 'consulting', but take very little notice of what has been said. As a result, distrust often develops if no ideas are ever supported and/or implemented. Another depowering tactic is where facilitators and/or planners appear to be consulting group members for their ideas; however, these ideas may be acknowledged verbally, but discreetly omitted from the wall minutes on flip chart paper, that is, ideas are eliminated and/or edited either at the first note-taking stage or later when they are typed.

5. **Placation**. At the placation level a hand-picked few 'worthy' workers or citizens are placed on committees and begin to have some degree of influence, usually small, and the power-holders retain the right to judge the legitimacy of the advice. Arnstein refers to informing, consultation and placation as degrees of tokenism because the ground rules allow the have-nots to advise, but the power-holders retain the continuous right to decide.
6. **Partnership**. When partnership occurs, power is redistributed through negotiation between workers or citizens and power-holders. They agree to share planning and decision-making responsibilities through such structures as joint policy boards, planning committees and mechanisms for resolving impasses. Groundrules are established and only changed with mutual consent.
7. **Delegated power**. The level of delegated power occurs when citizens achieve dominant decision-making authority through holding a majority of seats on committees and have power over a particular plan or programme, usually as a result of negotiation.
8. **Citizen/Worker control**. Finally, at this level community members and/or workers are given full autonomy over an area and are put in charge of policy making and managerial aspects of a decision, for example a neighbourhood corporation with no intermediaries between it and the source of funds, or a worker cooperative.

Arnstein's model is a useful tool for enabling administrators, facilitators and participants to understand more fully the concepts of participation and to make them aware of the pitfalls of tokenism. Consultation can imply varying degrees of effective power in decision making. She mentions that the ladder of citizen participation assumes two distinct groups, that is, the 'powerless have-nots' and the 'powerful haves'. However, in reality both groups are not identifiable as uniform groups. Nevertheless, she explains that in most instances each group perceives the other as homogeneous. Secondly, she cites, but does not explain, the road blocks of true citizen participation, for example racism, paternalism, resistance to power redistribution on the part of the power-holders, and feelings of distrust, alienation and inadequacies of most poor communities' socioeconomic infrastructure and knowledge base and organizing difficulty as primary barriers to participation on the part of citizens. Thirdly, Arnstein warns that token participation without the redistribution of power 'is an empty and frustrating process for the powerless' (1969: 176) and that participation without any real impact on outcomes is simply an 'empty ritual'. It enables those with power to maintain the status quo because they can claim that people are consulted. Fourthly, she points out that in the real world there might be 150 rungs of a participation ladder with less sharp distinctions between them. It was her view that in 1969 the level of participation in the majority of Community Action Programmes and Model City programmes in the USA was token participation.

With the above in mind, it may be prudent for facilitators to find out exactly what senior management or government officials intend so that participants can be told at workshops what levels of participation are invited. If the levels of participation are made visible to workers there is a basis for building trust. It is when there is a 'perceptual gap' of understanding between people that problems occur. Unfortunately, some senior management, in seeking to co-opt support for *their* views and ideas, are unlikely to want this degree of transparency.

Arnstein's ladder can be applied in numerous situations where some form of participation is sought, whether in education, industry or community programmes. In spite of the comments made earlier regarding the refinement of her ladder, it is still a useful simple model. I frequently use this model with groups involved in group decision making and immediately I get reactions like 'Now I understand why I got so annoyed, the manager was only consulting us, but we thought it was going to be a group decision.' Arnstein's model also inspired Elizabeth Rocha (1997) to develop a similar and very useful ladder of empowerment.

I will return to variations on Arnstein's ladder in Chapter XX. I now turn to the impact of writers from the development field who have influenced the field of participatory education.

No educational process is ever neutral

Some of the most powerful writings from the development field that have impacted on education came from Ivan Illich (an Austrian social and political thinker, 1926–) and Paulo Freire (a Brazilian lawyer, 1921–97) in the 1970s. Illich (1977) describes the teaching, medical, psychological, religious and legal professions as the 'depowering professions' which through their expert and legitimate power in the community consciously and/or unconsciously depower their clients. His main work, *Deschooling Society* (1971), advocates that not only institutions, but also society should be freed and 'deschooled'. He proposes that 'educational webs' should be established to heighten interconnectivity and opportunities for learning, sharing and caring. It would seem that his dream is in some ways being realized with the World Wide Web. Indeed the Web has enabled development workers in South America, Asia and Africa to discuss issues that would normally be channelled to their donor-host countries in the 'North'. The Web has also led to exciting developments in the facilitation field, that is, facilitation of electronic discussion groups in synchronous and asynchronous time (see Chapter 10).

Considering their own educational experiences, Ivan Illich and Paulo Freire attack the 'school' as a system of exploitation and destroyer of learning which should be lifelong and not confined to a fixed curriculum. Freire points out that people may develop a 'fear of freedom' which prevents them from responding to the underlying problems they face. To counteract this, he proposes the concept of 'conscientization', that is, a consciousness-raising process in which a facilitator dialogues with groups to deepen the awareness of learners of both the socio-cultural reality and the political arena that shapes their lives. This indicates the importance of the context in which learning takes place. The facilitator can then utilize the resulting internal motivation of learners (if it occurs) and develop their capacity to transform that reality through learning. The result of Freire's successful literacy programmes in Brazil was that peasants learnt to read and write and as a result, vote. This enabled them to take a stand against landowners and moneylenders they perceived as unjust. The government forced Freire to leave, but the impact of his writing lives on in the fields of development and education.

According to Freire (1972, 1974), governments have two alternatives regarding the goals of education. Either, education is designed to maintain the status quo and values and culture of the dominant class by 'domesticating' people, rather like animals, with the 'banking approach' to learning. Or, education can be designed to 'liberate' people, helping them to become critical, free, active and responsible members of society, that is, the 'problem-posing approach'.

Freire advocates starting from the inner motivation of people. In challenging the approach to learning, he compares the 'banking' to the more empowering or 'problem-posing' approach to learning (see Table 4.1). The problem-posing approach requires educators to let go of some of their position, legitimate and expert power. For some educators this approach is too threatening. Unfortunately, many institutions still keep to the 'banking approach' which often depowers learners. The latter approach also omits teaching learners how to learn (Downs, 1995) which would give them 'learning autonomy for life'.

An important consideration that these examples illustrate is who sets the limits and/or levels of power and how much empowerment is desired

Table 4.1 Banking and problem-posing approaches to learning

Banking approach	*Problem-posing approach*
Expert and/or teacher seen as possessing all essential knowledge and/or skills	Facilitator provides a framework for thinking, creative, active participants to consider common problems and find solutions
Learners regarded as 'empty vessels' needing to be filled with knowledge	Facilitator raises questions: why? how? who?
Expert and/or teacher talks and others listen passively, that is, monologue and silence respectively	Participants are active, describing, analysing, suggesting, deciding, planning

and by whom? Who decides who decides? How facilitators should be chosen and trained?

Development workers must answer these questions before embarking on programmes to enhance participation and empowerment. Refusal to do so may lead to confusion, distrust and disillusionment on the part of participants. It is important that power-holders are prepared to share power before the opportunity is offered. Once offered, any withdrawal will cause resentment.

Facilitation in developing and developed countries

I will now move on to the theme of facilitation and how it has evolved in development work in the so-called 'Third World' and then to an example in Western Australia.

On 20 January 1949, US President Truman in his inaugural speech (Sachs, 1995: 6) stated:

> We must embark on a bold new program for making the benefits of our scientific advances and industrial progress available for the improvement and growth of underdeveloped areas.
>
> The old imperialism – exploitation for foreign profit – has no place in our plans. What we envisage is a program of development based on the concepts of democratic fair dealing.

On that day two billion people suddenly were defined as the 'other'; they became seen as 'underdeveloped', a mirror image of what was perceived as ideal in the West. The word 'development' was a reminder of '*what they are not*. . . an undesirable, undignified condition. To escape from it, they need to be enslaved to others' experiences and dreams' (Esteva, 1995: 10). Western advisers from the USA, Australia and Europe poured into the 'Third World' as paternalistic, top-down and often well-meaning change agents to make 'them' more like 'us', that is, materialistic and subject to the gods of the 'market' and 'economic rationalism'.

Some projects were 'successful and sustainable', others were not. After considerable economic, political, environmental, cultural calamities and waste of public money, described in depth by Graham Hancock (1991) and Wolfgang Sachs (1995), there has been some movement away from this top-down approach to a more facilitative approach. This did not occur because of a change of heart by the paternalistic West. It grew from grassroots initiatives that occurred concurrently in East Africa, South America, India and South Asia. Dr Robert Chambers at the University of Sussex in the UK points out that researchers, scientists and administrators rarely appreciate the richness and validity of rural people's knowledge. He argues for a reversal in outsiders' learning, values and behaviour and gathering more realistic processes for tackling rural poverty. He describes the 'fear of involvement' of people from urban environments who became 'development tourists' using rapid rural appraisal (RRA) or quick and superficial questionnaires and date gathering techniques.

Robert Chambers has published widely over the past 20 years regarding 'putting rural people first' in the development process (whilst not over-romanticizing rural knowledge). His belief is that the role of the rural extension worker in the 'South' has changed from that of researcher-adviser to facilitator. A rural facilitator, he believes, should not be a detached investigator who conducts questionnaires and merely observes. Chambers argues that a rural facilitator should act as a catalyst for dynamic dialogue, learning exchanges and reflection that engages everyone in a community using a rich menu of visualization tools (eg participatory mapping and modelling), interviewing methods (eg focus groups and key informant interviews) and group work methods (in Scoones and Thompson, 1994). The International Institute for Environment and Development was established in 1971, in London, to promote the collection and dissemination of 'participatory rural appraisal' (PRA) facilitatory techniques and research and training into this area. Chambers is the first to admit that he did not invent PRA. When I observed him in a workshop in Nepal in 1995, I noted that he endeavoured to practise what he preached. He went out of his way to put Nepalese facilitators first and resist the accolades of a guru.

As a result, in development work it is now more common to find teams of male and female facilitators from different disciplines working with villagers. The aim of co-facilitation is to counteract possible manipulation of power by a single facilitator from a particular discipline (Long and

Villareal in Scoones and Thompson, 1994: 51). Also, in many areas women feel more at ease when speaking to female facilitators about their issues.

These participatory initiatives are also taking place in urban areas at government, organizational and NGO level so the terms RRA and PRA have now been replaced by 'Participatory Learning and Action' or PLA. In order to encourage the dispersion of grassroots initiatives, they are regularly documented in a journal entitled *Participatory Learning and Action* which is published three times a year by the International Institute for Environment and Development in London. NGOs have also combined and developed their own networks of facilitators, for example 'Nepan', the Nepal Participatory Action Network, and the Lao PDR Training Network. Aid agencies from the West, for example Oxfam, Danida, World Vision and Médecins Sans Frontières, are now attempting to work in partnership with local NGOs. This requires skilled facilitation, partnerships and power sharing rather than a top-down approach by the donor organizations (see Arnstein's ladder above).

Adult literacy and development

Adult literacy methods in the 'South' have been transformed by using facilitative 'reflect methods' developed by many NGOs, including Action Aid, whose base is in London (Phnuyal, Archer and Cottingham, 1997: 276). The process has been described in this chapter as the development of this programme, which has had not just an unprecedented impact on literacy levels, but also an impact on the communities involved:

> The reflect method is a structured participatory learning process which facilitates people's critical analysis of their environment placing empowerment at the heart of sustainable and equitable development. Through the creation of democratic spaces and the construction and interpretation of locally-generated texts, people build their own multidimensional analysis of local and global reality, challenging dominant development paradigms and redefining power relationships in both public and private spheres. Based on ongoing process of reflection and action, people empower themselves to work for a more just and equitable society.
>
> (Phnuyal, Archer and Cottingham, 1997: 29)

A locally trained person acts as a 'literacy facilitator'. The emphasis is on active writing and drawing about their own experiences and traditions rather than passive reading of imported texts. It incorporates the practical Participatory Rural Appraisal visual techniques described above with the written materials that are developed by each literacy circle, who construct their own maps, calendars and diagrams about their local reality and issues.

The Reflect method was first piloted in three action research projects in Uganda, Bangladesh and El Salvador in 1996. All the pilots were evaluated against traditional literacy classes which used 'primers' or traditional adult literacy texts. The conclusions were that:

> the Reflect approach was more effective: 60–70% of those enrolled learnt to read and write there was a link between literacy and empowerment, for example, in El Salvador 61% of learners took up positions of responsibility. In Bangladesh men took up more household work to free women for more farm work and more children were enrolled in school. The method was reasonably simple and cost effective.
>
> (Phnuyal, Archer and Cottingham, 1997)

The best practice from these action research projects was consolidated in a 'Reflect mother manual' published in 1996 by Action Aid. Much debate ensued as its designers wanted it to be a facilitator's guide, not a Bible, so that facilitators would feel free to adapt or develop their own processes and develop local manuals of tools and techniques.

Facilitation and the 'Theatre of the Oppressed'

Various forms of street theatre have now been used very successfully to raise issues of domestic violence, child labour and political oppression. Augusto Boal has travelled the world developing the 'Theatre of the Oppressed' since the 1970s. The aim of this kind of theatre is to stimulate debate (and later action), to show alternatives and to enable people 'to become protagonists in their own lives' (Boal, 1992: xxii). His workshops have been so powerful that he has been exiled twice from Brazil, his homeland. His method has been used in schools, factories, day centres, community centres and with groups of tenants, unemployed, homeless, disabled, ethnic minorities. The Theatre of the Oppressed consists of three main categories: Image Theatre, Invisible Theatre and Forum Theatre; each is orchestrated by a 'joker' or facilitator.

Image Theatre is based on the saying, 'a picture tells a thousand words', and consists of interactive exercises and games designed to uncover questions, contradictions about societies and cultures through mime. The participants make still images of their lives, experiences and oppressions. They then re-sculpt the static images as if they are Plasticine. As no words are used, the images communicate across language and cultural barriers.

Invisible Theatre is public theatre in which the general public is involved in the action without knowing it, as 'spect-actors', that is, active spectators. A group of actors perform a provocative scene and then engage the onlookers, who include a couple of *agent provocateur* actors mingling with the crowd to express extreme and/or opposite reactions to the performed events. The event appears to the onlookers as if it is a normal street incident, not a performance.

Forum Theatre is a theatrical game in which a controversial issue is shown in unsolved form and in which the spect-actors are invited to engage to solve the problem. The issue is always some form of oppression which is directly relevant to the lives of the spect-actors. The scene is shown once in full. It is then shown again until one spect-actor shouts 'stop' and takes the role of the protagonist and tries to defeat the oppressors.

Boal uses the term 'joker' to describe the person whose role is to teach the audience the 'rules' (although these can be changed at any time by anyone). Jokers are not allowed to manipulate or influence the audience who must draw their own conclusions from the discussions. Jokers must relay Socratic questions, doubts to the audience, for example, 'Would this solution work? Is it right or wrong?' They may interrupt proceedings and call 'magic' if they think that the proposed solution is cheating, impossible or inadequate. However, audiences sometimes override the joker if they believe that a solution is possible, that is, signalling their readiness for action. The joker is maieutic, like a midwife, helping people to identify ideas and actions.

The Theatre of the Oppressed borders on the frontier between fiction and reality. It enables the oppressed to create an alternative model to the current reality (a dynamic collection of images), to be subjects and to practise and train for action as protagonists, not spectators, of their lives. The tools and techniques are readily transferable to training and change situations in organizations and different countries. However, the use of such techniques would need to be handled with great care in certain regimes.

I now move on to addressing some key learning about facilitation and small business development in my own state of Western Australia. (For other examples of the use of theatre and facilitation see Book 2 Chapter 4).

Facilitation of small business development in rural areas

Development work is not just confined to so-called Third World countries. Ernesto Sirolli (1995) transferred what he learnt in Africa to community development in country towns in Western Australia. In the 1970s, Sirolli, working in Zambia, observed what he considered was wrong with development work, that is, outsiders (in this case Italians from the Italian Agency of Technical Cooperation) trying to motivate local people to undertake projects that they neither desired nor 'owned'. On returning to Fremantle, Western Australia, Sirolli observed local 'hippies' in the markets trying to sell their shoddy, home-made shoes. He looked for a skilled leather master who wanted to pass on his skills and invited the keenest young people to learn from the master (who specialized in orthopaedic boots). Sirolli got and received help from the local council and long-term jobs were created. In addition, as a result, a specialized craft was prevented from dying out.

Sirolli continued his ideas in 1985 in Esperance, a small rural community, over 900 kilometres southeast of Perth. With six months' funding, he set himself up in a small café in the main street and waited for people to come to him with their dreams for a small business. Word of his role slowly got around the community and after five days someone arrived with an idea. 'The Esperance Experience' was a resounding success and by 1995 more than 200 communities in three countries had adopted a similar 'Enterprise Facilitation Model'.

> Facilitation is based on the belief that it is human to dream and to desire... The skill of the facilitator is to become available to those who have the dream and to help them acquire the skills to transform it into meaningful and rewarding work. The skill of facilitation is therefore a communication skill with a twist. It isn't so much that they have to communicate to their client, rather they have to be the kind of person one likes to talk to.
>
> (Sirolli, 1995: 85)

In training enterprise facilitators to work one to one with people, Sirolli had two main rules: firstly, 'Don't ever initiate anything' and secondly, 'Don't ever motivate anyone'. Indeed one married couple came to him with the idea of mortgaging their house in order to set up a new small business on the high street. The night before they were due to sign the documents at the bank, they visited Sirolli and indicated they had 'cold feet'. He wrote that he made no attempt to bolster their flagging confidence; the decision and motivation to continue had to be theirs. They did not go ahead with their business plan. Considering that most people working in the development field are highly motivated about their work, this could appear odd. As Vogler (1992) states, 'The best mentor advice may be so simple. Breathe. Hang in there. You're doing fine. You've got what it takes to handle any situation, somewhere inside you.'

Development work requires many different approaches according to the individuals involved, available time and the situation. Sirolli's stance is too simplistic. At times, it is normal (and sometimes useful) to hesitate before taking a risk. Some people need encouragement and support from a facilitator or mentor. But there is a fine dividing line between encouragement and coercion and the dividing line between the two is a grey area and varies from person to person.

Conclusion

In this and previous chapters I have given an overview of the development of the concept of facilitation in management, education and training and community development.

Facilitators/managers/educators/development workers have to be aware of and alert others to the sources of power, skills and knowledge 'in and around' them. They need to be able to focus more on 'process' rather than on 'content'. To be effective they require process skills and knowledge to implement, monitor and evaluate participatory approaches whilst having a firm grasp of content, context, associated issues and some technical and/or local language.

People have always worked in groups, so what is different now? Hierarchies can function well in stable environments and deliver benefits, products and services very effectively. However, in 'turbulent' environments (Emery, 1974) it became difficult to make informed decisions without the cooperation of groups of people who were prepared to contribute information and exhibit appropriate personal behaviours. Facilitation has emerged to help groups clarify and solve problems resulting from dramatic social, cultural and technological change where old routines, customs and expectations were breaking down.

When I asked Bob Dick (a facilitator and author from Queensland) why he developed the 'Acts of God process' (described in Book 2 Chapter 6) to facilitate and handle angry negative groups, his response was, 'I was desperate, in one particular workshop, everything was going wrong' (Dick, 1997). Necessity was the mother of invention. The world has become so complex that many issues and decisions require the positive energies, synergy and collective wisdom of groups rather than individuals.

Likewise the development of new words and phrases; as facilitation is a relatively new field, it is understandable that a new vocabulary has evolved to describe models, processes and concepts of group dynamics, for example 'facilitation', 'nominal group technique', 'search conference', 'metaplanning', 'open space technology' and 'groupthink'.

I suggest that facilitation has developed out of desperation in that people needed to work together increasingly in groups, but the groups were not effective and valuable time was lost. The results of group work were often quick fixes with no long-term motivation to implement plans and some people were left feeling alienated, unheard and not valued.

Definitions and models used to understand facilitation will be described and critiqued in the next chapters. As 'facilitation' is an emerging field, there is no agreed definition. The art of facilitation is practised in many different ways: there will never be 'one right way' due to differences in context, participants, issues and facilitation style/s. Process development is emergent, often mutating in different ways at the same time in different parts of the globe. Facilitators have different philosophies, preferred methods and strategies. Fortunately, facilitators network and share their experiences in support groups, at conferences and over the Internet. The emergence of facilitation as a profession will be discussed in Chapter 11.

5

Definitions and metaphors of facilitation

Introduction

Having described the rise of facilitation, I now discuss attempts to understand the meaning of facilitation by analysing definitions and metaphors from a variety of authors and practising facilitators. I discuss what facilitation is and what it is not. I look at whom you facilitate and how.

Definitions and metaphors used to define facilitation

Laura Spencer, working in the USA for the Institute of Cultural Affairs, compared a facilitator to the conductor of an orchestra:

> The facilitator's role is to lead the group in drawing out answers, building a vision and developing plans that motivate everybody to achieve agreed upon goals – in short to win. . . The facilitator functions much like the conductor of a symphony, orchestrating and bringing forth the talents and contributions of others. The facilitator is also a communicator. Working with decentralized structures such as networks, small teams and cross-departmental task forces – which more firms are embracing as alternatives to the corporate hierarchy – the facilitator fosters communication and understanding between the units.
>
> (Spencer, 1989: 11–12)

Spencer lives and works in a highly individualistic, competitive society in the USA. I believe the role of the facilitator is not only to motivate people to 'win'. However, clarifying the criteria for 'winning' could be part of the facilitator's job. If Spencer is referring to the whole organization and 'winning' involves generating agreed upon goals, then the need 'to win' can be used as a means of fostering cooperation, not competition. However, if small groups within an organization are pitted against one another 'to win', I believe this strategy can have some detrimental results. In my own past experience in a university the division of groups by cost centres has led in some areas to the decline of interdisciplinary collaboration in curriculum design and research. Indeed the current reward system even militates against joint research amongst colleagues. A competitive focus can be, I believe, detrimental to the work of a group.

Mike Robson and Ciaran Beary in the UK devoted time and energy to the quality circles movement in the late 1970s. They see facilitators as change agents 'who, depending on their level of skill, and on the way they are deployed, work on helping individuals, groups and the organization as a whole to develop and improve performance' (Robson and Beary, 1995: vii).

Indeed facilitators, I believe, are catalysts for change, but not necessarily the instigators of change. Trevor Bentley, an English consultant and writer, focuses on the process and empowerment sides of facilitation: 'Facilitation is a word that describes an activity. It is something that someone does. It is a process. Yet it also includes non-action, silence and even the facilitator's absence. . . the empowerment of individuals to achieve for themselves. . . is for me the key to facilitation' (Bentley, 1994: 27). Likewise, John Heron in a later book (1999: 1) changed his definition of a facilitator to: 'a person who has the role of empowering participants to learn in an experiential group'.

However, I do not believe it is possible for facilitators to empower others. Facilitators can merely aim to provide some of the conditions for empowerment to occur by encouraging cooperative and autonomous modes in the workshop (Heron, 1999) and using legitimized authority and charismatic effect. But implicit in this debate is the fundamental right of individuals and their free will and right of 'choice' in deciding how to be and how and when to act. I develop this theme further in a book entitled *Facilitating Empowerment* (Hogan, 2000).

Hunter, Bailey and Taylor in New Zealand focus on the process role of facilitation using the metaphor of the dance:

> Effective group facilitation is an artful dance requiring rigorous discipline. The role of the facilitator offers an opportunity to dance with life on the edge of a sword – to be present and aware – to be with and for people in a way that cuts through to what enhances and fulfils life. A facilitator is a peaceful warrior.
>
> (Hunter *et al*, 1993: 1)

> Facilitation is about process – how you do something – rather than the content – what you do. A facilitator is a process guide; someone who

> makes a process easier or more convenient to use. Facilitation is about movement – moving from A to B. The facilitator helps to guide group members towards their chosen destination. Facilitation makes it easier to get to an agreed destination.
>
> (Hunter *et al*, 1993: 5)

The metaphor of the dance is effective since facilitators must always be on their toes, as when the dance is on between people, there is always a chance of serendipity. However, it is desirable for facilitator to have some knowledge of the content under discussion and an understanding of the work, internal language and key concepts of the group members.

Since facilitators are not therapists, they should, I contend, choose processes carefully. However, seemingly harmless exercises or comments can trigger catharsis in some individuals. Facilitators need to have the interpersonal skills to handle discharge of emotions appropriately and professionally.

Facilitators are like midwives: they are not present at conception, nor do they own the baby, nor are they present at the prize-givings to commemorate the successes of the child. Facilitators help groups with processes to enable them to reach their goals, but they are rarely there to see them come to fruition.

Warihay, a private consultant in the USA, brings the role of facilitator and team leader together: 'The facilitator is someone with exclusive responsibility for observing and keeping the group aware of their interpersonal process. . . in many cases, team leaders have "facilitator" responsibilities in addition to their responsibility for leading a meeting and guiding the team in the problem solving process' (Warihay, 1992: 60).

Certainly it is necessary for a facilitator to hold up a metaphorical mirror to a group to show them what is happening. However, it is often very difficult for a team leader to be objective enough to perform this role as he/she is often so enmeshed in the group process and is also often the main power-holder in the group. In some cases, also, the role of team leader can be in direct conflict with the role of facilitator. It is hard for a manager to stay removed or abstain from using his/her power to influence the outcome of a discussion. Likewise, it is hard for some team members not to be swayed by the position power of a manager, hence the usefulness of the differentiation of roles described by Doyle and Straus (1976) shown in Figure 5.1. In traditional meetings the chairperson (ie process) role was usually undertaken by the manager who, as the boss (ie power-holder) in the group, could influence the content and flow of the discussion. Doyle and Straus suggested splitting the role in half and asking a facilitator to guard the process and stay out of content. In this model the chairperson or manager is better able to be an active participant, but asked to use his/her power to remind participants of organizational rules, deadlines and to call for a vote if the group failed to come to a consensus decision.

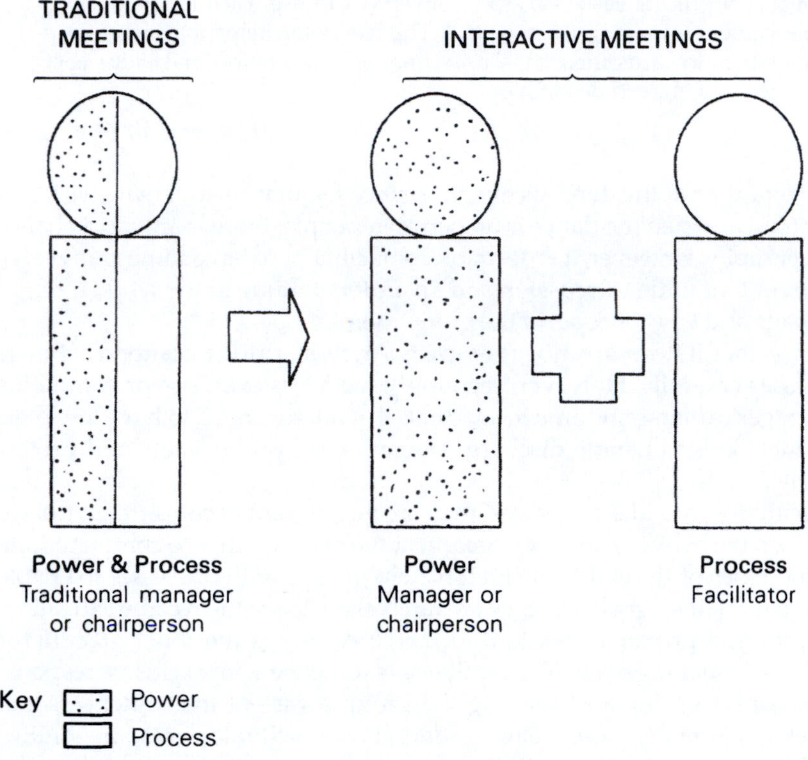

Figure 5.1 The roles of manager and facilitator
Source: Doyle and Straus (1976)

The fascinating aspect of facilitation is that there are few prescribed rules or ways of doing things. Indeed, another desired facilitator attribute is the ability to be flexible and creative. For example, 'Facilitation is an improvisatory art with an agreed negotiated structure. It is like jazz rather than classical music. Don't keep doing things in a certain way. Remember there is no one way or technique. Be flexible and stay awake' (Hunter, Bailey and Taylor, 1992: 75).

Heron takes the sleep metaphor further: 'Psychological somnambulism is a chronic habit in human behaviour; the tendency to fall asleep in interactions with others without awareness of one's behaviour, its effects and its motives. Hence we need, with much supportive rigour, to help each other wake up from time to time' (1989: 90).

Heron's sleep metaphor does not, however, acknowledge the advantage of routine activities in saving effort. It is impossible for a facilitator to be alert to everyone and everything that is happening in a group all the time.

Harrison Owen in the USA reacted against orchestrated conferences. He listened to the feedback that many people gave, namely that the chances to network at the breaks and lunchtimes are the best part of conferences. As a result, he developed the concept of 'Open Space Technology', first used in 1984, where groups come together with no pre-planned agenda in order to address, over a short period of time, a complex issue that they have in common. The process requires skilled facilitation and high levels of ownership and synergy on the part of the participants. The facilitator's key role is to 'hold the space', that is, to be fully present and allow the process to develop in a kind of meditative state. The facilitator does not join any of the discussion groups. Owen describes a number of stories (Owen, 1992, 1997) where not taking action was just as important as doing something: 'It is a curious role indeed, to the extent that if the facilitator becomes prescriptive, imposing time, space, and solutions, he or she will fail. The more that is done the less that will be accomplished. . . As the world would see it, the ultimate facilitator will do nothing and remain invisible' (Owen, 1992: 50–51).

This is an unusual role for the facilitator indeed. I have participated in an open space workshop. I observed the facilitator holding the space, but was alarmed when I observed patterns of dysfunctional behaviour, including male dominance of the discourse, repetition and attacking of ideas and people. Whilst there are many excellent ideas in open space technology, I believe a facilitator has to take a much more active role at times than just 'holding space'.

Roger Schwarz divides facilitation into two kinds, based on the objectives of the group. Firstly, 'basic facilitation' where the group 'uses a facilitator to temporarily improve its process in order to solve the substantive problem', and secondly, 'developmental facilitation' wherein a group 'seeks to permanently improve its process while solving a substantive problem' (1994: 6). The second level describes the more empowering aspect of the facilitation role, that is, to make oneself dispensable. This dichotomy is useful as it makes the role and responsibilities of the facilitator clear to both the facilitator and the client.

In Chapter 7 the concept of co-facilitation is introduced in which one mode utilizes the collaboration between internal and external facilitators. An evaluation of each type of facilitation is given in Table 5.1.

There are many forms of co-facilitation, including pairs or small groups of people who may comprise different gender, culture, age, background and experience (Knight and Scott, 1997; Schwarz, 1994; Pfeiffer and Jones, 1975; Cooper, 1980). Various types of co-facilitation are currently being investigated by Marie Martin (work in progress) using a phenomenological approach.

The concept of facilitation has been compared to that of a dancer, midwife, peaceful warrior, and orchestra conductor. It is a complex art and science.

Table 5.1 Comparison between external and internal facilitators (EF = External facilitator; IF = Internal facilitator)

	Pluses	*Minuses*
EF	• less biased, fewer initial stereotypes • easier to stay out of content • easier to concentrate on process • is not part of the political structure of the group • prevents proceedings being dominated by individuals and/or minority groups • can confront where necessary without fear of retaliation • can use apparently innocent 'naive observer' questions • results have more credibility both with participants and outsiders	• must be well briefed beforehand • must be chosen with care, not all facilitators, facilitate well! • more expensive • may be difficult for some participants to accept an outsider • needs to learn the language or concepts of the group • needs to learn the history of the group/organization • may not confront if only thinking of return work or wanting 'good' evaluations
IF	• less expensive • often quicker to brief because knows the history, the situation, politics and the people involved	• harder to stay out of content • harder to concentrate on process • harder to stay objective • may be difficult to confront individuals higher in the hierarchy • may be biased towards some individuals • may be put under pressure to manipulate the process

The context

During the writing of this book, it became clear to me that the 'underlying purpose' underpinning my facilitation work with clients and students is a deep-seated desire for peace. I believe that by teaching facilitation skills and theories to others and facilitating workshops, in my own small way I can contribute a little to world peace. Two weeks after writing this statement I came across the latest book by Hunter, Bailey and Taylor entitled *The Essence of Facilitation*. They recommend that facilitators consider the 'higher purpose' of their work (if any). I was interested to note their new definition of facilitation and the message that they published in bold type:

> Facilitation for us is not value-neutral. It is a body of knowledge and skills which seeks to empower groups of people **to work co-operatively towards creating a more co-operative and sustainable world.** Hunter *et al* (1999: 16)

Everything occurs in a context: the context of the group, organization, community and society. Facilitators are accountable to think about and take these layers into consideration. Everything we do is also value-laden. Facilitation is not value-free. By encouraging all members in a group to speak facilitators are valuing the input of everyone no matter what their status, experience or expertise. Facilitation has grown out of the bottom-up change process to create a more civil society and sustainable world.

What facilitation is not

Facilitation is not a fad or trendy label, nor is it therapy. Baxter (2000) made the following distinction: 'Therapy is a psychological process, that is looking at past issues of a person at a deep emotional level and working to resolve these issues. Facilitation, I feel, is helping people to understand how they think, interact and feel about specific topics that are related to specific roles in their lives, for example, work related.' This is a grey area since behaviour at work is often influenced by issues in a person's family and social roles. However, I believe it is important for facilitators to recognize the limits of their skills and knowledge and the boundaries of their work. It is necessary to limit the depth of interventions and/or refer participants to counselling help when and where necessary.

Hanson (cited in Burbidge, 1997: 236) postulates that the 'new profession of facilitation is rapidly taking its unique place alongside those of the consultant, coach, and trainer in organizational and community development'. Facilitation is certainly not 'touchy feely'. It does, at times, incorporate work involving participants and the facilitator in identifying and managing emotions. Some people find this very difficult and even threatening. They therefore block their own feelings and disown the impact that feelings have on themselves and others. Yet as human beings, feelings permeate everything we do. Managing one's own feelings and other people's anger and frustration that evolve naturally out of participatory work is not for the faint-hearted. Facilitation is not some 'New Age' doctrine of unstructured, self-centred permissiveness. Rather it involves the utilization of everyone's skills and perceptions, generally for a common purpose.

Whom do you facilitate: self and others?

According to the New Zealand facilitators, Hunter, Bailey and Taylor (1993), there are many levels at which you can facilitate:

> You can facilitate yourself, another person or a group... to facilitate groups effectively you need to facilitate yourself – your own processes (external and internal). And you need to be able to facilitate others, individuals as well (coaching or one-to-one facilitation) as groups are made up of individual people who come together to fulfil a particular purpose... you need to train yourself in self-facilitation, the facilitation of others and the facilitation of a group.
>
> (Hunter *et al*, 1993: 5)

I believe Hunter *et al* are on the right track, but facilitation is more complex than they have depicted. Facilitators have to be self-aware. They must be constantly looking inwards to their inner beings so that they are aware of prejudices and self-talk, and outwards to the group. But I concur that it is difficult to facilitate others until you can facilitate yourself, that is, facilitators need to be 'fully present' (ie centred in the here and now) and authentic with group members. It is important that facilitators minimize and manage egos, that is, they need to be confident, but not attention seeking. They need to be sensitive and compassionate, but not susceptible to internalizing the toxicities of organizational distress (Frost and Robinson, 1999). They need to be able to manage their own feelings and/or past distress patterns. I will discuss this further in Chapter 11.

Hunter *et al* (1993) further comment:

> It's not so much what you do or what you say, because words can be said in so many different ways. It's more to do with who you are and who you are being for the group you're working with. There are different ways of saying that: where you are coming from or what your attitude is. The relationship you develop with the group is the key to effective facilitation. There is a body of skills, but the bottom line is: 'Who are you for the group?'
>
> (Hunter *et al*, 1993: 199)

Facilitation is also about who you are for yourself. The ongoing personal development of the facilitator is crucial if s/he is to be effective in the development of groups. Regarding the moderating of ego, Lao Tzu, one of the political leaders of ancient China, wrote in the 'Tao Te Ching' in the fifth century BC: 'The wise leader settles for good work and then lets others have the floor. The leader does not take all the credit for what happens and has no need for fame. A moderate ego demonstrates wisdom' (Heider, 1986: 17).

According to Keltner (1989), there are three different ways in which individuals may take on a facilitative role. Firstly, a sensitive 'group member' may intervene in content discussion to raise awareness on process issues. However, some members may perceive this as attempting to control a discussion or influencing the nature of a decision. Secondly, a 'group leader (formal, appointed or assumed) may take on a facilitative role; however, again influence on process may be suspected as process interventions may influence decisions. Thirdly, there is the 'facilitator specialist' who does not deal with group content, but functions as a non-group member or as a member whose role is restricted to process consultation. Regarding this third category Keltner comments: 'There are risks the facilitator must take at every stage of the process. Alternative choices are always present for the skilled facilitator' (1989: 24). I will return to the issues of risks and choices of facilitation again in Chapter 11.

How do I define facilitation?

This all leads me to clarify both how I define facilitation and to describe critical factors embedded in this. I define a facilitator as

A self-reflective, process-person who has a variety of human, process, technical skills and knowledge, together with a variety of experiences to assist groups of people to journey together to reach their goals.

I see facilitation as an art, science, craft and profession. I believe elements of facilitation may be intuitive and/or learnt at a young age. As mentioned previously, a facilitator is similar to a 'dancer'. At one minute the facilitator is leading, setting the step and the pace; at others, individuals or the group lead the dance. The dance involves working every day with dilemmas, choices and decisions. They are not straightforward black and white decisions as there are many shades of grey.

Yet for all of that it is a most exciting movement in which to be involved.

Conclusion

The definitions and metaphors produced so far indicate that the concept of 'facilitation' is complex. Whereas facilitation is becoming a specialized field of practice and study, and to some extent professionalized, nevertheless facilitation is a role that anyone may take: manager, leader, parent, child, farm worker or factory worker.

I believe that if the world has more people who are willing and able to think and act as facilitators, conflict will be managed and/or 'provented' (sic) (Burton, 1990) and ultimately I hope we will have a world whose peoples are more at peace with themselves and each other. However, facilitation without its integral ethical component is unlikely to foster such an outcome.

Facilitation involves incorporating a range of communication, process skills and participatory values into one's life. A workshop is an interactive social process and all parties have a degree of ownership and responsibility for both success and/or failure of the event. A facilitator does not take exclusive or foremost credit for outcomes of a workshop and should acknowledge the group members' efforts and accomplishments. As Lao Tse wrote, 'When the job is done the people will say we did it ourselves' (in Heider, 1986). However, if a workshop goes wrong neither the group nor the facilitator should be scapegoated. A careful debriefing is required to spot errors (which often stem from the planning stage) so that learning from all perspectives is gleaned and some sort of remedial action is taken if required so that such occurrences do not happen again.

The definitions and metaphors discussed here give different and at times overlapping interpretations of what facilitation is about.

In Book 2, Chapter 4 I describe how facilitators may use metaphors in their work. In the next chapter I describe several models of facilitation, noting their various emphases. Further consideration of models relating to facilitation and technology will be undertaken in Chapter 10.

6

Models of facilitation

Introduction

In this chapter I describe models of facilitation and then describe how I came to develop two models. In books on facilitation I have read, authors rarely divulge the processes involved in developing a model. I believe the process of development is important in understanding how knowledge is constructed and depicted. I have called the first model a 'Living frame of facilitation' in that it depicts my view of facilitation at this time. The second is a classificatory grid of varieties of technologies directly useful for facilitation with individuals, groups and/or networks and is located in Chapter 10.

Models

Like theories, models summarize and direct our attention to concepts regarded as important. One can ask many questions in order to understand the purpose and potential uses of models. All the models described enable us to understand the phenomenon of facilitation more easily, but none 'map the territory' completely. They each provide different lenses with which we may view facilitation or parts thereof. They all challenge our thinking about the topic in varying degrees and therefore have potential to have an impact on practice. Table 6.1 includes a summary as a basis for comparing the models.

Models are produced throughout the social sciences and business and management fields and there is little agreement on the definition of a model. A key reason for this disagreement is that models vary as to their aims, functions, modes of construction and the extent to which they are dynamic. Suffice to say here that all the facilitation models described below are simple classificatory devices. They are little more than summaries or *aides-mémoire*

Directive	Nondirective
Interpretative	Noninterpretative
Confronting	Nonconfronting
Cathartic	Noncathartic
Structuring	Unstructuring
Disclosing	Nondisclosing

Figure 6.1 Six dimensions of facilitation (Heron, 1977: 3)

which on occasion generate new insights through cross-classification. They seek to construct simplified representations of the key elements of that which is being studied, that is, they try to simplify reality so that we may understand complex reality and/or concepts more easily. Also, as Emory and Cooper (1991) note, they often represent a phenomenon by use of an analogy.

I will describe five models of facilitation: how they were developed and how they may be used by facilitators for self, peer and participant evaluation of facilitation. The first was designed by John Heron in the UK, between 1977 and 1993 (1989, 1993). The second was designed through discussion on the Internet between members of the International Association of Facilitators (IAF) and the Institute of Cultural Affairs (ICA) 1995–2000 (in the USA and across the world) (Pierce, Cheesebrow and Braun, 2000). (At the time of writing there are over 900 subscribers to this discussion group from 32 countries.) The third was designed by A Glenn Kiser and takes a more linear approach to the stages of facilitation (Kiser, 1998). The fourth was developed by Hunter, Bailey and Taylor (1999) in New Zealand and lastly I offer a personal Living Frame of Facilitation (2001).

The Heron model of facilitation styles

John Heron is a major author in the facilitation field. He developed a model of 'facilitator styles' first in 1977. His model emerged from one-to-one counselling work where a counsellor-facilitator would hierarchically choose what interventions to make with a client. His facilitation model grew out of his Six Category Intervention Analysis (Heron, 1975) for counsellors. The six dimensions for facilitators (Heron, 1977) are shown in Figure 6.1.

To begin with he saw these dimensions as types of facilitator intervention, that is, options and strategies. I will return to these issues later in Book 2, Chapter 6 when I describe facilitator choices. Heron later modified this basic bi-polar model to incorporate 18 possible styles of facilitation. He explained the catalyst for the change by e-mail:

> I think it was at a radical education workshop which I ran at the University of Surrey sometime in the mid eighties. A whole day or more of the programme was devoted to an autonomy lab, in which I was a participant along with everyone else. One of the sheets I posted at the start of the lab was about my needs to clarify facilitation issues. Several other people signed up and we had a long session sharing views and perspectives. I had for some time been aware that the bipolar model, which I had used in many training workshops and in self and peer assessment, was effective as far as it went, but that the X–non X scheme missed out too much. The broad outlines of the new scheme clarified in my mind as I was taking my turn in the autonomy lab subgroup.
>
> (Heron, 1997)

A two-dimensional model emerged incorporating 18 possible styles of facilitation (see Figure 6.2). In this model Heron adds a second dimension: that of power and how it may be allocated or distributed in a group via hierarchical, cooperative and autonomous decision modes:

- **Hierarchical mode: direction**. The facilitator directs the learning and group process and does things *for* the group. For example, s/he makes decisions about planning and objectives, interprets the meaning of key concepts, confronts resistance, manages feelings, develops structures for learning events and values participants' contributions. All these decisions are made by the facilitator.
- **Cooperative mode: negotiation**. Here the power is shared between the facilitator and the group members. The facilitator works *with* the group and ideas are shared.
- **Autonomous mode: delegation**. Here the power is shifted to the participants to take responsibility for the six dimensions: 'This does not mean abdication of responsibility. It is the subtle art of creating conditions within which people can exercise full self-determination' (Heron, 1989: 17). It may occur in one of three ways. Autonomy may be conferred by the facilitator to the group, or it may evolve by negotiations between the facilitator and the group, or it may be seized by the group (Heron, 1999).

There are many styles of facilitation that emanate from a person's personality. Some facilitators are very reflective, others more dynamic. Hunter, Bailey and Taylor state that 'As a facilitator, you will be most effective when you are being your natural self and allowing your own personality to be expressed' (1992: 72). The main thing, as Heron points out, is to be flexible:

DIMENSIONS / MODES	Planning	Meaning	Confronting	Feeling	Structuring	Valuing
Hierarchical ie direction: facilitator alone						
Cooperative ie negotiation: facilitator and participants						
Autonomous ie delegation: participants alone						

Figure 6.2 Heron's facilitation style model (1999)

at times a more reflective person may have to be dynamic and a dynamic person more reflective.

A brief explanation of Heron's interpretation of each dimension follows:

- **The planning dimension** is goal-oriented, that is, the overall aims and objectives of the group.
- **The meaning dimension** is the cognitive aspect relating to understanding concepts, making sense of experience and actions of group members.
- **The confronting dimension** is to do with raising awareness about resistance to or avoidance of issues that need to be faced and dealt with.
- **The feeling dimension** is the affective aspect of facilitation.
- **The structuring dimension** is to do with the design of experiences in a workshop.
- **The valuing dimension** is to do with creating a supportive climate that honours and celebrates each individual.

The whole system of dimensions and modes, according to Heron (1989, 1999), is linked to the level of human intention based on ethical values, norms and principles which he elaborates in his seven 'criteria of excellence' by which the competency of a facilitator may be judged:

1. **Authority**. Facilitators should be able to use 'distress-free authority' when making group interventions; ie without displacing his/her own pathology on the individual or group.
2. **Confrontation**. Facilitators can supportively confront individuals and/or the group when necessary about defensive or rigid behaviour.

3. **Orientation**. Orientation means the ability to give a clear conceptual orientation to experiential work when appropriate.
4. **Care**. Having a caring, empathic, genuine manner is important for facilitators.
5. **Range of methods**. Heron suggests that facilitators should be able to handle deep regression and catharsis and transpersonal work. He adds that a repertoire of techniques and exercises is also desirable.
6. **Respect for persons**. Facilitators must respect 'the autonomy of the individual and the right of the individual to choose when to change and grow' (1999: 340).
7. **Flexibility of intervention**. Facilitators need to be able to move within the modes and dimensions described in his model, shown in Figure 6.2.

In 1993, Heron again built on his thesis about facilitation in *Group Facilitation: Theories and Models for Practice*. In this book, Heron points to the paradox of the facilitator-teacher who has to pass on a body of knowledge and skills (which is ever changing) through processes that develop the autonomy and wholeness of learners. This is exacerbated, he argues, as we are at a watershed of two educational cultures (especially at tertiary level): one, authoritarian, is most widespread and sometimes may incorporate using oppressive forms of teacher authority, the other involves student autonomy, a freer, more holistic and integrative approach to learning.

Heron introduced the concept of three types of authority available to the facilitator-teacher: tutelary, political and charismatic. The first is *tutelary authority* of the facilitator-teacher as someone who has 'mastery of some body of knowledge and skill and of appropriate methods for passing it on, effective communication to learners through the written and spoken word and other presentations, competent care for learners and guardianship of their needs and interests' (Heron, 1993: 17).

In this role a facilitator-teacher, according to Heron, is involved in a variety of tutelary activities. These include open learning and self-pacing of material; active learning (role plays, simulations); real learning (projects, fieldwork, real case studies); peer learning (student cooperation); multi-stranded curriculum (the interconnectedness of subjects and how it relates to the student as a whole person); contract learning (students learn to plan what and how they will learn); resource consultant (the teacher is more of a resource-consultant to clarify, discuss and support); guardianship (the facilitator cares for and watches over students as a guardian, opens up new areas and reminds them of commitments and contracts).

The second is *political authority* and relates to the decisions made by the facilitator-teacher regarding the content, methods and timing of learning. The three modes are shown in Figure 6.3 (direction, negotiation and delegation), but Heron strongly advocates that facilitator-teachers involve students in a meta-discussion of the potential modes of decisions, that is, who decides who decides?

The third is *charismatic authority* or personal power: 'I do not mean by such power the ability to control and dominate others, to be a source of oppression. I mean the very opposite: the ability to be empowered by one's own inner resources, the wellspring within, and the ability thereby to elicit empowerment in others' (Heron 1993: 32). He suggests that the facilitator influences learners and the learning process by his/her presence, style and manner. He argues that facilitators can learn to centre their physical being by being 'fully present' and describes centring and charismatic exercises to develop this state. He also differentiates between two sorts of speaking time available to a facilitator, that is, 'clock time' and 'charismatic time'. In clock time speech is fast, urgent and tense; in charismatic time the facilitator uses deep, slow rhythmic speech and intentional pauses and silence. The latter is anxiety-free and may be used for setting groundrules or referring to them if broken, for handling critical incidents, for example comforting a distressed participant, or for confronting a group or a participant who breaks ground rules.

In 1993, Heron adapted his model of facilitation for teaching-learning situations as shown in Figure 6.3. In 1999 he added 'evaluation'.

In this model Heron notes the potential for involving learners in planning, devising learning methods, choosing and finding resources and the development of assessment procedures. He omits, however, the broader level of evaluation. I return to this issue in Book 2 Chapter 16.

Evaluation of Heron's model

When considering the worth of this model I should acknowledge that John Heron is a credible author, having published over 50 articles and four books on facilitation and group work. Personally, I now find his work easier to

	Objectives	Programme	Methods	Resources	Assessment	Evaluation
Hierarchy Facilitator alone						
Co-operation Facilitator and the group						
Autonomy Group alone						

Figure 6.3 Decision-modes for planning learning

Source: Heron (1999: 74)

understand, though I recall in 1990 finding the abstract language very bewildering. I have used his model with students of facilitation since 1992. Many students grapple with the model (and Heron's language) when they first read it. As a result, I have created a variety of techniques to 'bring it to life', including building a mythical story around it. Once students apply the model to their own facilitation work, in an assignment, they all show that they understand it and they can apply it to their own work.

Once internalized, Heron's model of facilitation is a useful tool to enable a facilitator to be 'transparent' with a group and indicate to participants how power is being used and/or shared in the group. The model can also be a useful aid in planning of facilitation workshops. It can also be used to show participants when they are relinquishing their own empowerment, for example when they resist taking control and attempt to give back power to the facilitator.

Heron's model invites facilitators to think about how they use and/or share power in groups whether in 'hierarchical', 'cooperative' or 'autonomous' mode. It provides a lens that facilitators may use to analyse their approaches to power sharing. Ideally facilitators should be aiming at making themselves dispensable, culminating with a group being self-directing in autonomy mode. The six dimensions of the model also challenge facilitators to investigate areas they need to develop, for example to manage feelings: their own and those of others; to confront and encourage participants to confront each other; to value participants; to plan and to structure interactive processes; and to determine how 'meaning' is made and interpreted. It gives facilitators a framework within which to examine their practice and to use when planning and structuring a workshop.

Heron's model and accompanying texts omit three emerging areas of facilitation: firstly, co-facilitation, whereby two facilitators work in close and complementary ways with a group; secondly, the issues raised when facilitating cross-cultural groups; and thirdly, technology as a tool for facilitators.

In summary, then, Heron's main contribution is a classificatory conceptual analysis of various aspects of facilitation. His approach is in the Weberian tradition of the 'ideal type' model. 'Ideal', not in the sense of morally desirable, but in directing our attention to important sets of concepts for further analysis. These are not necessarily directly research-based, although they are likely to rest on experiences. They can lead to fruitful research and practice.

Heron's explanations have a strong psychosocial orientation, with an emphasis on personal and interpersonal dynamics, and especially personal development.

A central and persistent theme in his work on facilitation has been that of power and authority, and how these are allocated and handled, both personally and within groups.

In his more recent writings (1999) he has reiterated his earlier conceptual analysis but gives greater attention to facilitation in groups, especially within teams, located within large organizations. Peer support and peer review audits are included here, along with ideas for the assessment of individual performances.

In terms of covering the area under discussion, I believe that Heron's model requires the addition of evaluation as a separate dimension, that is, to determine a sense of the 'value' or 'worth' of a workshop and its components (including the facilitator). Evaluation processes are usually generated by the facilitator, but it is useful to involve participants in the design of evaluation. Also, as evaluation is often the 'poor relation' when it comes to workshop design (ie it is often left until last), I believe it is useful to give it prominence in a model. Heron (1989) argues that it is included in the meaning dimension and in 1999 in planning dimension. However, I think adding 'evaluation' to the model would give it the attention it deserves. I believe it is a worthwhile exercise to ask participants, 'How will you know if you/we were successful?' in the planning stages, and then to revisit the questions at the end of the facilitation.

I make the distinction here between assessment and evaluation. I see assessment as subset of evaluation, a much larger concept (Kirkpatrick, 1975). Evaluation, I believe, is important and methods for measuring the 'value' or 'worth' of a programme should be devised at the planning stage to enable 'formative' as well as 'summative' and 'long-term' evaluation to take place. Also, Heron focuses on peer review of participants and self-evaluation of facilitators (according to his 18 styles and 7 criteria for excellence) but does not in his later works discuss processes nor the role of participants in evaluation of the facilitator. This is despite his attention to feedback from group members in his 1977 work.

More recently (1999), whilst retaining his earlier formulations, Heron has ventured into the realms of management, and in doing so, has devoted an appendix to the idea of 'manager as facilitator'. Along with this there is also some attention to wider issues in society. Whilst it is useful for managers to have facilitative skills as described by Quinn *et al* (1990), Heron ignores the potential conflict of interest if managers attempt to facilitate their own team meetings as illustrated by Doyle and Straus (1976) and described in Chapter 5. Essentially, however, Heron's main focus and contribution is in the analysis of styles of facilitation.

The IAF competency model of facilitation

Since 1990, the International Association of Facilitators (IAF), in conjunction with the Institute of Cultural Affairs (ICA), has orchestrated discussion across the world on Facilitator Competencies. The resulting model published by Pierce, Cheesebrow and Braun (2000) is the result of discussions at the IAF and ICA conferences in the USA and Canada, e-mail discussions and literature reviews. (See Figure 6.4.)

The purpose of the model is to formulate both what facilitators value and what they do. There is a strong emphasis on professional growth, in terms of promoting the profession, standards of practice, and assessment procedures. The model categorizes desirable skills, knowledge, and attitudes in relations to facilitation. The scope of the classification is comprehensive. For instance, it includes collaborative working with groups, participative procedures, multi-sensory learning, co-facilitation, the importance of trust, creativity, learning styles, ethics, possible misuse of group methods, the recognition and management of conflict, the relevance of cultural diversity, and the importance of considering time and space dimensions when designing facilitation procedures.

Although this model was constructed as a basis for assessing facilitator competencies, it is useful for designing academic courses in facilitation. As a checklist for facilitator workshops, it is overly complex. A similar point can be made for its general classroom use. Indeed, many new facilitators and students regard the model as quite daunting and impossible for one person to achieve all the competencies in a lifetime. Nevertheless, it is a relevant reference, which recognizes and illustrates the complexities of facilitation.

Evaluation of the IAF competency model

Pierce *et al* also suggest that the competency model could be used for some form of formal registration. The assessment of competencies is an integral part of the process of professionalization in so far as trades and professions have long used the assessment of competencies as a basis for registration. Facilitation is only now emerging as a professional discipline and the establishment of agreed-upon and assessable competencies is now becoming an urgent requirement. The issues surrounding professionalization of a discipline are discussed more fully in Chapter 11.

The model is an all-encompassing coverage of the area. It includes a section on commitment to personal growth, as does Heron (1999). But this is hardly a competency, more a desired goal. 'Competence is measured with a snapshot; professionalism is measured with video' (Schwarz, 2000: 33). Likewise a commitment to a life of integrity and participation in a facilitation network, whilst desirable, are not in themselves competencies. A section on values and beliefs that guide integrity in the facilitation role would be more appropriate. All these attributes, however, do, as Wilkinson (2000) points out, answer the question, 'What does a competent facilitator do?' A commitment to a life of integrity and participation in facilitation networks are values and activities which support the achievement and ongoing development of facilitator competencies.

Figure 6.4 Facilitator competency model of facilitation

Source: Pierce, Cheesebrow and Braun (2000: 26)

A **Engage in professional growth**	B **Create collaborative partnerships**	C **Create an environment of participation**	D **Utilize multi-sensory approaches**	E **Orchestrate the group journey**	F **Commit to a life of integrity**
1. Maintain a base of knowledge • Knowledgeable in management, organizational systems and development, group development, psychology, and training • Understand dynamics of change • Understand learning theory	1. Develop working partnerships with those served • Identify authentic client needs • Clarify mutual commitment • Promote the value and use of facilitation	1. Demonstrate effective interpersonal communication skills • Demonstrate effective verbal communication skills • Develop rapport with participants • Practise active listening • Demonstrate ability to observe and provide feedback to participants	1. Evoke group creativity, blending all learning and thinking styles • Be aware of individual learning/thinking styles • Communicate with all styles • Draw out participants of all styles • Encourage creative thinking • Accept all ideas	1. Guide the group with clear methods and processes • Establish clear context • Apply a variety of participatory processes • Manage small and large group process • Know consequences of misuse of group methods	1. Ask the depth questions of oneself and others • Uncover the profound insights of a group • Articulate one's own life purpose • Elicit root issues
2. Contrast facilitation methods • Know a range of processes • Distinguish process from task and content	2. Create and maintain professional collegial relationships • Design services cooperatively • Demonstrate team values and processes	2. Honour and recognize diversity, ensuring inclusiveness • Encourage positive regard for the experience and perception	2. Employ multi-sensory processes • Assess group sensory needs and abilities • Select from a wide variety of sensory approaches	2. Facilitate group self-awareness • Keep the group moving • Recognize tangents and redirect to the task • Listen, question and summarize	2. Model profound affirmation • Articulate the possibility of transformation in all situations • Approach situations with self-

A Engage in professional growth	B Create collaborative partnerships	C Create an environment of participation	D Utilize multi-sensory approaches	E Orchestrate the group journey	F Commit to a life of integrity
	• Support co-facilitation during delivery of service	of all participants • Create a climate of safety and trust • Bring forth the diversity of the group • Know the impact of culture	• Use approaches that best fit needs and abilities of the group • Awaken group energy	to elicit the sense of the group • Assist the group in reflection on its experience	confidence and an affirmative attitude • Model professional boundaries and ethics, eg confidentiality
3. Maintain professional standing • Engage in ongoing study • Practice reflection and learning • Participate in a facilitation network or organization	3. Co-design and customize applications to meet client needs • Design customized constructs • Define a quality product • Assess/evaluate client satisfaction	3. Facilitate group conflict • Recognize conflict • Provide safe environment for conflict to surface • Manage disruptive group behaviour • Mediate conflict	3. Use time and space to support group process • Arrange space to meet the purpose of the meeting • Plan and monitor effective use of time • Know when to move the group and when to stay • Manage symbolic aspects of meetings	3. Guide the group to consensus and desired outcomes • Know a variety of approaches to meet group objectives • Adapt processes to changing situations • Assess and communicate group process • Assist with task completion	3. Trust group's potential and model neutrality • Honour the wisdom of the group • Encourage trust in the capacity and experience of others • Set aside personal opinions • Maintain an objective, non-defensive, non-judgmental stance

The ability to select the most appropriate method to suit client needs is desirable yet there is little rigorous research which would enable facilitators to make such an informed decision. Mongeau and Morr (1999) compared brainstorming, nominal group technique and brainwriting in face-to-face and electronic settings, but highlights the need for further research into the outputs of different techniques and the social benefits of a group interacting together versus individuals generating ideas alone. Bookshops abound with collations of icebreakers, games, role-plays and simulations for facilitators but few offer evaluations of these tools. Clearly there is need for further research into the comparison and results of facilitative tools and techniques.

The IAF model advocates care and respect for the client in addressing disruptive behaviour, but as illustrated in the Flores and Smith case studies there is little agreed-upon specific behaviours within the profession. As such, it would be interesting to find out if the examining board of the IAF would 'pass' such facilitative behaviours.

One missing competency is the ability to reflect on practice and identify gaps between espoused value/beliefs and facilitative actions. Accreditation alone will not ensure professional behaviour throughout a career. Also missing is a section on the integrity of sharing valid, but negative, information which may not affirm the client and may indicate difficulties for the client and/or the facilitator (Schwarz, 2000: 33).

Despite the comments made above, the competency model does serve as a significant tool for curriculum design, self-development and the furthering of the facilitation profession.

The Kiser masterful model of facilitation

Kiser (1998) presents a very different model of facilitation, taking a more linear, time-oriented approach; his model is a variant of an action research design. Objectives are clarified and decided upon prior to the facilitative intervention. After the intervention, the actual outcomes are evaluated against the specific goals. Like many action research models, there is a feedback loop in the design where consideration of results is fed back to clarify objectives in a continuing investigative process.

Kiser's model draws attention to the fact that different functions are allocated to different stages of the process, of which facilitating a group is but a part. (However, a facilitator actually starts facilitating during the first negotiating meetings with a client.) The five-phase typology shown in Figure 6.5 is described below.

Although not exclusively so, Kiser's main focus is on working with groups or teams within larger organizations. As such, he gives considerable attention to the organizational context within which group facilitation is to take place. When discussing actual facilitation, he provides many useful

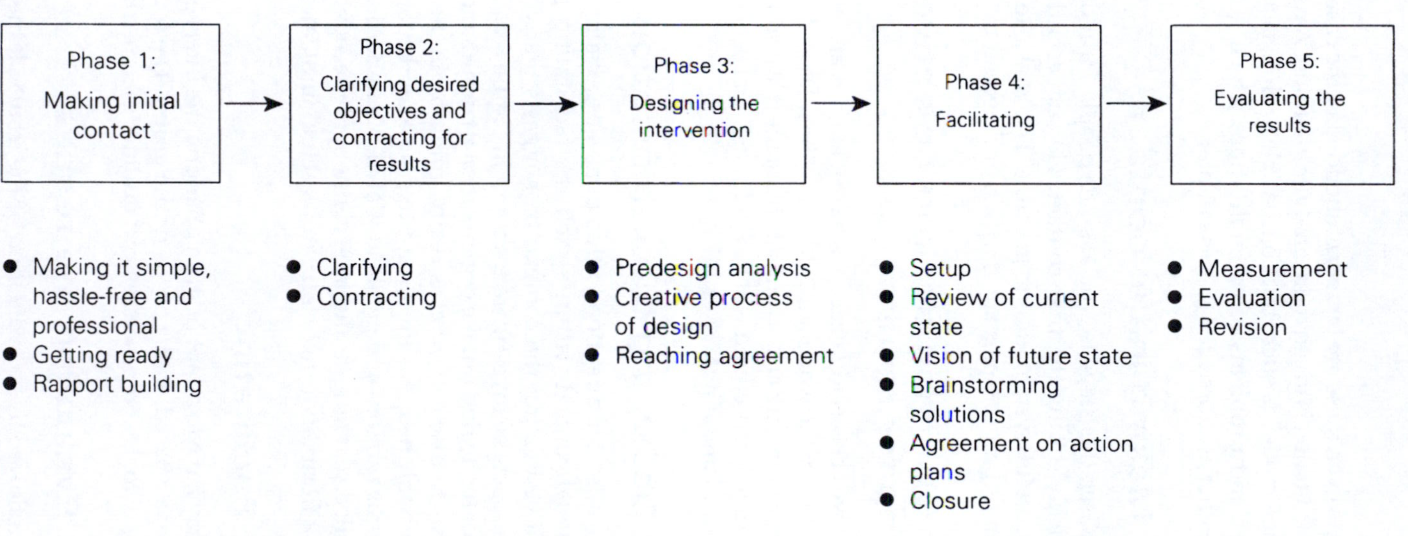

Figure 6.5 The masterful facilitation model

Source: Kiser (1998: 29)

suggestions; however, these are largely embedded in the case material. The evaluation of facilitation is given more analytic attention. A useful addition, not built into the model as such, but compatible with it, is a discussion of the advantages and problems of co-facilitation, which gets little or no mention from other authors cited in this chapter.

Phase 1: Making initial contact

According to Kiser, this stage is crucial since people form opinions about facilitators quickly during the first contact. He suggests that facilitators should be purposeful, systematic and genuine. The goal is to build rapport with the person or group. Goals are clarified and agreed upon.

Phase 2: Clarifying desired objectives and contracting for results

This stage involves clarifying exactly what outcomes are wanted, that is, what is the purpose of the workshop? What are the roles and responsibilities of the facilitator, organizers and so on? At this stage it is important to decide how the facilitative intervention will be evaluated, that is, were the desired outcomes achieved and if not why not?

Phase 3: Designing the intervention

Kiser gives considerable attention to this phase, especially to finding out the organizational context within which the facilitating group will be operating. In investigating the context, he suggests that where possible, the following aspects be investigated, shown in Figure 6.6.

The facilitator has to find out the organizational context and then conduct a needs analysis to discover what is really going on in the group. When that has been established, it is important to plan a workshop (if that is the most suitable intervention) and get it circulated. He underlines the importance of a detailed planning of the intervention. He recognizes, however, that a degree of flexibility is necessary in its actual implementation.

Phase 4: Facilitating

A facilitator may have to adapt or even abandon the intervention strategy planned in Phase 3 based on the needs of the group. The facilitator makes use of a variety of tools and processes and outlines their use in case studies.

Phase 5: Evaluating the results

Facilitation is followed by an evaluation of the results. If the facilitator did a thorough job at the clarifying stage, the evaluation should be straightforward and may lead to a further clarification of objectives for the next workshop. (Indeed evaluation should also be discussed at the planning stage.) Evaluation is regarded as integral to the facilitation process. Kiser suggests a number of criteria, namely:

- Evaluating the effectiveness of the facilitation activity through comparing outcomes and objectives.
- Evaluating the process of facilitation itself, that is, how well it was done.
- Improved interpersonal relationships. Did relationships improve during facilitation?
- 'Self-sufficiency', that is, to what extent are the participants no longer dependent on the facilitator?
- 'Masterful facilitation', that is, masterful here refers to professional skill. In assessing this, Kiser refers to two components: firstly, client satisfaction, and secondly, facilitator competence. He uses the facilitator's own assessments as well as those of others.

Kiser's model is based on the standard teaching model from needs analysis to evaluation. I will return to this issue in Chapters 10 and 13 where I discuss ethical issues of facilitation.

Evaluation of the Kiser masterful facilitation model

Kiser provides a useful linear, time-oriented model. Its advantage is its apparent simplicity. It views facilitation as an adaptable process in which

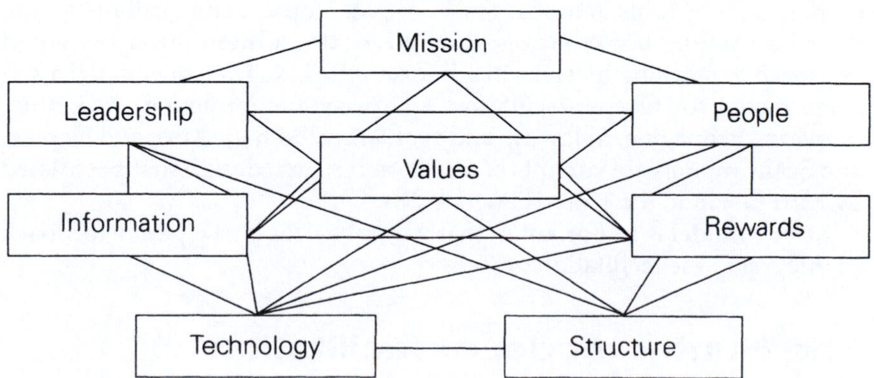

Figure 6.6 Organizational processes to consider when designing an intervention

Source: Kiser (1998: 57)

preliminary planning, clarification of objectives, feedback and evaluation are integral. It provides a useful overview. In content, greater attention to the complexities of facilitating itself (Phase 4) would have been an advantage.

During Kiser's first phase (illustrated above) in which he describes making contact and building rapport with clients, I would add the need for a greater appreciation of context. Also in Phase 3 a short history of the organization and/or department in question may be desirable. To Kiser's credit, organizational context is taken into account in Phase 3 in designing the appropriate strategies for intervention. However, placing contextual investigation earlier can clarify whether the facilitation project should take place at all. Kiser omits to describe the choices that facilitators and clients have, that is, to go ahead or not depending on their values and/or the level of skills and needs of the client and the nature of the job in hand. A 'no go' choice should always be an option for both facilitators and clients. To leave it until later can cause disappointments.

Kiser describes several forms of evaluation, but the concept needs further elaboration. I believe evaluation is far too important to be left until the end of facilitation or teaching processes. At the contracting phase facilitators need to build in opportunities for self and other evaluation, formative evaluation (from participants, for example, after the first day of a long programme), summative evaluation (at the end of the programme) (Scriven, 1967) and long-term evaluation (after say six months). I will return to this issue in Chapter 11 where I discuss ethical issues of facilitation.

It appears somewhat unfortunate in today's gender-sensitive climate that Kiser uses the term 'masterful' to describe his model. However, it appears he was using the term in the sense of the Medieval guilds and Master craftsmen. I am surprised that Kiser makes no reference to preceding models on which his is based. For example, Hopson and Scally (1981) in their best-selling books successfully advocated a more group-oriented approach to teaching lifeskills in schools in the UK. They developed a six-stage model for teacher-facilitators comprising: contracting, designing, preparing, managing, follow-up and evaluating. Both the Kiser and Hopson and Scally models are variants of an action research design first postulated by Kurt Lewin in the 1940s (Lewin, 1958).

Kiser's model is important in that it emphasizes participative feedback as integral to the facilitation process.

The Hunter model of facilitation

Hunter, Bailey and Taylor (1999) in New Zealand developed a model to illustrate the essence of facilitation, distinguishing between purpose (ie direction) and culture (ie process). It takes into account the internal and external context. The triangle represents the links between facilitating self, one to one and one to group. The apex of the triangle (Figure 6.7) is the facilitator's role to help the group to achieve its purpose, which is often neglected. Hunter *et al* emphasize the need for facilitators to focus on purpose at pre-planning meetings, at the beginning/middle of workshops and to make use interventions during workshops such as:

- Where are we?
- Where do we go from here?
- Why are we here?
- What results are we here to achieve?

Personally, I prefer to use 'you' rather than 'we', ie 'Where are you?', to verbally reinforce the divide between the facilitator and the group and to ensure that the facilitator stays out of content all the time. Hunter *et al's* emphasis to get the group to put its purpose in its own words is a useful tool to focus the group.

The model addresses the need for facilitators to ask questions related to culture setting (ie contracting for desirable group norms or behavioural rules).

Evaluation of the Hunter model of facilitation

The Hunter *et al* model is clear and simple, easy to recall and therefore to use in practice. A facilitator who is unsure of what is happening in a group could utilize the model for self-facilitation or with the group to analyse

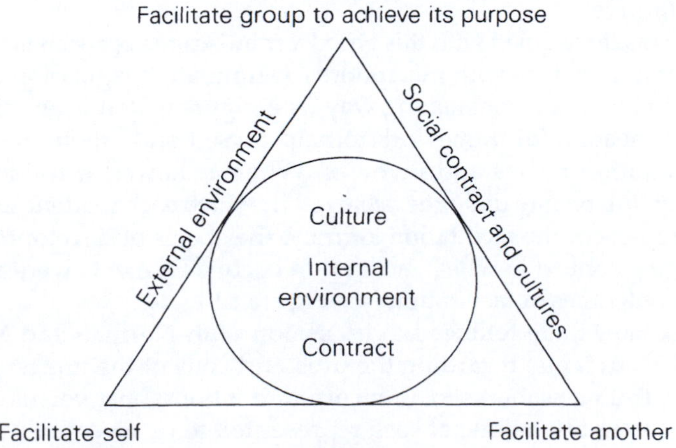

Figure 6.7 The Hunter *et al* model of facilitation

Source: Hunter, Bailey and Taylor (1999: 18)

what is happening. Hunter *et al* emphasize the need to make distinctions between purpose and culture. Their model takes into account the formal and informal influences of the external environment which impact on us as citizens from different cultures and organizations.

The base of the triangle, ie 'facilitate self' and 'facilitate another', may also represent co-facilitators (see Chapter 7).

The four books by Hunter, Bailey and Taylor (1999, 1992, 1993, 1997) have made a significant contribution to simplifying and demystifying facilitation. Dale Hunter is currently completing a PhD on facilitation ethics.

The Hogan living frame of facilitation

I developed a working/living frame of reference which is useful in directing attention to what I regard as important dimensions in facilitation. Initially I drew the model as a system of boxes (see Figure 6.8), to direct attention to relevant categories. In trying to indicate the linkages between the boxes, the two-dimensional nature of these interactions made the diagram of less use than I had hoped. I then changed the title to a 'living frame' since it is my frame or lens of my practice of facilitation at this stage of my career. The concept was to create a framework to enhance self-sustaining, self-regulatory, facilitation.

Because the dynamic interactions are difficult to portray without a great deal of verbal description, it meant that this representation was not adequate for my purposes, although it helped clarify those issues which should be included. To me a box-type representation looks more 'final', more 'definitive'.

Since I was dissatisfied with this I tried a mindscape approach (Margulies, 1992), that is, a picture with metaphors to stimulate imagination and self-examination in a non-threatening way (see Figure 6.9). It is an attempt to develop a meaningful framework to help myself and others understand what facilitation means and involves. When I showed it to facilitation students an interesting dialogue occurred in which each student suggested ways to represent the facilitation journey, the stages of development and the changing context in which facilitation occurs. Elements were added to show the outcomes of facilitation (see Figure 6.9).

A week later there followed a discussion with Norman and Margaret (facilitation students) regarding the pros and cons of the imagery for the facilitator: from a seahorse to a unicorn and a houseboat versus a sailing yacht versus an ark and what each represented to us. Eventually I settled on the metaphor of the ark/houseboat as a stable boat and long-standing 'archetype' of stability successfully riding the storms of nature.

So what was happening here? I have always loved the idea of serendipity and here, I believe, is a good illustration of it. Students and colleagues were

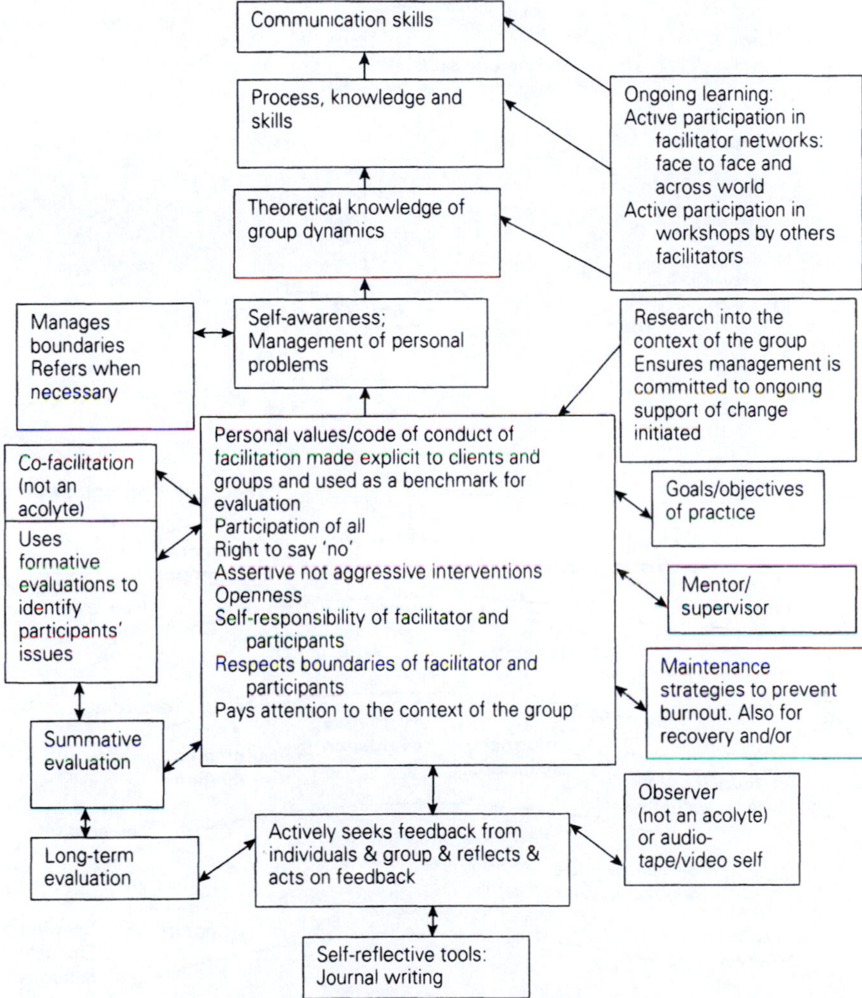

Figure 6.8 Model in progress, since discarded

excited and talked freely about the model and what it triggered for them. I was getting very different responses from facilitation students. Normally when I ask them to critique models I sense a reticence from some, perhaps due to reverence and awe, 'Who are we to critique this?', and a lack of confidence, 'What do I know compared to him/her?'. Because I showed it to them in a raw form, as a hand-drawn diagram, they perceived it as an open-ended and potentially creative task and responded in an enthusiastic manner. Inadvertently, the framework had become user-friendly and

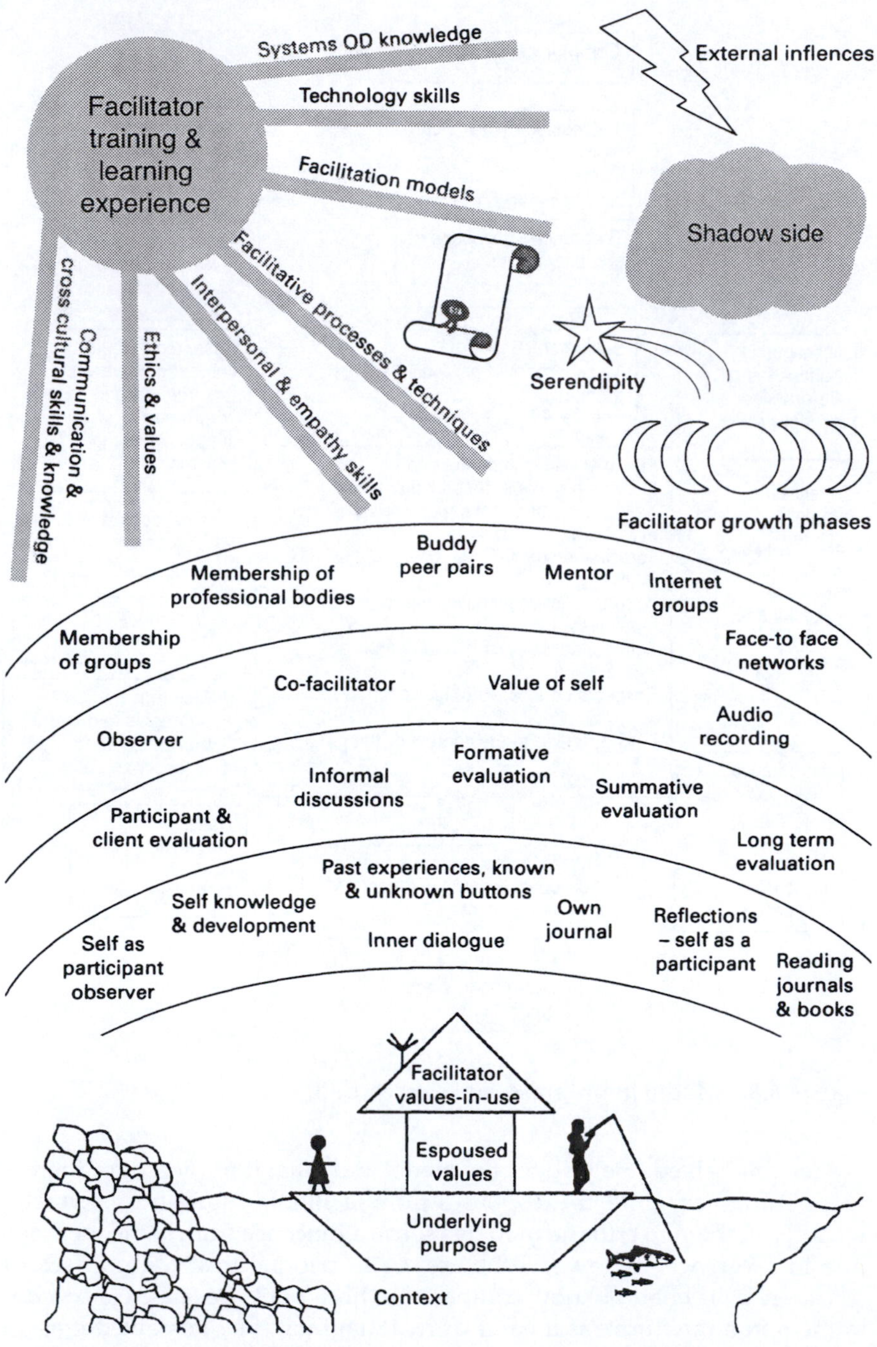

Figure 6.9 A living frame of facilitation

playful and others had become drawn into its construction. I realized I had more chances of getting students of facilitation to draw their own frameworks of facilitation if I showed them my unfinished version rather than a highly polished, professionally drawn version. What I realized was that I had inadvertently developed a partly projective technique of getting students directly involved and committed in model making, thereby demystifying the process. It also helped students to elicit, confront and think about issues of relevance in facilitation.

Later, I added more detail to the model, for example an aerial sticking out of the boat to represent technology (which I expanded into a separate model because of its complexity), and a certificate to represent education and training in facilitation.

My interpretation of the framework

People use and interpret this framework in different ways; however, below I will give some illustrations of how I interpret the model's iconography.

The facilitator in the boat is fishing, representing the need to keep a balance in life. There is another person in the boat, representing a co-facilitator or critical friend or supervisor.

External influences may be positive and/or negative. They may come from the past or from the immediate context, or be worldwide trends or a mix of all of these. The lightning of serendipity, that is, positive unusual combinations or unexpected events (and negative surprises) indicates the need for facilitators to be able to utilize such comets positively.

The sea of context may be calm and positive or rough and negative, representing the cultural, societal and organizational contexts in which the facilitation takes place. The waters may contain fish, mermaids and sea horses that represent the varieties of friendly supports, critical friends and mentors. But there also may be snakes, crocodiles and sharks to watch out for. There are islands of different shapes, climates and cultures that the facilitator may visit in order to work with the inhabitants. Before docking at each, the facilitator needs to investigate the environment carefully, and on arrival needs to listen and to watch carefully.

The design of the ark/houseboat will vary according to the facilitator's current culture and/or *cultural background, gender and experiences*. The foundations of the ark represent *the facilitator's 'higher purpose'*, his/her deep-seated rationale for facilitating (Hunter, Bailey and Taylor, 1999). The more aware he/she is of these, the deeper the hull and the more stable the boat. The houseboat itself includes the *facilitator's 'espoused theories' or values* (Argyris, 1990; Argyris and Schön 1994). These may differ from one facilitator to another according to his/her facilitation styles (but there are some 'common values' as exemplified in the Declaration of Human Rights). These 'espoused theories'/values should be made explicit for clients when they are deciding whether or not to recruit the services of the facilitator *and* when evaluating services. (See also Chapter 11 for further discussion on values and ethics.)

The roof of the houseboat represents the *facilitator's 'theory in action'*, that is, how the facilitator behaves under pressure and the gaps between what he/she espouses and what happens in practice. The aerial protruding from the roof of the ark represents the many *applications of technology* for facilitators. The facilitator is holding a fishing line, representing ways of gaining *nurturance* from the seas around and the occasional *recreational breaks* when the facilitator needs to put up a metaphorical sign 'Gone Fishing'. Facilitators, like counsellors, need a variety of activities outside their work to enable them to maintain equilibrium and recharge energies. There is a certificate, which represents formal course learning and/or accreditation, that is, symbols of the *professionalization of facilitation*. There is another figure in the boat who could represent either a *co-facilitator or a mentor*.

The islands represent the *various groups* that the facilitator works with in different cultures, climates, latitudes, longitudes, elevations and depths. Some islands have welcoming harbours, others do not. The *rainbow* represents the need for *life-long reflexivity*. The layers of the rainbow are like different coloured mirrors that are held up in front of us: *self knowledge and development and ways of monitoring our learning;* participation and client evaluations; co-facilitator and/or observers (not acolytes) and lastly feedback from facilitator groups: buddies, mentors, face-to-face support groups, Internet groups and professional bodies. All these contribute to our work as facilitators.

The *sun and its rays* represent *life-long learning about facilitation*: awareness of ethics and values, communication and cross-cultural skills and knowledge; interpersonal and empathy skills; facilitative processes and techniques, models; knowledge of organizational systems, development and change.

The *facilitator growth phases* are represented by the cycles of the moon, though they are more erratic than the regular waxing and waning of the moon, indicating the stages in the development of a facilitator. The cloud represents our *shadow side*. The cloud can grow and cover the sun if we are not careful. It links to the bottom band of the rainbow and continuing self-development.

Application of the framework

How may the model be used? Is the framework viable? Models vary and are designed to do a diversity of things. Does it aid understanding? Does it add anything to an understanding of facilitation? Is a framework useful? In order to give some illustrations of how I use the model I will refer briefly to a case study described in Chapter 11 describing the work of Fernando Flores.

Flores in the hull of his 'boat' espouses his *raison d'être* as having 'had enough of the bullshit'. He advocates that talk is the source of executives' failures and promotes 'speech acts', blunt language rituals that he says build trust. I believe his 'values-in-use' are different to his 'espoused values'. He espouses that absolute openness develops trust without thinking about the *degrees* of openness and *how and where* open messages are best given. He appears not to listen to feedback: 'Tell my critics, I am not dangerous enough.' He seems to be playing games. He invokes the rainbow and invites feedback from participants in front of their peers, 'Tomas stand up and tell me honestly what you think of me. This is how you develop trust.' Then he pretends to accept the feedback according to his formal 'Thank you very much for your assessment, Tomas, I appreciate your sincerity. Now here is my assessment of you. You are an arsehole...' He rejects participants' thoughts and scares them into submission to his ways of giving and receiving feedback whether they like it or not. Thus they have no choice, a most de-powering place to be in. He also coerces participants to do things his way: 'If you agree to be trained and don't follow my lead, I will kill you.' This is not facilitation, this is bullying.

Evaluation of the living framework

The living frame of facilitation provides an alternative way of illustrating the complexities of facilitation. The use of visual imagery and colour will be of particular interest to people who are visual learners, but also because people generally are now far more used to sending and receiving information through pictures through the use of computer graphics programs like PowerPoint and Sketch (Horn, 1998: 56).

Like the other models, the individual items need further elaboration; it is a summary of ideas. As it is in a different format to the other models produced to date it is also memorable. Research by Margulies (1992) pointed out that mindscapes are memorable.

The model does not include a time dimension apart from the waxing and waning of the moon to illustrate the development stages of a facilitator who may experience cycles of growth and energies. However, context is given attention with the different islands, lightning and serendipity.

Comparison of models

Like theories, models summarize and direct our attention to aspects regarded as important. One can ask many questions in order to understand the purpose and potential uses of models. All the models described above enable us to understand the phenomenon of facilitation more easily, but none 'map the territory' completely. They each provide different lenses with

Table 6.1 Comparison of facilitation models

Model	*Author/s Date/place*	*Type of model*	*What does the model summarize?*	*What are its main emphases?*	*What are its main uses?*
1. Facilitator styles model	Heron 1977–2000 UK/Italy (Heron, 1989,1993, 1977, 1999)	Classificatory grid	● Three modes and six dimensions of facilitation ● Personal development	● Power & authority ● Personal development ● Facilitator styles ● Politics of learning	● Self and peer assessment ● Aid for planning workshops ● Teaching ● Facilitator checklist of 18 possible facilitator style/s
2. Facilitator competency model	International Association of Facilitators (IAF), Institute of Cultural Affairs (ICA), USA. E-mail discussions 1996–98. (Pierce, Cheesebrow and Braun, 2000)	Classificatory grid	Desirable knowledge, skills, attitudes of facilitators	● Professional growth ● Growth of facilitation profession ● Multi-sensory learning ● Conflict ● Diversity ● Ethics and values	● Competencies as a basis for formal registration for the profession ● Course construction ● Assessment design ● Facilitator selection

Model	*Author/s Date/place*	*Type of model*	*What does the model summarize?*	*What are its main emphases?*	*What are its main uses?*
3. The masterful facilitation model	(Kiser, 1998) USA. Based on teaching model by (Hopson and Scally, 1981) and action research by (Lewin, 1958)	Linear, time stage model	Stages in the facilitation process	● Planning initial contact ● Clarifying objectives ● Facilitation is part of a process ● Evaluation	Aid for new facilitators/ consultants in that it simplifies complex stages
4. A model of facilitation	(Hunter, Bailey and Taylor, 1999)	Simple geometric representation of essence of facilitation	Three possible areas to facilitate: self, one to one and one to group. Group purpose	Need to align internal culture and external context and the group purpose The relationship between the end and the means	To enable facilitators to distinguish between the various aspects of what they are doing with a group
5. Living frame of facilitation	Hogan (2001), Australia	Pictorial, mindscape A model representing one person's frame of facilitation at one point in time	Items regarded as important in facilitation & for the training of and learning by facilitators Does not include time and space except the growth phases of a facilitator	● Facilitation skills ● Self knowledge ● Group supports ● Personal development ● Ethics and values ● Ongoing evaluation ● Technologies ● Context ● Cross-cultural issues	For teaching facilitation and personal evaluation – an *aide mémoire*

which we may view facilitation or parts thereof. They all challenge our thinking about the topic in varying degrees and therefore have potential to have an impact on practice. Table 6.1 includes a summary as a basis for comparing the models.

A comparison of the models of facilitation and technology appears in Chapter 10.

Conclusion

In this chapter I have briefly illuminated four models of facilitation and the background of their development. All the models described above help to make the more covert roles of a facilitator explicit.

The Heron model is power-based. The IAF model is competency-based and indicates the breadth and depth of skills and knowledge perceived to be important for a facilitator and for the professionalization of the facilitation field. The Kiser model is stage-based, although the label of 'masterful' for his model indicates an underlying power base, whether explicit or implicit. In today's world we are becoming far more attuned to the gender issues raised in language usage and the title 'masterful' facilitation might also be called into question. The Hunter *et al* Model of Facilitation emphasizes the 'essence of facilitation' and that facilitators need to distinguish between the group's purpose, internal and external context. The Hogan Living Framework offers a personal view of facilitation at the time of writing. I encourage you to map your own mental frameworks of facilitation.

The future is hard and impossible to predict as the speed of technological change is still showing signs of speeding up. Suffice to say facilitators have always embraced varying types of technology as a significant tool in their profession. See Chapter 10 for discussion and models of facilitation and technology.

7

Definitions of co-facilitation

Introduction

This chapter was written by Marie Martin, a long-term friend and colleague whose facilitation work I have greatly admired over the years. She has kindly summarized below some of the results of her current PhD research with a variety of co-facilitators. I am indebted to her for the following contribution to this book.

The chapter covers definitions, requirements and outcomes of co-facilitation. There are tips to help maximize the benefits and minimize the disadvantages. Based on discussion with co-facilitators, there are models of different types of co-facilitation relationships and a discussion of the stages of co-facilitation. The chapter finishes with suggestions for co-facilitators of ways of working with each other and the group and discussion of the contribution that co-facilitation has for the profession as a whole.

Definitions of co-facilitation

So what is co-facilitation, how does co-facilitation work and what does it have to offer? Knight and Scott (1997: 11) devised the following definition of co-facilitation:

> Two or more facilitators working *in partnership* to enable a *group and its individual members* to reach an agreed outcome in a way that *maximizes* their own and others' *learning*, through the *active involvement* of all (authors' italics).

This is an inclusive definition. It includes many people in different settings: teachers or teachers and assistants working with children, mediators working with contesting parties to resolve conflicts, therapists working in group psychodrama or with support groups, leaders working with teams, managers working with employees in a department or agency, counsellors working with families, directors working with actors to perform a play or facilitators supporting group decision making. The definition does not limit the kind of partnership that will be undertaken and whether all roles will be equally shared. It identifies the need for a group comprised of individuals, but does not specify a disciplinary area. It focuses on an agreed outcome, but does not specify whether that outcome is a decision, a process, a set of minutes, an advertisement, a business plan, a project or a performance. It requires learning for all involved, but does not describe whether that learning will be in knowledge, skills or attitudes. Lastly, it invites activity from all involved, but does not specify what kind of activity or equal levels of activity. The advantage of such a broad definition is that it allows all of these people, in all of these settings, to rethink their relationship in terms of 'co-facilitation' and at the heart of this is 'facilitation' with all of the complexity previously described. It also focuses on the additional complexity of relationships, partnerships, working together and with the group and achieving outcomes for all.

Fundamentally, the difference between facilitation and co-facilitation is the addition of another co-facilitator or co-facilitators. It is a *relationship* between *two or more people* working with a group *to facilitate a group* process, product, project or performance. Like facilitation, co-facilitation focuses on the group. Co-facilitation, however, is about making things easier for the group *and the facilitators*.

Requirements for co-facilitation

Co-facilitation assumes that each co-facilitator is competent as a facilitator. Therefore, each individual facilitator needs to be:

- effective in using core methods;
- able to manage relationships with the group;
- thoroughly prepared;
- able to use time and space intentionally;
- able to evoke participation and creativity;
- practised in honouring the group and affirming its wisdom;
- capable of maintaining objectivity;
- skilled in reading the underlying dynamics of the group;
- able to develop rapport and orchestrate or choreograph processes;
- able to keep people helpfully focused on the topic and issue;
- able to adapt to the changing situation;
- responsible for the group journey;
- able to produce powerful documentation of the group's insights;
- professional, self-confident and authentic;
- reliable and honest. (Stanfield, 2001)

In addition, co-facilitation requires other competencies, including:

- developing and maintaining a relationship with the co-facilitator;
- supporting the co-facilitator's relationship with the group;
- developing and maintaining a relationship with individual members of the group in the presence of another co-facilitator;
- coping with the additional scrutiny of another skilled peer.

When co-facilitation works, it achieves the goals of making things easier for the group and easier for the facilitators. When it doesn't work very well it makes things harder for the group or harder for the facilitators. Unfortunately there are also times when co-facilitation makes things harder for the group and harder for the facilitators. In this chapter I will explore some of the layers of co-facilitation and discuss ways of supporting co-facilitators in making things 'easier and easier'.

Choosing co-facilitation

Co-facilitation is often chosen as an alternative to solo facilitation when the complexity of the problem, the long-term needs for skill or knowledge development, the number of people involved, and/or the length of time required suggest that the process will be difficult for one facilitator to manage alone. In these complex and potentially difficult situations, facilitators need to work together to ensure that they 'make things easier' for the group and for themselves.

A CO-FACILITATION STORY: EASIER AND HARDER

Co-facilitating is different from facilitating. When it works it's easier and harder. I don't have to do everything, I can rely on my co-facilitator to do some stuff and there's less pressure. So it's easier. The harder part is that while having a focus on the group, part of my focus has to be on my co-facilitator. It's like an L-shape. Here I am at the join, and there's the clients, customers, whatever, and here's the co-facilitator.

If it doesn't work it's just harder and harder. If it doesn't work it's terrible. It's like there's a block here, or there's some sort of struggle going on, and I feel tighter, and it doesn't work.

So how is that different to solo facilitation? As a solo facilitator I have to rely more on myself. At every single level, at every single minute, I'm relying on myself. If I work with a co-facilitator it's easier because it's shared. Even if it's a total disaster, some of it is shared. Whereas if I did it completely on my own and it's a disaster, I wear all of that.

The outcomes of co-facilitation: easier or harder?

Co-facilitation can make things both easier and harder for facilitators, groups, participants, the organizations and communities they work with and the facilitation profession.

Making things easier for the facilitators

From a common-sense point of view it is reasonable that co-facilitation can make things easier for the facilitators. The task of facilitation is difficult and complex and sharing that complexity should alleviate some of the difficulties.

Co-facilitation can enable less skilled facilitators to gain knowledge and experience by working with skilled facilitators. It can also support the personal and professional development of skilled facilitators, particularly when co-facilitators experience the synergistic feeling of adding to their own, each other's and the group's experience. Through observing other ways of working and by trying different strategies with the support of another facilitator, co-facilitators can increase their skills and experience.

Co-facilitation can combine the skills, insights and talents of people with different strengths, knowledge, skills and personalities which can increase creativity through the professional exchange of ideas and strategies. Sharing the workload can also avoid the sense of isolation that facilitators can experience when they are working alone.

Co-facilitation can help facilitators to stay objective and reduce their need to respond, rescue or intervene in the group process. It can help to reduce the risk of facilitator burnout by sharing the responsibility for attending and responding to the issues and thinking of appropriate responses. Co-facilitators may be better able to monitor and facilitate group development because there are more minds addressing issues and problems, and there can be a greater awareness of the group process as well as individual dynamics.

Co-facilitation can enable facilitators to identify the best person to intervene in a situation according to their skills, relationship with the group and individuals, gender, theoretical background and experience. It is possible to address simultaneous issues and increases the capacity to work with complex issues. Co-facilitation can also enable one facilitator to work with one or two 'emotional' people while the other facilitator continues working with the whole group, maintaining the focus on the issues or task.

Co-facilitation can reduce self-induced pressure to perform and relieve the intensity of coping with group members' difficulties. Opportunities for rest periods can be made, especially if a difficult intervention suddenly leaves one facilitator tired or even drained and in need of 'space'.

Co-facilitators may be able to use each other as a sounding board, helping each other to analyse the group process and determine appropriate interventions. Supported reflection on a session can help co-facilitators to challenge each other's point of view and to uncover biases and assumptions.

Making things easier for the group

For the group, there may be advantages in co-facilitation. They have two people with whom they can relate, enabling then to match their needs with the person whose background, gender, age, skills, experiences, background or personality most complements theirs. Facilitators have their own pace and style, which can support or focus the group on the topic and help to sustain the energy of the group. There is often a sharper focus on issues because there are two viewpoints. Co-facilitation can enable a group to continue to focus on the work needing to be done if one facilitator needs to leave the group.

Having two or more facilitators can help to reduce or dissipate individual participants' responses to authority figures and reduce dependency.

Co-facilitation can model different leadership styles, appropriate interpersonal behaviours and ways of resolving conflict. Pfeiffer and Jones (1975) even suggest that there is an increased likelihood that skills learnt in a group session may be transferred into the real-life situation of group participants' daily lives because they are more 'true to life'.

Making things harder for the facilitators

In each of the above beneficial examples, I have used words such as 'can' and 'may'. Co-facilitation is not always a positive experience for the facilitators or for the group. Spinks and Clements (1983: 156) actually 'strongly recommend that [people] do not actually facilitate together, in the sense that you share the leading of a discussion or share the responsibility of guiding the group through the process at a given point'.

As in any shared task, one or both facilitators can feel that the workload is unequally distributed. This can be due to factors such as different response times, different theoretical perspectives, different technical expertise, different personalities or different styles or orientations in working with a group. There may also be a perception that there is less of a need to be committed to achieving the group goals and purposes because the responsibility is shared (social loafing).

Co-facilitation requires maintaining energy for each other as well as the group. Co-facilitators need to be careful not to cut across or undermine the other facilitator's interventions. There is the potential for disagreement over topics, structure and applications. Co-facilitators may be unwilling to confront or challenge each other, so that instead of getting the best from each other, weaknesses are sustained.

Co-facilitation may also be touted as a 'quicker' way of facilitating a group process. This is simply not true. It takes much longer to plan a group process because different perspectives and approaches need to be blended. The implementation of the process takes just as long as in individual facilitation, and possibly longer if there are different perspectives to be presented. Finally, the reflection and debrief following the process require additional time in order to evaluate the group process and the working relationship.

Making things harder for the group

Co-facilitators may reinforce each other's assumptions, leading to a lack of responsiveness to the group and a support of each other's blind spots. They can vie with each other for the attention of the group or stifle group participation and learning by intervening too much.

Groups may perceive the need for two facilitators negatively, as an indication that 'this is a big problem' or 'we are a difficult group'. It is also easier for groups to receive conflicting messages when two people are delivering information or guiding a process.

Particularly when the co-facilitators are not working well together, a group may see poor or ineffective modelling of communication, negotiation and conflict resolution which may reinforce existing communication patterns. Poor co-facilitation may impact on the effectiveness of the group facilitation process.

Making things easier (or harder) for the organization or community contracting the facilitation

An organization or community may elect to have a process co-facilitated for many reasons. Co-facilitation is a way of training employees and developing their organizational knowledge and skills. It can enable people to develop specific facilitation skills, also building the skills of the organization or community.

Co-facilitation can support the development of a product, programme or project since there are two or more perspectives and two or more reviewers. Co-facilitators are able to arrange for one person to take notes about the effective and ineffective aspects of the programme, the group responses and the outcomes achieved while the other delivers the programme, guides the process or develops the project. The organization or community benefits from a more robust programme that has been more thoroughly reviewed.

Co-facilitation can provide a collegial team that provides new challenges for employees or citizens, develop a team to act as a model for other teams, develop mentoring skills to enable members of the team to support members of other teams, or initiate change in one area that attracts attention from other areas. For the organization or community, the skills required to co-facilitate effectively can be shared by others.

Harder for the group **Easier for the facilitators**	**Easier for the group** **Easier for the facilitators**
The group members are unsure of who is in charge, who to pay attention to. Facilitators seem to cut across one another, to give mixed messages and ask people to do different things. Both facilitators provide 'input' to group discussions or intervention, sharing the responsibility and complexity of the group, but the process results in a group that is 'over-facilitated'.	Facilitators work together seamlessly, providing multiple perspectives, skills, knowledge and experience to group discussions in a way that makes them complementary rather than repetitive or confusing to the participants. The group is supported through difficulties in interactions and decision making through appropriate intervention and a positive model of communication and conflict resolution.
Harder for the group **Harder for the facilitators**	**Easier for the group** **Harder for the facilitators**
The group members are aware that the facilitators do not like one another. Facilitators leave the room from time to time, leaving the group feeling dislocated and interrupting the flow of the session. Facilitators do not stick to the session plan but 'detour' at whim and without consultation. Facilitators appear to be working at cross-purposes. Facilitators are unsure of what the other is doing and why. Facilitators jockey for power. Questions are treated as challenges and confrontations.	The group members are able to achieve their objectives and feel supported by the facilitators. Facilitators feel constrained by the other facilitator and feel less able to respond to the group needs and change directions as required.

Figure 7.1 Co-facilitation: easier or harder?

A small, strong, motivated partnership or team working effectively together and with groups of people throughout an organization or community can, however, pose potential problems. As the co-facilitators work together they may develop a power base that can undermine other groups, or lead others in a direction unsupported by the organization.

It may be highly advantageous to engage a facilitator from outside an organization and/or community to work with an internal facilitator. An internal facilitator knows the history, biases, politics and characters. An external facilitator provides a fresh face, is not involved in the politics and as a result can ask 'naive questions', and may more easily confront power-holders and/or play the role of devil's advocate.

There can also be a difficulty of expectations. Co-facilitators are often brought in when the problem, task or process is more difficult from the outset or when an issue has reached the desperate stage. The scales are already tipped toward incompletion (at best), inadequacy, or confusion. There can be an expectation that two people can do more, address more problems, solve more difficulties and achieve better outcomes, particularly since there is usually an additional cost in having two or more co-facilitators. These expectations can place a burden on the co-facilitators and, perhaps, limit the effectiveness of their work.

Making things easier for the profession

There is another level of 'ease' yet to be discussed: supporting the professionalism of co-facilitation. Co-facilitation can help to maintain quality control and professional standards by encouraging peers to review each other's performances and provide constructive criticism. In a field that is difficult to moderate, co-facilitation enables peer scrutiny and evaluation.

Maximizing the advantages and minimizing the disadvantages of co-facilitation

The literature on facilitation and co-facilitation suggests many aspects of co-facilitation to which co-facilitators should attend. These include:

- power positions, projection and transference (Knight and Scott, 1997);
- coping with differences in style and orientation (Paulson, Burroughs and Gelb, 1976), including:
  - co-facilitators' concepts of their role in relation to the group (Heron, 1993);

  - preferences for working independently or interdependently and negotiating or compromising (Bruffee, 1993; Hill and Hill, 1990);
  - preferred learning styles (Mumford and Honey, 1992);
  - the 'multiple intelligences' of each co-facilitator (Gardner, 1982);
- dividing the work according to the qualities and skills of the facilitator (Ward, 1993);
- coordinating roles, taking into account:
  - the particular processes chosen for the group to undertake;
  - the ways in which co-facilitators support each other's interventions (the 'zone of deference or indifference' (Barnard, 1938, cited in Schwarz, 1994);
- dealing with tension, including:
  - the effectiveness of the group in terms of productivity;
  - feelings of reward and the cohesion of the group over time (Gallegher, Kraut and Egiolo, 1990);
  - management skills such as setting objectives, clear communication, delegation and leadership (Allen, 1995);
  - collaboration skills such as developing understanding in a shared space over a finite period of time (Shrage, 1995);
  - conflict management skills (Dick, 1991);
  - identifying appropriate feedback mechanisms (Cross and Angelo, 1988).

In the remainder of this chapter, I will focus on four aspects of these areas: choosing whether and how to co-facilitate, developing ways of working with the group, developing ways of working together and resolving conflicts.

Choosing whether and how to co-facilitate

Many facilitators prefer to facilitate alone. Many prefer to co-facilitate. Having experienced the positive effects of co-facilitation they seek opportunities to co-facilitate. There are many ways in which co-facilitators work that can be described as 'co' facilitation, each of which evolves, in part, from:

- the reasons for working together;
- the co-facilitation model chosen;
- the complementarity of the facilitators;
- the facilitators' capacity to manage the complex factors surrounding the co-facilitation task.

Reasons for working together

Co-facilitation may occur because the facilitators have a formal working relationship. It can occur serendipitously in being present in the same place and time for the same purpose. It can occur because facilitators wish to maximize the known advantages of co-facilitation. It may be imposed through the establishment of organizational codes of practice, or the allocation of particular staff to a task. It may also occur because a complex task is contracted and the contracted facilitator determines a need for a co-facilitator.

From whichever of these evolutionary beginnings, co-facilitators will need to choose how they will co-facilitate, and keep in mind many factors that will affect the co-facilitation experience.

Models of co-facilitation

Co-facilitation is most effectively employed when the needs of the group are matched with the skills, experience, expertise and knowledge of the co-facilitators.

Facilitators recognize that they adopt many roles when they facilitate a group. These may include some, or all, of the 'group and task maintenance functions'. Group task functions help the group to achieve the objectives and to complete any tasks. These roles include:

- giving information and opinions;
- seeking information and opinions;
- proposing goals and suggesting ways of initiating action;
- giving directions and developing plans on how to proceed;
- summarizing related ideas, suggestions and major points discussed;
- linking ideas and activities by relating them to each other;
- diagnosing sources of difficulties the group has in working effectively;
- stimulating a higher quality of work from the group;
- examining the practicality and workability of ideas, evaluating alternative solutions, and applying them to real situations to see how they will work;
- evaluating group decisions and accomplishments.

Group maintenance functions assist the group to keep operating on an interpersonal level. These functions include:

- encouraging everyone to participate;
- helping communication;
- supporting the emotional climate of the group;

- observing and supporting the process by which the group is working;
- helping the group be aware of standards and goals and the progress being made toward the goal;
- actively listening to others' ideas;
- building trust, reinforcing risk taking and encouraging individuality;
- easing tension;
- persuading and supporting people to reconcile disagreements;
- solving problems.

There are a variety of ways that these roles can be combined so that co-facilitators share these roles and functions. Richardson and Anderson (1995) suggested that there are five roles needed to enable a group to be effective, and these roles need to be undertaken by at least two facilitators:

- facilitator – a highly visible person who elicits and draws out knowledge and pays attention to the group process and the roles individuals are playing in the group;
- modeller/reflector – someone who focuses on the model being formulated, ensuring that it reflects and crystallizes the information provided;
- process coach – someone who focuses on the dynamics between the individuals and sub-groups;
- recorder – who reconstructs the thinking of the group and records what decisions are made;
- gatekeeper – a person related to the group, who initiates the group work, helps frame the problem, identifies appropriate participants and keeps decision making 'grounded' in the real-world experience of the group.

In Table 7.1, I have summarized some of the ways in which co-facilitators might share roles and responsibilities, combining some of the task and group maintenance functions and the five systems roles described by Richard and Anderson. There are many other ways these roles and functions can be combined according to the needs and abilities of the facilitators, the group, the organization and the wider community.

Where skills, expertise, experience, backgrounds and personalities are complementary, facilitators may choose a '*seamless*' model with both facilitators sharing responsibility for all aspects of the facilitation. Facilitators in this model do not explicitly allocate roles and operate intuitively to share responsibilities with each other (Schwarz, 1997: 219). Knight and Scott describe this as an 'equal' model, but in many respects it is more a sharing of the responsibilities and functions rather than necessarily requiring equal input, time with the group, power or intervention.

Facilitators may choose to have a 'task' person and a 'people' person (Schwarz's 'task/relationship' model), enabling one facilitator to concentrate on the group task or the creation of a product and the other to focus

Table 7.1 Models of co-facilitation

Models of co-facilitation	*Roles of facilitators*
Seamless	Both facilitators share responsibility for all aspects of the facilitation.
Equal	One facilitators focuses on the task and the other on the group relationships or one facilitator focuses on the content while the other focuses on the group process.
Team	Roles and responsibilities are defined by the facilitators and assigned according to the match of the facilitator's skills, experience and expertise with the group needs.
Tandem	Facilitators take it in turns to work with the group. When they are not 'on' they may leave the room or sit quietly without intervention.
Unequal	Facilitators have different levels of responsibility. One person may focus on the intervention while the other provides the leader with information about the group reactions. Or, one facilitator has main responsibility for all aspects of the facilitation and the other facilitator provides support for the facilitator or the group. Or, one facilitator is learning from the other beginning with a large observing role and slowly accepting more responsibility for the group process, with the coach ready to support or intervene if required.
Intervenor/ Recorder	One person facilitates the process and product, the other records the outcomes, processes and decisions.
Mature	Facilitators plan a session together, one facilitator delivers the session with phone contact with the other facilitator, both facilitators debrief the session and determine next directions for the group.

on the group process or the interpersonal dynamics of the group. This model can be especially effective where one facilitator is needed to concentrate on the specific needs of an individual or small group (Schwarz's 'intervention/ reaction' model). I have used the term *'equal'* to describe each of these situations because the roles are not the same but they are of equal significance. In the 'seamless' model, each facilitator moves in and out of the roles. In the 'equal' model, facilitators retain basic roles or functions which complement each other and support the group.

Facilitators may plan the group process and then decide which facilitator will support which aspects of the process according to their strengths. Knight and Scott acknowledge the need for this model particularly in *'team'* facilitation situations where there are three or more facilitators (1997: 133).

Co-facilitators may choose to take turns and share the time and responsibility in *'tandem'*. This model enables one person to rest or observe while the other is 'on' (Schwarz's 'on-line/off-line' model). It is also a model that evolves when people share the facilitation role but allocate specific responsibilities (a shared leadership model) or where two people share a specific job.

In situations where one facilitator has greater skills or has more experience in facilitating a particular process, the other may assume a minor role so that they can learn from their skilled peer. This *'unequal'* model includes a 'learner/coach' relationship where one facilitator is actively learning from the other or a 'primary/secondary' model where one facilitator takes primary responsibility for the group task and process and the other provides support.

It can also be beneficial to have one person essentially silent but recording the decisions and processes of the group while the other actively leads the session (an *'intervenor/recorder'* model). The recorder role is not passive. Recorders function, as described above, to ensure that there is a complete and accurate record of the decisions, products and/or processes of the group.

Most co-facilitators report that the roles and responsibilities that they negotiate prior to the session do not remain fixed. A facilitator may go from being the passive observer or recorder to assuming a more active team role if a particular skill is required. They may intend to work in tandem but find they move into a seamless interchange of roles and responsibilities. On the other hand, facilitators may have intended to work seamlessly but find that the match between the skills of the facilitators and the needs of the group result in one person being more active and the other facilitator assuming a more passive role. Co-facilitation can also require two interconnected models. For example, a co-facilitation relationship may be unequal in tandem with one facilitator 'on' at a time but with one facilitator having more 'on' time than the other.

The *mature* model described in the table borders, for many facilitators, on not being co-facilitation at all. In this model the facilitators plan their co-work and determine that one facilitator will not be present during some part or all of the facilitation of the group. This situation may arise because one facilitator is unable to attend the actual group session but both facilitators feel their joint expertise is beneficial to the group and one facilitator feels able to reflect that combined experience. With the added expense of having two facilitators, a group may be unable to afford to have co-facilitators but the co-facilitators themselves may prefer to plan and evaluate the work together. It may also arise negatively during a session, with one facilitator effectively being sidelined, and receiving no recognition of their work, ideas or input, or more positively if one facilitator is called away in an emergency or needs to work independently with one member of the group. The ability to thoroughly co-plan a session that may be delivered by one person, to recognize the collaboration of both facilitators, to 'represent' a different point of view, to respond effectively to the group in this way and to jointly take responsibility for the outcomes even though only one facilitator is actually visible to the group requires 'maturity'. This 'maturity' may also appear to the group as a tandem, unequal or seamless model.

Whichever model of co-facilitation is employed (in planning and in practice), facilitators need to be prepared to respond to the group needs as they arise, to change roles and to assume additional responsibilities. Facilitators who work together regularly also describe differences in the ways in which they co-facilitate depending on the group, the purpose of the facilitation and their relationship. The story that follows uses metaphor as a way of explaining some of these differences.

A STORY OF CO-FACILITATION: METAPHORS FOR CO-FACILITATION

Our working relationship can be described variously as:

- coleslaw – various bits and pieces and some of them spiky;
- stereo – the audience get one side and then the other, two perspectives on the same issue;
- a sonata – no highs and lows but working well together;
- a violin/piano duet – picking up the themes and revisiting them in different register or in a different order or elaborated in different ways – like with Mozart, in particular, where there are little trills and additions;
- a vocal duet – two voices weaving in and out together, equally important, not always equally obvious to the audience, but without the other it would be thinner;
- a jazz rendition – with one picking up on the other;
- mince – jumbled up, savoury, but with very good quality beef, onions, maybe garlic, spices, herbs, sauces, not very glamorous;
- strawberry sponge cake with cream – gentle and unstressed, two layers, but eaten as a whole with cream and strawberries supporting or holding the thing between that makes the sponge cake taste better;
- stew and dumplings – with the audience as the dumplings.

> Co-facilitation is a different experience depending on us, the audience and the topic, so some analogies are more appropriate at some times in some circumstances than in others. There are some occasions that the co-facilitation experience is not really a sonata (because there aren't high soaring bits) but certainly isn't coleslaw because there are no sharp bits either. Any time people co-facilitate it's a combination of how each of them comes at the time, which includes the history, but also their current issues, concerns and relationship. But it also includes the participants because with different audiences there are different outcomes. Inevitably facilitators, either individually or jointly, respond to their audiences.
>
> The context is also very important even though the facilitators don't always know what this is. We have had to respond to staff anger over cancellation of a winery tour, a cyclone demolishing the homes of people in the workshop and teachers trying to attend professional development the day after a massacre. These factors, over which facilitators have no control, have a significant effect – and can't be ignored – they have to be worked with. Perhaps we need to enlarge our food analogies to include a description of the buffet, party, wake or afternoon tea at which it is being served and our music analogies to describe the scout hall, garden, sound shell or concert hall in which our compositions are heard.

Complementarity

One of the advantages of co-facilitation is the variety and diversity that different perspectives can bring to the work, both for the group and the co-facilitator. Having people who know different aspects of the topic, have different skills and experience, have different personalities and different strengths brings more to the table. Facilitators report advantages in 'complementarity rather than duplication'.

Complementarity, however, implies difference, and difference can lead to conflict. It is helpful when facilitators discuss their differences, and the advantages these differences offer to the group and to each other.

Stages of the co-facilitation relationship

There are many models of group development that describe 'stages', 'phases', 'periods' or 'modes' through which groups progress as they work together, building trust, developing structures and processes, resolving conflicts and achieving outcomes (Smith, 2001). It has been suggested that the co-facilitation team is a similar group that also undergoes 'stages' of development.

Knight and Scott describe three stages in the co-facilitation relationship:

1. the initial stage;
2. the developing stage;
3. partnership stage.

These stages 'represent a qualitative shift in the nature of the working relationship between the co-facilitators' (1994: 88). They suggest that not all relationships will undergo these three stages since some will cease before they have had a chance to develop and some may operate at a low level even though the co-facilitators work together over a long period of time.

During Knight and Scott's 'initial stage', co-facilitators explore philosophical beliefs and values, ways of approaching the group, ways in which they like to work as facilitators, and their backgrounds, experiences and personal viewpoints. In the 'developing' stage, co-facilitators increase their understanding of each other and the ways in which each works. This stage is marked by the development of conflicts and ways of resolving them. Where the relationship develops positively, co-facilitators explore individual and interpersonal issues, analyse their interventions with a group, take risks and experiment with different ways of working and model effective ways of resolving conflicts when they are working with a group. In the 'partnership stage' there is a high level of trust, support and challenge. Co-facilitators expect issues and conflicts to arise, and draw on their complementary skills to resolve them in a way which contributes to the effectiveness of the group and to their own personal learning. Knight and Scott also acknowledge that relationships may 'run their course' at any of these stages.

My own work suggests that co-facilitation is not as simple as this. Co-facilitators can achieve a 'partnership stage' early and easily, rising to challenges and difficulties due to a commonality with each other and ease with the group that is not sustainable in another setting. Some co-facilitators argue that they progress back and forth through these stages in any one session, let alone through multiple experiences together. The metaphor story above indicates this variability and unpredictability.

Like many of the advocates of a cyclical or non-sequential model of facilitation (see Smith, 2001), co-facilitation requires, I think, awareness of the variety of relationships between facilitators, between facilitators and the group, between members of the group, between the group and the task and between the group and the wider organization or community. Other factors such as the length of time for the group process, the time of the day, previous experience with the task and the external requirements for performance also affect the group structure, the degree of involvement of individuals, leadership roles and ways in which agreement can and will be reached. In turn, these aspects influence the 'development' of the co-facilitation relationship.

Ways of working: with the group

Many facilitators (eg Pfeiffer and Jones, 1975; Knight and Scott, 1997; Schwarz, 1994) suggest that co-facilitators develop a contract or working agreement that includes discussing such elements as personal philosophy, previous positive and negative experiences of co-facilitation, how the work will be divided, individual roles, ground rules, ways in which information will be delivered to the group, how changes might be managed, when and how the other facilitator might intervene if things are not going as expected, when the group processes will be reviewed and the way feedback will be given. These focuses are the 'outer elements' of co-facilitation (Knight and Scott, 1997).

Knight and Scott also suggest that facilitators need to address the 'inner elements' of co-facilitation, which include being open at all times, being aware of the dynamics of power and the ability to manage it. They describe a process of setting boundaries so that facilitators only interfere if a group member will suffer harm, the intervention is inconsistent with core values and ground rules, if it changes the facilitator's role, or if it prevents the group from accomplishing its goals. They ask facilitators to be aware of 'projections' where they attribute to the co-facilitator thoughts, feelings and behaviours which are actually part of themselves, and 'transferences' where they react to their co-facilitator as if he/she is a significant person from the past. They suggest that facilitators reflect on their values and personal objectives, be aware of differences as rich sources of learning and balance their challenges with support. They invite facilitators to think about their willingness to learn and change and their individual interest in the co-facilitation. Finally, they encourage facilitators to strive for quality contact with their co-facilitator involving all aspects of themselves.

Pfeiffer and Jones recommend a three-step process for negotiating a working relationship: an initial interview prior to the group session, a 'clinic' after each part of a session, and a 'debrief'. The 'initial interview' enables facilitators to share their pervious experiences, describe issues that have arisen in previous co-facilitation experiences, define goals for the group, decide roles and responsibilities, decide how, when and where to deal with conflicts, issues and disagreements with each other or between members of the group and to discuss ethical considerations. The 'clinic' enables facilitators to diagnose how things are going with the group, provide feedback about each other's work and renegotiate the task, process or guidelines with the group and with each other as required. In the 'debrief' co-facilitators review the goals achieved, their individual learning and goals for their future learning and discuss ways in which their work together could be improved at a future time.

In preliminary work to my PhD, I tried to develop a 'framework for co-facilitation' that enabled people to address a set of questions related to their individual philosophies, ways in which they established trust of and with each other, ways of working together, ways of resolving conflicts and ways of evaluating their successes. The framework was developed with teachers and assistants who facilitate the learning of children over the period of a year and who need to maintain a working relationship on a daily basis for this length of time. Some of the questions from the framework that are generalizable to other fields of work and settings are included in Figure 7.2.

Four findings emerged from my work with these teachers and assistants. Firstly, just talking about these things is not enough; conflicts do happen, things do go wrong and working together is often challenging. Secondly, it isn't enough to go through these sorts of questions once. The questions are not more relevant at any one 'stage' in the relationship. Rather, they need to be addressed each time people are working together. Thirdly, in order to work together people develop ways of working. They may not be conscious of these ways, and the ways may be ineffective, but nevertheless there are guidelines and processes in place. Articulating and making explicit ways of working can support the facilitators as they work with the group by providing a framework for the session and their roles, preventing them from leaving things out that are important or making assumptions about who will do what, when, where, how and why. Lastly, ways of working need to remain flexible so that they do not constrain the ability of the facilitators to work effectively and respond to emerging needs.

Ways of working: together

Most co-facilitators discuss some or all of their ways of working in relation to the group. They articulate ground rules that they hope individuals in the group will follow, plan structures and processes for the group to undertake and identify who will take responsibility for which sections. Many co-facilitators also talk about 'walking the talk', doing the same things with each other that they do with the group. When asked to compare the ways of working with the group with their ways of working with each other, however, most co-facilitators interviewed find they do not walk all of their talk all of the time.

Philosophy

- What are our individual understandings of 'facilitating' and 'being a facilitator'?
- Which do we each value most: 'product/content' or 'process', when and why?
- What are our responsibilities if a participant has a psychological, social, emotional or family difficulty?
- What is non-negotiable for each of us in working with a group?
- How much of our behaviour will be determined before the group process, and how much will be responsive to the situation?

Setting the climate

- What helps us to trust others or to be comfortable?
- How can we create a climate of trust and cooperation every day?
- What is the place of laughter in the group process?
- What are our individual and collective 'missions' – what are we trying to achieve?
- What are our attitudes to mistakes – our own, the participants' and others'?
- What are our individual learning styles? What does this mean for the ways in which we act and react? What does this mean for the ways in which we give and receive information?
- What are our individual reactions to conflict?

Planning

- What are the community or workplace's expectations of us? What do these expectations imply for our roles and responsibilities?
- What do we hope to achieve – for the participants, ourselves, each other and our relationship?
- What are our long-term goals for this group? What are our roles in the achievement of these goals?
- How can we best describe these goals to ourselves, each other, the workplace, the community and the participants?
- What are our individual and collective strengths? How can we use these effectively in the programme?
- When will we make time for reflection and evaluation?

Working together

- What do we each think we are expected to do in our role in the group?
- What do we each think we should do in our role in the group?
- What do we expect of each other in our role in the group?
- What differences are there in our responsibilities and why do these differences exist?
- How can we more effectively listen to each other, the participants and the workplace?
- How will we intervene if we think the other person is doing or saying something wrong? Will we correct each other in front of the group?
- When and how can we appropriately intervene and/or support each other as we work with the group?
- In the event of a conflict: What is the conflict about? How can we map it?
- Are there other ways of working which might be effective?
- How can we continue to work together whilst disagreeing about an issue?

Evaluation

- What kind of feedback do we each want?
- In what format and at what intervals will we give feedback?

Figure 7.2 A framework for co-facilitation – questions to ask and answer

A STORY OF CO-FACILITATION: CO-FACILITATING A CONFERENCE

A team of psychologists, psychotherapists and social workers met together to plan a conference with a difference. They wanted to reflect on the guidelines, structures and processes they developed as a group, recognizing that each of the conference planning team would somehow encapsulate the experience of some participants in the conference. Over time they identified ways in which they were:

- beginning meetings with personal conversation and encouraging social connections;
- reporting new information they had gathered;
- trying to envision a dynamic and interpersonal conference;
- develop action to assist them in their journey towards making this happen;
- reflecting on the discussions of the meeting in order to allocate new responsibilities.

The conference programme reflected these structures and the team gave each structure a name:

- openings;
- perspectives;
- provocations;
- links to practice;
- reflection.

The planning time for the conference lengthened, and the nitty gritty of conference management mired the team in reporting on the actions they had taken since the previous meeting. Meetings got longer and longer, and all felt they were less and less productive. When they stopped to think about what was happening they realized that they had lost the dynamism and hope of a conference with a difference. They were still *opening* their meetings with interpersonal connections, and the perceptivity of one committee member in ensuring that food and drinks were provided to support communication was a vital ingredient in having people attend the meetings at all. But the *perspectives* were now only provided by two people (who were doing most of the work) and they were reports only of the action. The meetings had become too long for *provocations*, *links to practice* or *reflection*.

As a team, they needed ways to abbreviate the reporting time and to enlarge reporting to perspectives, to ensure that time was allocated for provocations so that the conference vision was held in mind, to constantly make the connections between the planning processes and the conference processes and to celebrate achievements and successes.

Co-facilitators are well advised to discuss the ways in which they will work together and to develop guidelines, structures and processes. The conference story describes the structures that this group had put in place as ways of working together and some of the challenges they found in developing and maintaining them. Establishing the structures helps co-facilitators to describe their 'ideal' way of working, to develop a framework through which they can audit their planning and working processes and to develop a process for reviewing and evaluating the effectiveness of their work.

Developing and making explicit guidelines, structures and processes does not mean, however, rigidly following them. The constant requirement of co-facilitation is to meet the needs of the group and make their tasks or processes easier while also making things easier for the co-facilitator. At times this will require co-facilitators to 'give up the script'.

STORY OF CO-FACILITATION: GIVING UP THE SCRIPT

Some of our most successful co-facilitation experiences have been times when we planned for all identified eventualities and then 'given up the script' in order to respond to the emerging needs of the group. Some of these occasions were 'formal' in that, during the workshop, we discussed the direction of the workshop and the needs of the audience and decided together to change our planned activities. Sometimes we 'gave up the script' informally. One of us would decide that we needed to add information, do a different exercise or change direction and we would just do it. We were aware of each other, but not constrained by each other. It was like seeing a car coming in the rear vision mirror and pulling over. We don't take turns. Something tells us that the other has something to add or we need to do something different.

Managing differences

One of the greatest challenges of co-facilitation is managing the differences between facilitators in such a way that these *differences* make things easier for the group and easier for each other. Managing differences requires facilitators, firstly, to recognize them as assets and strengths rather than feeling confronted or defensive. Exploring the differences can assist the group to clarify issues and hear different points of view while helping the co-facilitators to think more creatively, inclusively or expansively.

Co-facilitators act as a model for negotiation and conflict resolution. It can be helpful to determine a process for negotiating and resolving conflicts in the early stages of establishing the relationship and practising

Table 7.2 Developing 'co' while facilitating a group

	Choosing to co-facilitate	*Choosing a co-facilitator*	*Establishing a working relationship*	*Planning a group session*	*Establishing a climate for daily working*	*Working together*	*Managing differences*	*Debriefing the group session*	*Evaluating the working relationship*
Description of the step	Initial contact is made with a group, organization or community and preliminary goals for the group session are discussed. Through the discussion it is evident that the group process will be complex in terms of individual agendas, perspectives to be considered, skills required, time to complete, number of people involved.	Lists are created of knowledge, experience, skills, personality traits, personal qualities needed to enable the group to achieve their goals. Co-facilitator/s are approached and availability ensured.	Co-facilitators conduct a preliminary meeting to discuss the group session, the goals and the background to the session. Co-facilitators share personal experiences and expectations.	Co-facilitators meet to plan the group session. Consultation with the organization or group may occur at this step. Roles and responsibilities are accepted. Co-facilitators individually complete tasks and preparation for the group process. Additional meetings may be required.	Co-facilitators meet an hour before the scheduled session. They share personal baggage, review the processes for the session, ensure personal preparedness. They set up the space, considering lighting, groupings, mood and personal safety.	Co-facilitators quietly discuss the group processes as required, calling for whole group intervention or discussion of problems as required. Co-facilitators remain open to the group and each other, observing processes and interpersonal dynamics, supporting discussion and facilitating decision making.	Differences of opinion are shared openly and without rancour. Co-facilitators keep the focus on the group process and/or product.	Co-facilitators discuss the successes of the session and any areas of concern. They use a 'we' approach to problems.	Co-facilitators discuss their personal learning, aspects of the facilitation that benefited them personally and professionally and identify future areas for growth and learning.

	Choosing to co-facilitate	*Choosing a co-facilitator*	*Establishing a working relationship*	*Planning a group session*	*Establishing a climate for daily working*	*Working together*	*Managing differences*	*Debriefing the group session*	*Evaluating the working relationship*
Dos	Discuss the benefits of co-facilitation for the group and the organization or community.	Look for people who complement each other. Look for people who the group can and will trust.	Be honest, open and direct. Clearly state aspects of the task each of you can contribute to. Acknowledge skills, strengths, personality, gender, age, experience and knowledge. Meet as many times as you need to establish trust and confidence in each other	Develop a broad array of possible structures before choosing the 'best fit' for this particular group. Identify working guidelines or ground rules for the group.	Take time to stop, look at each other, share coffee or tea (or the equivalent), talk about aspects of your personal lives and share any baggage you are carrying that may impact on your performance in this session. Keep the review of the plan short. Talk about any environmental preparations you feel are important. Set the environment, recognizing the changes that may be required to your plan.	Help the group focus on the task and process of the session. Vary the pace of the session, using the different voices of the facilitators as a way of avoiding repetition and routine.	Speak only from personal experience. Remain silent unless you can forward the discussion. Appreciate difference and celebrate your and your co-facilitator's ability to voice dissension. Remember that conflict only matters when the relationship matters — celebrate that this is a relationship that matters. Record differences between you and your co-facilitator to discuss at a break (if it is urgent) or in the debrief.	Rejoice in and celebrate successes.	Remember that this experience (positive or negative) was a complex interaction of many factors. Try to articulate all of these.

Table 7.2 Developing 'co' while facilitating a group *(continued)*

	Choosing to co-facilitate	*Choosing a co-facilitator*	*Establishing a working relationship*	*Planning a group session*	*Establishing a climate for daily working*	*Working together*	*Managing differences*	*Debriefing the group session*	*Evaluating the working relationship*
Don'ts	Be careful not to under-estimate or minimize the time planning, delivery and evaluation will require.	Don't get stuck on one model of co-facilitation. A different model may meet the needs better and help your own learning.	Avoid defensiveness. Recognize tensions and mentally (or physically) list them. Discuss tensions prior to beginning your work with the group.	Avoid using a single method just because that is the only one you have used before. Don't get hung up on who does what and for how long.	Don't get stuck on your plans. The day, climate and environment may require changes.	Avoid cutting across your co-facilitator's interventions. Work within the guidelines you have set. Avoid competing with your co-facilitator. Avoid projections and transferences. Avoid defensiveness and blame.	Avoid defensiveness. Avoid blame.	Avoid dwelling on issues as negatives and treat them as learning points.	Avoid defensiveness and blame.
Questions to ask	What does the group, organization or community hope to achieve? What agendas may arise? How many people will be involved? Over what length of time?	Can this person: ● Anticipate problems? ● Support the task and the process? What are our individual and collective strengths?	What are our individual understandings of 'facilitating' and 'being a facilitator'? Which do we each value most: 'product/ content' or 'process', when and	What are the community or workplace's expectations of us? What do these expectations imply for our roles and responsibilities? What do we hope to achieve – for	What are our individual and collective 'missions' – what are we trying to achieve? How can we create a climate of trust and cooperation today?	What differences are there in our responsibilities and why do these differences exist? How can we more effectively listen to each other, the	What is the conflict about? How can we map it? Are there other ways of working which might be effective? How can we continue to work	What kind of feedback do we each want? In what format and at what intervals will we give feedback? What worked in this session for the group, for individual members of	What have we learnt about co-facilitation, facilitation, ourselves and our relationship? What are our future goals for our learning?

Choosing to co-facilitate	*Choosing a co-facilitator*	*Establishing a working relationship*	*Planning a group session*	*Establishing a climate for daily working*	*Working together*	*Managing differences*	*Debriefing the group session*	*Evaluating the working relationship*
How many session are required or expected?	How can we use these effectively in the programme?	why? What are our responsibilities if a participant has a psychological, social, emotional or family difficulty? What is non-negotiable for each of us in working with a group? How much of our behaviour will be determined before the group process, and how much will be responsive to the situation? What helps us to trust others or to be comfortable? What is the place of laughter in the group process?	the participants, ourselves, each other and our relationship? What are our long-term goals for this group? What are our roles in the achievement of these goals? What do we each think we are expected to do in our role in the group? What do we each think we should do in our role in the group? What do we expect of each other in our role in the group? How will we intervene if we think the other person is		participants and the workplace? When and how can we appropriately intervene and/or support each other as we work with the group?	together while disagreeing about an issue?	the group, for us individually and for us as a working group? What further action is required?	

Table 7.2 Developing 'co' while facilitating a group *(continued)*

	Choosing to co-facilitate	*Choosing a co-facilitator*	*Establishing a working relationship*	*Planning a group session*	*Establishing a climate for daily working*	*Working together*	*Managing differences*	*Debriefing the group session*	*Evaluating the working relationship*
				doing or saying something wrong? Will we correct each other in front of the group? When will we make time for reflection and evaluation? What are our attitudes to mistakes – our own, the participants' and others'? What are our individual learning styles? What does this mean for the ways in which we act and react? What does this mean for the					

	Choosing to co-facilitate	*Choosing a co-facilitator*	*Establishing a working relationship*	*Planning a group session*	*Establishing a climate for daily working*	*Working together*	*Managing differences*	*Debriefing the group session*	*Evaluating the working relationship*
Tips	Be prepared to negotiate a price if you are convinced of the benefit of co-facilitation.	A co-facilitator who is very different from you may help your learning more. Choose your degree of fit according to the complexity of the task. A very difficult and complex task may provide sufficient learning opportunities.	Be open, honest and direct. If there are difficulties at this point in the negotiations that are not resolved they are likely to surface again (publicly and more uncomfortably) in the facilitation.	ways in which we give and receive information? What are our individual reactions to conflict? Initially, keep the focus on the group's needs not the facilitators'. Identify personal goals after the group needs are discussed.	Trust requires active construction every day. Begin from a position of trust and actively develop that trust in everything you do and say.	Ascertain the group's goals and keep the focus on achieving them. See obstacles as 'opportunities through which to realize the future' (Epps, 2001).	Intervene in such a way that the group's thinking is recorded and open for all to see and the group processes are brought to their attention. Summarize and reorganize information in such a way that it clarifies the difficulties – and whether they are differences over the content or the processes of the group decision making.	Problems and issues are firstly our own. Solutions are developed together.	Whether you will work together again or not, this relationship becomes part of your experience of co-facilitation. If you are feeling 'I'll never do this again' it is very important that each discusses why. If you are feeling 'that was magic' articulating what made it so will help you replicate it on another occasion.

them in planning sessions. Conflict resolution strategies such as 'principled negotiation' or a 'solution focused approach' can be useful (Fisher and Ury, 1988).

When agreement cannot be reached, co-facilitators need a way to privately and publicly agree to disagree or 'disagree agreeably' (Bennett, Rolheiser and Stevahn, 1991).

Conclusion

Being professional as co-facilitators

Co-facilitators need to have an intensive focus and commitment to facilitation, retaining a primary focus on the group and the relationships within it, and remaining constantly aware that their task is to 'make things easier for the group'. Co-facilitators simultaneously need to maintain an awareness of each other, the relationship of their co-facilitator with the group and ways of supporting each other. Co-facilitation occurs within the setting of the group, organization or community and co-facilitators have a responsibility at this level. Finally, co-facilitators have a responsibility to other co-facilitators. Co-facilitation, as a more expensive option, needs to bear significant benefits for all involved in order for it to remain an option for group work. Each co-facilitation experience sets a precedent for the next – for all involved.

Co-facilitators need to present a professional face to the client, organization and group. Roles and responsibilities, ways of working with the group, ways of working together and ways of managing difficulties need to be discussed, developed and reviewed. Flexibility remains a requirement in responding to the needs of the group and the other facilitator in order to make things 'easier and easier'.

Table 7.2 aims to help facilitators set in place a professional relationship. While it summarizes the points made in this chapter, it is not intended as a recipe for co-facilitation. In short, there is no recipe. The table weaves together aspects of facilitation and co-facilitation, threading the development of a working relationship between co-facilitators with the work of facilitating a group. It is neither comprehensive of all the steps required nor complete in its analysis of the things that co-facilitators should or should not do. My aim is to provide a tool for reflection. I encourage you to add your own ideas, questions and tips to it.

8

Basic theories and concepts of group work

> There is nothing so practical as a good theory.
>
> Kurt Lewin

Introduction

This chapter is designed to give some background to the basic theories of group work. As copious tomes have been written on this topic, I have had to be selective and have chosen theories and concepts that have been useful to me in my facilitation work. I have also chosen models that are easy to recall and hence easy to put into practice.

The chapter is organized like a V-shape. It starts with the general issues of contexts, systems and diversity, then narrows down to communication through dialogue rather than debate. Then there is a summary of stages of group development and team roles. Individual behaviour and needs are discussed along with the impact of size of groups and large group interventions.

All groups are involved in informal learning, even if they are not educational groups per se. An outline of adult learning theories, experiential learning and learning models is given.

Contexts and systems

In setting up workshops, facilitators have always been encouraged to investigate the organizational context (see Kiser and Hunter models in Chapter 4). However, there is a need for facilitators to research wider contexts than merely the organizational background. Emery (1976) encouraged organizations to discuss desirable and non-desirable future environments in the first stages of Search Conferences (a participatory planning process devised by F Emery and M Emery). However, the emerging tensions arising from living in 'turbulent environments' (Emery, 1974) and increasingly complex organizations illustrated the need for a more comprehensive approach (Senge, 1990; Dorner, 1996).

Urie Bronfenbrenner (1979) developed a useful ecological theory of development which shows a systems model of human behaviour and identified several layers of context or ecology (Figure 8.1):

- microsystem – the most immediate and earliest influences such as family, school, religion and peer groups;
- mesosystem – an intermediate level of influence such as local neighbourhood or community, social institution and culture;
- macrosystem – the most removed influence, such as international, regional or global changes.

It shows how human behaviour, thought, spirit and health are interconnected with the concentric rings of community, society, region and globe.

How can managers manage the interface and tensions between all these areas? How can facilitators help organizations to take more interest in the environment, natural resources and potential and actual disputes over them, along with social movements which are growing in relation to these matters? Likewise the political contexts as I have noted in more totalitarian regimes: how does a facilitator work within political environments that may at local level wish to stimulate individual empowerment and group decision making, but be uneasy with empowerment and democracy at high community levels? (Rocha, 1997).

As facilitators, what can we do to stay aware not just of the organizations and cultures that we are working with, but of changes on the world scene which are impacting on us and our participants?

Web sites
http://chiron.valdosta.edu/whuitt/materials/sysmdlc.html
http://www.psy.pdx.edu/PsiCafe/KeyTheorists/Bronfenbrenner.htm#Research

Facilitators can help groups build different future scenarios and hypothetical questions, 'What would happen if you did. . .?', and then to pursue the potential ramifications of each scenario with an open and creative mind (see Book 2 Chapter 9). Alternatively simulations like the 'Beer Game' are useful for demonstrating the effects of change on systems (see Chapter 10).

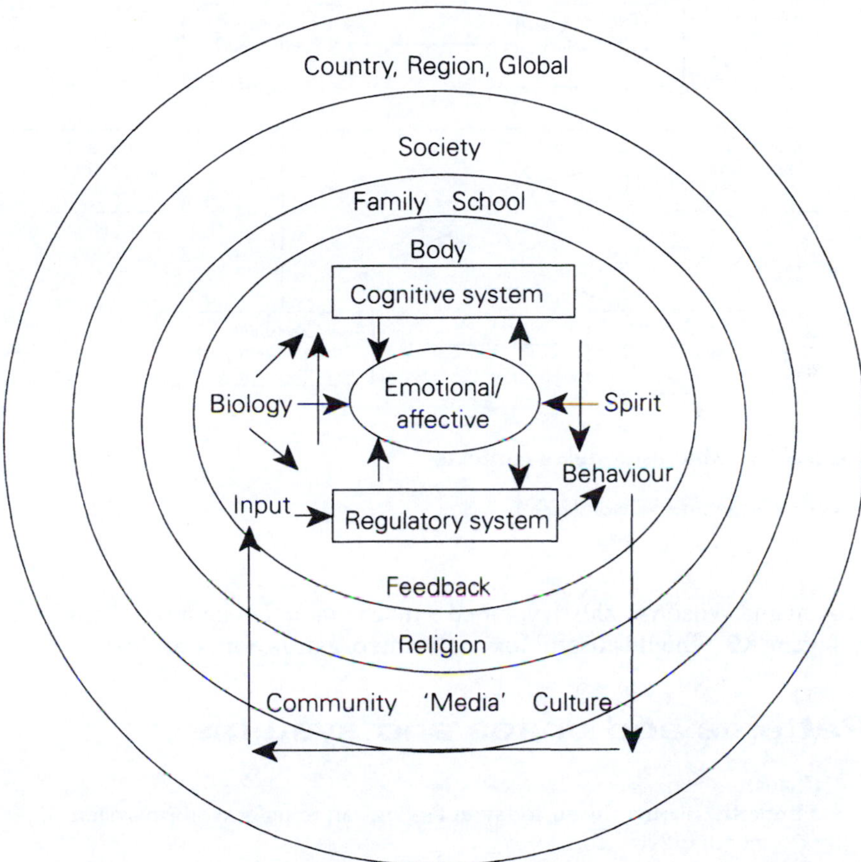

Figure 8.1 Systems model of human behaviour

Source: Adapted from W G Huitt (1994), Bronfenbrenner (1979) and Norman (1980) on Web site: http://chiron.valdosta.edu/whuitt/materials/sysmdlc. html, downloaded January 2002

Macro-model of contexts

Small, incremental changes may reach critical or flashpoints where the nature of various systems radically alters. Examples include: the terrorist attacks of 11 September 2001, the recent riots against corporatism and globalization, the reactions of consumers against mega companies like Coca-Cola, McDonald's and Nike; increasing disputes over water rights in the Mekong and Ganges river systems, India's Narmada Dam, the salination of the Murray-Darling River system (Beckett, 2000; Caulfield, 1996/1998).

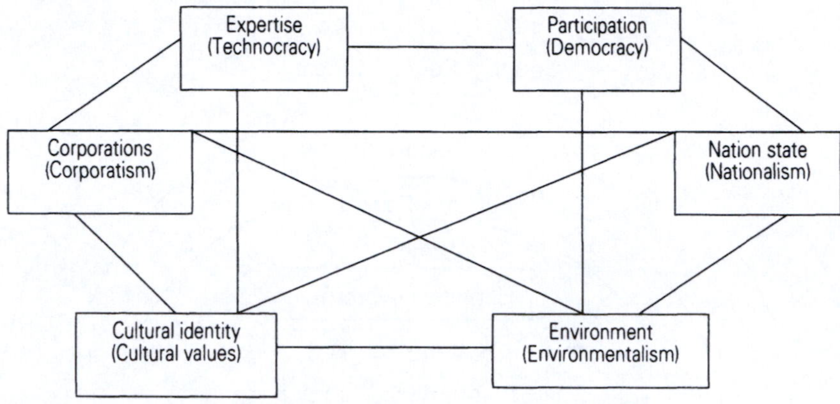

Figure 8.2 Macro-model of contexts

Source: Wilson and Wilson (2000)

Wilson and Wilson (2000) developed a macro-model of contexts illustrated in Figure 8.2, which is useful for analysing organizational contexts.

Patterns and chaos and systems

> Chaos. . .
> a butterfly stirring the air today in Peking can transform storm systems next month in New York.
>
> (Lorenze, 1964: 8)

Luckily for facilitators, groups do show some patterns of behaviour (see sections on group theory later in this chapter). But at times they plunge into chaos or dis-equilibrium or in Kurt Lewin's terms they 'unfreeze' (McClure, 1998).

Groups are open, complex systems (within concentric and interlinked circles of larger systems: organizations, society at large) and managers and facilitators need to think about interventions holistically. Changing one thing in a system will cause all sorts of ramifications in other parts, some seen, some invisible.

Figure 8.3 Behaviour fluctuation in groups

Story

A couple of years ago a disastrous fire broke out on board a large naval ship in the Indian Ocean, off the coast of Western Australia.

A workshop participant arrived late and looked pale and haggard. The news of the disaster had not yet broken. I asked what was wrong. He immediately started to tell us of his colleagues and friends and what it felt like to be 'on a ship which is like floating on top of three full petrol stations. Every sailor dreads fire. . .'

The group dynamics immediately changed and focused on his fears and pain. . .

Workshop groups are microcosms of bigger community groups like 'fractals' or geometrical figures, each part of which has the same shape or statistical character as the whole. For more detail on these ideas see (McClure, 1998). As the world took in the ramifications of 11 September 2001, a group I facilitated the next day huddled in a close circle. I played 'Give peace a chance' by John Lennon, some wept and then together we 'held the space and the silence' so people could speak in turn, like a Quaker session, as the need arose.

Diversity

A group is a microcosm of the sum of the individuals' history and experiences, organization, families, communities, future, society (and its prior history if it is an ongoing group). See Figure 8.4. From this we have our own values, dreams, ways of speaking, being and doing, mental models, levels of tolerance, and worldview, sometimes called 'baggage', which filter how we perceive and react to our world.

Thinking points for facilitators (Hunter, Bailey and Taylor, 1992) include:

- Am I aware of some of my baggage? (Some is in our 'blind spot')
- Am I comfortable with my baggage? (That is, do I need to do some personal development?)
- Do I allow room for the baggage of others?

How much 'baggage' to unpack?

How much a facilitator delves into these layers depends on the relevance of the information to the purpose of the group (Gill Baxter, 2000).

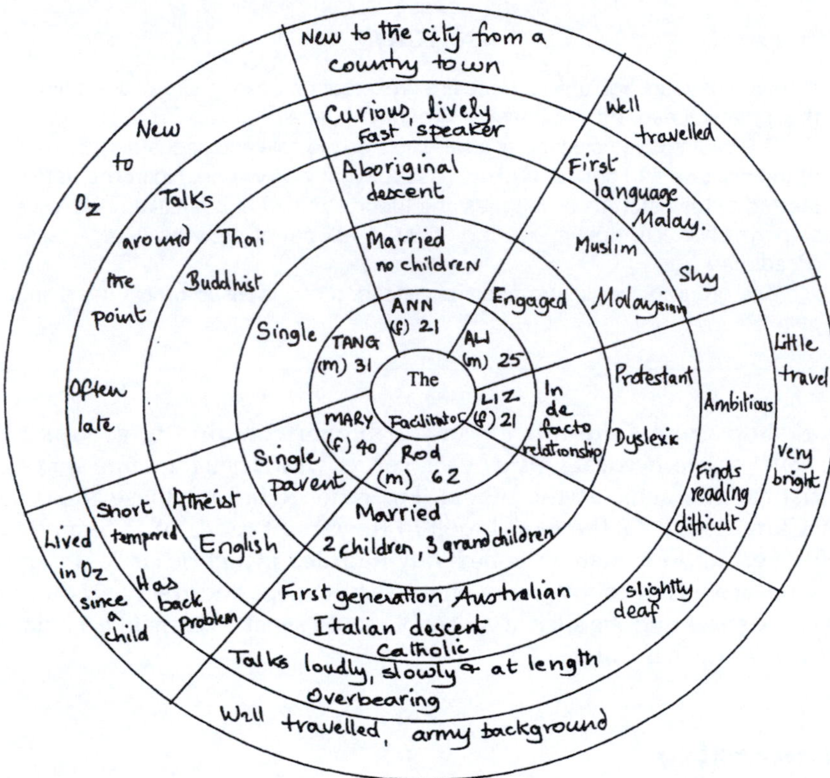

Figure 8.4 The diversity of group members

For example, in a 1–2-day short workshop on problem-solving strategies, comprising individuals from different organizations, it may not be necessary to spend one hour on introductions and life stories when the individuals may never see each other again. A useful question to ask is: What processes/interventions are appropriate to the goals, the group, the time, and space?

Inclusivity: working with difference

Part of a facilitator's job is to help people feel included in a group. Just as organizations are taking more notice of people's different dietary needs for workshops, so we need to think about what we can do for people's physiological needs. Whilst watching a group, facilitators may notice behaviour they can't explain and as such need to be alert to the possibility of health issues and/or disabilities that may or may not be disclosed or obvious. Being isolated in a group or scapegoated because of difference can be the most demoralizing experience. We have a duty of care, though the boundaries of this are unclear.

Covert disability

Many disabilities are not obvious at first and tactful facilitative interventions are required. At a break a facilitator could give a gentle invitation for disclosure, eg 'I noticed you squeezing up your eyes to read the flip chart paper – should I write larger, or would you like to sit closer?' (ie state the observation) or 'Is something going on for you at the moment?'

If you have deaf people in a group, do not stand in front of a bright window, as the back lighting will make lip reading more difficult. Beards and moustaches may be a problem and it helps to pin back long hair away from the face, speak normally, don't walk around, and 'make your face available to them'. It helps if hearing-impaired people sit next to a buddy who will whisper anything that has been missed.

Formats of materials

Participants are now understandably exerting their rights to access learning and/or have their needs met. Some organizations are starting to add on advertising brochures:

> This workshop uses written handouts; if for reason of disability you require printed materials enlarged please let us know at least one week prior to the workshop.

Also, there are now AV companies who will dub videos on request.

Gender of facilitators

There are still a lot of unknowns regarding the impact of the gender of facilitators on groups. There appear to be a majority of females entering the facilitation profession, yet the literature so far is dominated by male, Anglo writers.

When there are co-facilitators and one is female and the other male, a large majority of participants (both male and female) tend to assume that the male is the lead facilitator, most skilled/experienced, etc, even when the opposite has been described in the introductions. As a result, the Quaker facilitators I met in London, who had a policy for mixed gender dyads, always ensured that the female facilitator started the group and engaged the group in major issues, not just 'housekeeping' introductions.

There is some debate as to whether or not males would be less likely to confront female facilitators (as it could appear unmanly). It is hard to generalize. In some all-male, blue-collar environments, I have found I have had to prove myself. I usually throw in references to 'past work with hardened criminals in Fremantle jail'. However, once I have established my credibility, I find all male groups easy in that I am not a threat to them.

Assertive women are often perceived as being aggressive by males.

Gender composition of groups

Group composition varies: all female, all male, equal male–female, male dominated, female dominated. How does the gender mix impact on behaviour? Some men do find it hard to talk about feelings, but so do some women. But there are now many men's groups that focus on developing this side of themselves.

In some instances it may be more 'appropriate' to have all women or all men, either culturally, eg Moslem women, or because, for example, women who have been abused may be more comfortable initially with women and with female facilitators. Men who are exploring issues of 'maleness' may prefer to be with all men. In some Aboriginal groups there is differentiation between genders for 'secret men's business' and 'secret women's business'. These terms have now been taken up by the wider population (see gender issues and outdoor learning in Book 2 Chapter 13).

All female groups (as in the playground behaviours of girls) tend to spend more time building relationships and/or clearing the air before concentrating on tasks. I have noted in female groups with only one or two males that the females tend to check if the men are OK. I have not noted the same behaviour in male groups with only one or two women.

Of course there are related issues regarding touch and sexual attraction. If someone is upset I now ask permission to give him/her a hug along the lines of 'Oh you look upset, do you need a hug?' Or I just sit beside them and listen.

Facilitators, like teachers and managers, occupy power roles and group members immediately sense and understandably resent overt flirting which is both unprofessional and totally unacceptable in the facilitation profession.

Communication: dualistic thinking

> Communication is not a matter of being right, but of starting a flow of energy between two people that can result in mutual understanding.
>
> John Sanford

Much of western thinking is limited by Aristotelian 'dualistic' thinking. Examples include right–wrong, private–public, winner–loser, amateur–professional, cognitive–affective, teaching–learning and cooperation–competition. One of the main tasks of facilitators is to ask questions that stimulate thought and elicit information that has not been previously shared.

'Dialogue' rather than 'argument'

One of the goals of facilitation is to enhance 'dialogue' rather than 'argument'. The word 'dialogue' comes from the Greek 'dialogos' (dia = through, logos = word) and is more like a dance of words. Our political system is based on opposing parties who meet each other to argue and 'debate'. Yet these terms are analogous of a fight, ie win–lose. Heated debates can generate a great deal of angst but stop people reaching a useful understanding of one another's issues. Facilitators have many processes and tools to harness the ideas of the group members. In the USA 'talking circles' are used to explore complex issues. To ensure that only one person speaks at a time a 'talking stick', feather or stone is passed around (similar to the conch shell in *The Lord of the Flies*).

The summary in Table 8.1 includes ideas from:

1) 'Common Ground Network for Life & Choice' (Web site: http://www.searchfor commonground. org) and
2) 'Conflict Resolution Network' (Web site: http://www.crnhq.org/govt2.html).

See also David Bohm's concept of dialogue:

1) http://world.std.com/~lo/bohm/0000.html and
2) http://world.std.com/~lo/bohm/0001.html.

Group theory: stages of group development

The behaviour of groups varies all the time. It is normal for some:

- individuals, sub-groups or the group to challenge the purpose of the workshop;
- individuals, sub-groups or the group to challenge the role of the facilitator;
- interpersonal or intergroup conflict to occur;
- external factors to impact on a group.

Table 8.1 The differences between dialogue and argument

Dialogue	*Argument: is like a fight*
Pre-meeting communication between facilitator and participants and between participants	Minimal communication beforehand
Facilitator gains agreement and commitment to agreed ground rules, builds trust, and a safe environment to allow new ideas to emerge	No ground rules set. Implicit rules are shouting and interruptions are ok; repetition of ideas; survival of the fittest, no new ideas
Exploratory atmosphere. Clearly negotiated ground rules enforced by facilitator and participants. It is safe to disagree and voice concerns	Sometimes threatening atmosphere
Both–and	Win–lose
Understanding and being understood	Dualistic thinking: I'm right, they're wrong; I won/they lost
Searching for common ground	Warlike narrative of argument: 'I shot down their arguments in flames'
Searching for concerns, beliefs and values that are shared	'Your point is indefensible'
Looking at difference with fresh eyes; trying to walk in their moccasins	'Don't attack my argument'
Paraphrasing their main points before you add your point	His/her point is right on target
New information comes to surface and/or new ways of thinking are generated	Non-negotiable convictions; arguments polarize thinking
Voice uncertainties as well as deeply held beliefs	Ideas are voiced as proven facts
Genuine questions used as tools to open up thinking, probing, 'What would it take for us to…? Assumes continuum of views; people speak for their own point of view, ie use 'I' not 'we'	Questions used to score points or mask suggestions: 'Why don't we do…?' Polarized views, stereotyping. Assumes unity of views between people of each 'side'

The 'group dynamic' or the mental, emotional and physical energy of the group is constantly changing (Heron, 1999). This can be very confusing, but there are some discernible patterns of behaviour which have been described in models to simplify complex reality.

I once heard that there are over 100 models of the stages of group development. The problem is that most models were developed by studying short-term laboratory or therapy groups. The good news is there are similarities of stages amongst the developmental models; what we need is a common language.

Table 8.2 is a composite of the main group development theories based on the work of Tuckman and Jensen* (1977), McClure~ (1998), Schutz+ (1972) and Heron^ (1999). Symbols have been used to allow you to see the source of terminology used.

Groups may not go through stages sequentially, some stages may be skipped and/or they may get stuck in others or go round in cycles. Many factors impact on a group. For example, new people join a group and people leave; available resources fluctuate; external events impact on productivity. Table 8.2 is a merely guide to help summarize key stages and the issues and associated facilitation skills needed at these stages.

Beginning a group

> Both ice breakers and endings should be **relevant and appropriate** to the purpose of the group.
>
> Gill Baxter

It is not in our nature to come together as human beings and immediately get down to a task. However, I have noted that some facilitators take inordinately long periods of time for introductions when a group is only coming together for a short period. Perhaps this is caused by the facilitator's need to prevent any surprises or even to use up time? On the other hand, some introductions are necessary (see Book 2 Chapter 2). Gill Baxter's quote is apt: 'Both ice breakers and endings should be relevant and appropriate to the purpose of the group.' It is the responsibility of a facilitator to make the atmosphere as inviting and conducive as possible for the type of participant and the task at hand.

Storming stage

The source of most concern for some participants and some facilitators and the area least understood is the storming or conflict stage. McClure (1998) maintains there are two main causes: 1) intermember differences; 2) anger

Table 8.2 Stages of group development (P = Participant; F = Facilitator)

Stages	*Issues*	*Facilitation skills*
PREFORMING~	P 'Shall I join the group or not?' 'Do I have to go?' P 'I'm far too busy' 'Oh not another of those workshops'	Contracting, needs analysis to check **real purpose of the group** Check who has been left out that should be invited Find suitable venue Consider what the size of group should be to get the job done
FORMING* **INCLUSION+** **WINTER: Stage of defensiveness^** **UNITY~**	P 'Will I be heard?' P 'Will they like me?' P 'Do I want to be a member of this group?' P 'What are the others like?' P 'Will I be able to cope with the work?' P 'Can I trust them?' 'I feel anxious' Polite rather than open behaviour Covert and overt anxiety	Active listening Building trust, allaying fears Risk taking Establishing rapport and empathy Gate keeping (ie inviting quieter members to speak) Sorting out logistics (time and place of meetings, resources) Negotiating desirable group norms
STORMING* **POWER, CONTROL & INFLUENCE+** **SPRING: Stage of working through defensiveness^**	P 'Who is in charge here?' P 'Do I have any influence?' P 'Is everyone heard?' P 'Who is dominating?' P 'I don't need/want to be here... this is not relevant/ waste of time. . .' P 'I'll fold my arms and glare' (passive aggressive) P 'Who is this facilitator anyway? I'll challenge him/her' Boundary testing	Active listening Continued norm setting and re-negotiation Understanding group process Negotiating skills Resolving conflict Confronting skills

Stages	*Issues*	*Facilitation skills*
NORMING* **AFFECTION+**	P 'I'm not happy, but I'll stay quiet' P 'Why rock the boat? There only X hours/X weeks to go so I'll sit it out' Concern about cohesion rather than dealing with issues A need for each member to be open about his/her concerns Superficial unity Illusion of harmony. Backbiting in private	Active listening Self-disclosure Sharing information. Willingness to change behaviour if necessary, eg to speak less or to speak more Referring back to ground rules Getting on with the task See the Abilene Paradox story later in this chapter
PERFORMING*~ **CONTROL/ INCLUSION+** **SUMMER: The stage of authentic behaviour^**	Increased cohesion and mutual support and trust. 'Let's get the job done' 'Let's be as open with one another as possible' Task as well as process oriented Authentic caring and sharing of ideas Acceptance of individual differences and emotions Creative and constructive disagreements and conflict Diversity is valued and used to create synergy Increased self-acceptance and self-disclosures and risk taking	Active listening Giving and receiving positive and constructive/change feedback Teamwork using the varying strengths of different individuals Creativity and authentic humour Pull back and let the group manage itself
ADJOURNING* **MOURNING** **AUTUMN: Closure^**	Finishing the task Pride in accomplishments Resolving past differences: tie up loose ends Possible nostalgia and regret Celebration of each other and what has been achieved. Saying warm and friendly farewells in the group and one to one If group still at storming stage, there are feelings of relief	Active listening Self- and group evaluation of learning Accepting consequences of past actions or in actions Letting go and moving on
POST-TERMINATION	Some individuals may feel lost without the group Some groups or sub-groups autonomously organize reunions or maintain contact via e-mail	

at the leader because she is held responsible for the group and the workshop. Participants may vent their frustration without thought for her well-being and feelings (especially in large community meetings where the facilitator is seen as representing large companies and/or government bureaucracies). A third reason may be 'transference', ie participants transfer their frustrations with an organization or government department on to the facilitator.

McClure divides the conflict stage into three sections:

1. disunity: the inability of the group or the leader to satisfy member expectations;
2. conflict/confrontation, where there are attacks on the facilitator role based on transference;
3. disharmony: member disagreements surface fully and norms for the expression of conflict and conflict resolution are established.

The 'conflict stage' is of course culture bound in that displays of open conflict are frowned on in many countries in Asia. Indeed exhibitions of frustration and/or anger may cause considerable loss of face. Dissatisfaction with the facilitator in some parts of Asia may be communicated via trusted messengers or notes. (See cross-cultural issues in Chapter 9 and Book 2, Chapter 6.)

Norming stage

Sometimes highly cohesive groups, ie at the 'norming' stage (Tuckman and Jensen 1977), become 'stuck' and narrow in their way of thinking, leading to characteristics which Irving Janis (1972) called 'groupthink'. This 'condition' has a variety of symptoms which will be described in turn below and in Table 8.3. We are often oblivious to groupthink and when appropriate it is part of a facilitator's role to help groups to learn to identify it, accept if it is happening and take action to prevent it.

Groupthink: it's a question of degree

It is wonderful to see or be part of highly cohesive groups of people feeling a sense of pride in their work and accomplishments and enjoying each other's company in and out of the workplace:

Positive cohesion ______________________________ Negative over-cohesion

However, if the cohesion and bonding lead to an over-commitment to restrict norms and enforce people to agree for agreement's sake and/or the suppression of dissent then someone has to 'blow the whistle'. The person who does this is often punished, ostracized, scapegoated and/or labelled for being 'negative' or 'subversive'. People who wish to preserve the status quo spend inordinate amounts of energy in denial that there is something wrong and in maintaining 'business as usual'.

Groupthink or 'stuck' or 'blinkered' thinking can occur on societal, organizational and group levels and we ignore it at our peril, as the following examples illustrate.

Groupthink at societal level

The media, as we now experience it, is often based on 'grabs' of a few seconds. This results in a kind of 'shorthand', and encourages 'groupthink'. For example, directly after 11 September 2001, the media equated all Muslims with 'terrorists', regardless of nuances and shades of meaning. In Australia, at the time of writing (January 2002), politicians denigrate asylum seekers, saying 'some could be dangerous or criminals', the implication being that asylum seeker = dangerous criminal. Thus it may be important for facilitators to tease out ideas, encourage alternative views, encourage more creative ways of thinking, and encourage participants to looks at context and 'scenario build'. In other words, what if the conventional 'wisdom' is not adequate to deal with this issue?

In totalitarian regimes the facilitator's job may be even harder. For example, in one communist country I worked in, conventional wisdom maintained that not only was it important to make plans, but also to stick to them. To change a plan was seen by the system as 'failure'. Having a common purpose once a plan of action is decided is important. However, in the planning stage it is important to draw out the creative ideas of participants and not just rely on the ideas of a few. Likewise in the implementation stage, people often need to be 'given permission' to adapt; deviation from a plan should not be seen as failure (as the *Challenger* space disaster proved).

Any form of economic and/or political propaganda encourages simplification of issues and groupthink, for example:

- 'Privatization is more efficient' (resulting in many train crashes in the UK, due to insufficient funds spent by small companies on regular line maintenance).
- 'Where there is a need, the market will provide' (not if you are poor and starving in a village in the 'South').
- 'Globalization is good' (like any massive change in human history, it has both positive and negative impacts (Roddick, 2001)).
- 'You are either with us or against us' (George Bush, 2001).

'Groupthink is the basis of all "isms" – racism, sexism, ageism, homophobia – and all wars. We need to objectify other groups if we are going to kill people we don't even know' (Hunter, Bailey and Taylor, 1997: 72). Political correctness can also be oppressive and limiting. Any form of extreme fundamentalist beliefs leads to a one-eyed view of the world called the 'tyranny of absolutes' where people believe that their beliefs are the truth.

In the aftermath of 11 September 2001, some people became stuck in overly long periods of fear and anger and stopped their normal lives and travel whilst others mourned loss, discussed fears and anger and then moved on to start thinking about how can we listen better to the needs of other countries. How can we deal with terrorism? How can we change to ensure this does not happen again?

Groupthink has also occurred at organizational level. In the UK, Margaret Thatcher preached the gospel of economic rationalism and reportedly said to a group of England's best scientists: 'Gentlemen,. . . pause. . . gentlemen. . . pause. . . I have one word to say to you. . . pause. . . profit, profit.'

In the early days of Australian colonial history, there was a commonly held belief (groupthink) in 'terra nullius', ie that Australia was an empty land with no inhabitants, completely ignoring the Aboriginal peoples with their long, diverse and complex cultures and traditions.

In Medieval times, the Church maintained that 'the earth is flat' and 'the sun moves around the earth'. People who questioned such strongly held beliefs did so at their peril.

Group think at organizational level

Managers need to be aware of the dangers of surrounding themselves with 'yes' people. On the one hand, 'yes' people give them political support and power but managers cannot always rely on them as their main information source. One manager commented to my friend who is an external consultant: 'Oh I like to have you around because you are straight and tell me "as it is". My team, I fear, only tell me what they think I want to hear.'

Consider the following examples:

- 'Restructuring/downsizing will increase cost effectiveness' (leading to a loss of organizational stories/networks and informal information. You can only downsize so often, resulting in no staff left and/or no staff to deal with an upturn in business).
- 'Internal competition will make us more efficient and effective' (resulting in duplication of courses in different departments in universities and resulting confusion and negative impact on staff and student morale, leading to a decrease in collaboration and increase in distrust).

These 'perceived wisdoms' are like the story of the Emperor's New Clothes (see Book 2 Chapter 4).

Table 8.3 Groupthink symptoms (adapted from Janis, 1972)

Symptom	*Description*	*Examples*
Illusion of invulnerability	Ignoring dangers, overly optimistic, taking extreme risks A group may feel over-confident believing that they are bound to win, or are so necessary that they cannot lose or no one would dare to cut their funding	'The Titanic will never sink' Admiral Kimmel's group maintained that the Japanese would not dare to attack Pearl Harbour right up to 7 December 1941. 'The Japanese will never take Singapore' (World War Two). 'The West is invulnerable' (prior to 11 September 2001)
Collective rationalization	Discrediting or ignoring warning signals that run contrary to group thinking	'Don't rock the boat' *Challenger* Flight 51-L disaster – problems with 'O'-rings suppressed
Unquestioned morality	Believing that the group's position is ethical and moral and that others are wrong and/or evil, eg the use of napalm bombs on civilians and large areas of farmland in South Vietnam	'Bombing Afghanistan is the only way to deal with terrorists' 'If we don't stop the Reds in South Vietnam, tomorrow they will be in Hawaii and next week they will be in San Francisco'
Excessive negative stereotyping	Viewing the opposing side as being too negative to warrant serious consideration, eg the others are evil and won't listen to reason	Before the US Bay of Pigs invasion of Cuba fiasco, President Kennedy's advisers completely underestimated Fidel Castro's air force and army All the Afghan people are responsible for harbouring Osama Bin Laden
Strong conformity pressure	Discouraging the expression of dissension options under threat of expulsion from the group for disloyalty	If someone disagrees frequently they are pressured by people saying 'don't rock the boat' 'You are either with us or against us' – President George Bush as he announced the invasion of Afghanistan, 2001
Self-censorship of dissenting ideas	Keeping dissenting ideas to oneself (as a result of the strong conformity pressure)	'It's more than my job's worth to speak out on this issue' Individuals feel threatened, learn to stay quiet rather than 'blow the whistle'

Table 8.3 *(continued)*

Symptom	*Description*	*Examples*
Illusion of unanimity	Shared false belief that everyone in the group agrees. Air of assumed consensus	People all superficially pretend to agree
Self-appointed mindguards	Mind guards protect the group from negative threatening information	'You don't need to know this', or 'Don't worry the boss at the moment, he/she is very stressed'

Story: Organizational groupthink, *Challenger* Space Shuttle

In January 1986, the world watched on TV as the *Challenger* Space Shuttle took off from Kennedy Space Center at Cape Canaveral and exploded seconds later. Why? There was a push to launch on time (for political kudos) and a failure to listen to qualms about the temperature tolerance of the 'O-rings' that sealed joints. The Presidential Commission later concluded that the disaster was caused by NASA's 'flawed' decision-making process in the application of so-called 'management science' focusing on commercial and political factors rather than human concerns and issues raised before the launch (McConnell, 1988). Hence it was a managerial/organizational failure as well as an engineering failure and a classic example of 'groupthink'.

Table 8.3 illustrates the symptoms and examples of groupthink.

There are many strategies for preventing and managing groupthink included in Book 2 Chapter 11.

Performing stage

During the 'performing stage' energies rise to accomplish the purpose of the group and group members will pull together to get the task done, sometimes at the last minute. However:

> There is nothing wrong with the last minute.
>
> Reg Bolton

Table 8.4 Comparison of a car and a group

	Task	*Maintenance*
Group	Purpose: to get group from present to some place, ie CONTENT	Fostering group development, cohesion, sorting relationships, raising hidden agendas, ie PROCESS
Car	To transport you from A to B	Adjustments of parts, inputs of oil, water, petrol, air in tyres

Endings

The last stage or mourning was at first ignored (and still is in some areas) partly because in western society ending rituals (including funerals) were not well dealt with. Indeed the early model devised by Tuckman and Jensen in 1965 was devised by observing groups in laboratory situations and did not include a 'termination' stage. They added this later in 1977 as society in general became more conscious of the human need to grieve and mourn loss through the work of Elizabeth Kubler-Ross (1970). (See Book 2 Chapter 15 for details of ending activities.)

For a comprehensive review of the models of group development see Smith (2001).

Task and maintenance roles

Facilitators and participants play many different roles in groups; some assigned and formal, others informal and seized.

A group is a bit like car which needs maintenance in order to get from A to B. Like a group, it is also an open system with inputs, processes and outputs.

Benne and Sheats (1948) conducted a study and identified many task and maintenance roles which have been added to in Table 8.5. These roles may be performed by the facilitator and/or group members. Later, defensive and dysfunctional roles were added. Whilst the roles have been categorized under four headings for convenience, there are some inherence contradictions since many roles have a positive and negative side. For example, a critical evaluator or devil's advocate is a useful role which may prevent groupthink. However, if overly negative the role could be regarded as a 'pessimist in the dysfunctional category'.

Table 8.5 Roles that participants play in groups

Task roles: *Help the work of the group*	***Maintenance roles:*** *Help relationships between participants*	***Defensive roles:*** *Protect the group from anxiety*	***Dysfunctional roles:*** *Block progress to get jobs done, focus on own needs, not group's*
Starter Initiates new/different ways of doing things	***Encourager*** Give praise and encouragement	***Tension reliever*** Fill silences, suggests breaks to diffuse tense atmosphere	***Lobbyist*** Uses the group to focus on own issues
Information and opinion seeker and/or giver Ask others for ideas, facts, feelings. Expresses ideas, facts, feelings	***Gatekeeper*** Helps quieter members to speak, retrains dominators	***Court jester*** Tells jokes, invents puns or shows the funny side of things to stop groups getting too 'heavy'	***Playboy/girl*** Naughty child behaviour, whispering, doing something else
Coordinator Organizes ideas and people	***Communication helper*** Requests people to speak louder, reflects back	***Scapegoat*** A person is isolated	***Recognition seeker*** Seeks praise or attention
Summarizer Lists achievements and issues	***Mediator/harmonizer*** Steps in when needed as a go-between		***Blocker*** Rambles off the point, raises irrelevant issues
Energizer Encourages people	***Trust builder*** Values other who take risks and openness		***Pessimist*** Expresses negative opinions and feelings. 'It won't work, we've done it before'
Diagnoser/analyser	***Process observer*** Offers observations on how the group is working or how it could work better		***Aggressor*** Attacks, criticizes

Task roles: *Help the work of the group*	*Maintenance roles:* *Help relationships between participants*	*Defensive roles:* *Protect the group from anxiety*	*Dysfunctional roles:* *Block progress to get jobs done, focus on own needs, not group's*
Reality tester Checks ideas in practice and what is going on in group	***Cultural translator*** Acts as a go-between to enhance understanding between people of different ethnicity		***Rebel*** Challenges facilitator and authority figures for the sake of it, breaks group norms
Consensus tester Calls for straw vote	***Cultural adviser*** Gives information about the ways things are done in other cultures/countries		
Critical evaluator or devil's advocate	***Nurturer*** Nurtures group with warmth and food and goodies		
Technician Helps re material distribution, seating, tables, technology, etc			
Scribe/recorder Manages group memory			
Spokesperson Raises issues on behalf of the group			
Wise person Points out wisdom in confusing information			

Table 8.6 Examples of group behaviours

Fight behaviour verbal and non-verbal conflict	If a group switches into a fight mode, learning is inhibited by playing win/lose battles. Participants may 'fight' and challenge the facilitator
Flight behaviour jokes, red herrings, anecdotes	In the flight mode, joking can be productive in defusing tension. On the other hand, it can be a delaying tactic or defensive technique for putting off the task at hand
Dependency behaviour Dependence on the facilitator	In the dependent mode, participants feel no dependence on each other for learning, but want to rely totally on the facilitator and regard her/him as an expert who has all the answers to their problems. Facilitators are not content 'experts'

Individual behaviours and needs

All behaviour is caused. As human beings we have learnt basic ways of handling difficult situations. A whole group, parts of a group or individuals may exhibit certain behaviours. See Table 8.6.

When a group of people come together, the participation and/or learning of some individuals may be inhibited by psychological defensiveness. It is useful to understand the possible causes of defensive behaviours. See Figure 8.5.

The diagram is a little confusing in that the arrows of cause and effect are not just vertical. For example, a person whose repressed anger is triggered may behave submissively rather than aggressively. Participants who are embarrassed may just smirk and/or giggle. When I first entered Fremantle Jail School as a tutor, my three male students giggled for some time. I just ignored the behaviour and carried on and it finally ceased once they had got used to me and realized I was there to help them.

Facilitators are not required to delve into the causes of archaic anxiety (hence the bold dividing line) unless they are trained therapists facilitating a group advertised as a therapy group. However, if there is a cathartic outburst from a participant it *may* be useful to know why it has happened and have strategies to manage it.

The art of 'good' facilitating is to be sensitive to the moods of the groups and to use a variety of tactics to keep participants on the task. Facilitators need to recognize that it is natural for groups to:

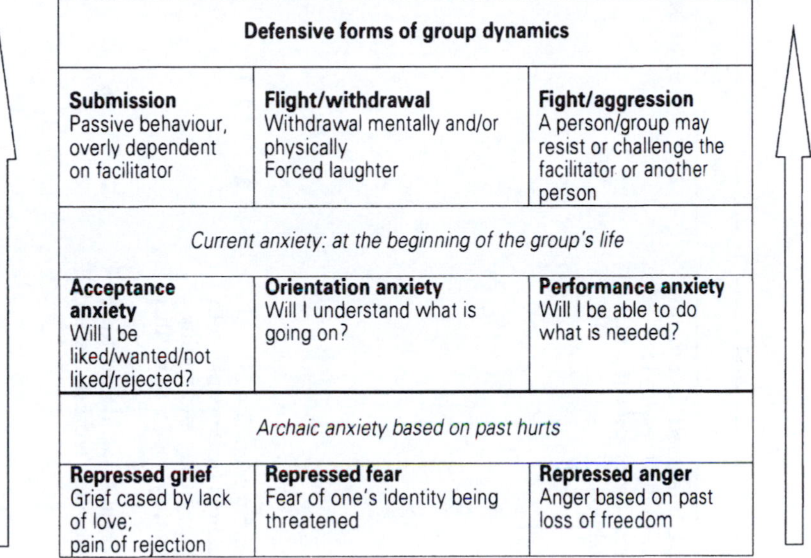

Figure 8.5 Causes of defensiveness of participants

Source: Adapted from Heron (1999: 63)

- work at a varying pace and in different ways;
- work in fits and starts;
- reach plateaux at times and need time for reflection – a short summary from the facilitator at these times helps to reassure the group and restore confidence;
- experience phases of confusion;
- go round in circles or off on tangents;
- be very noisy at times – Merrelyn Emery commented that 'creativity has a disturbing resemblance to madness' (Emery, 1976).

Maslow's hierarchy of needs

Our behaviours are also influenced by our needs. Facilitators are involved in enhancing the behaviour and motivation of groups to achieve their goals. Participants are also responsible for their own motivation of course and this may be enhanced if their needs are met (eg if they are comfortable, in bright surroundings, with food and drinks available). Abraham Maslow developed a 'hierarchy of needs', a rather simplistic model which, however, has stood the test of time. It provides a simple checklist and a basis for many facilitation activities and responsibilities (Maslow, 1943, 1954).

Table 8.7 Maslow's hierarchy of needs

Needs	*Maslow's categories*	*Facilitator's responsibilities*	*Book*	*Chapters*
'Being' needs	**Self-actualization** Desire to become whatever you are capable of becoming Opportunities for new learning, adventure creativity, innovation, trying new things Determining and creating your own lifestyle/s Challenging projects and taking new risks Making a difference, helping society, environment Independence for some (interdependence for others) Feeling empowered (having choices)	Self-actualization needs relate self-fulfilment and realizing ones potential. It relates to self-development, career development and lifestyle change workshops	**2**	**7, 9, 10, 11,12**
'Doing' needs	**Self-esteem** Recognition Feeling worthwhile Respected Being recognized for achievements/contributions Being involved in important projects	Issues of self-esteem and recognition are involved in how facilitators treat people with respect at the beginning, during and ending of workshops and how they ensure that others do the same	**2**	**2, 15**
		Checks and balances on how facilitators treat people are kept by evaluating workshops and facilitators	**2**	**16**

Needs	Maslow's categories	Facilitator's responsibilities	Book	Chapters
	Belonging Love (in its many different forms) Acceptance by co-workers, peers, management, customers Feeling part of the group/s	Belonging needs relate to how facilitators manage issues of diversity and exclusivity	**1** **2**	9 **5,12**
		Technology enables people to be part of wider groups than ever before. Does not replace the joy of being face to face with real flesh and blood!	**1** **2**	**8** **14**
		Issues of self-esteem and recognition are involved in how facilitators model and treat people with respect at the beginning, during and ending of workshops and how they ensure that others do the same		
		Checks and balances on how facilitators treat people are kept by evaluating workshops and facilitators		
'Having needs'	**Safety** Protection from physical and psychological threat, danger Living in peace Feeling safe to take risks Safe working environment Job security	Safety needs underpin contracting for ground safe rules, methods of confronting	**2**	**2, 6**
		Ethical issues	**1**	**11**
		It is important how facilitators begin and end workshops	**2**	**2,15**
	Physiological Food, water Shelter Comfortable temperature (good ventilation, adjustable heating, air conditioning) Welcoming ambience Comfortable workspace, seating	Physiological needs underpin the preparation work undertaken by facilitators and clients regarding choice of venue, etc	**2**	**1 and 2**
		In outdoor learning facilitators choose less comfortable environments within safe limits and with backup.	**2**	**13**

I will briefly explain each level of the model and how it relates to facilitation. In Table 8.7 there is a column which links each section to the practice of facilitation and the relevant chapters in Books 1 and 2.

Physiological needs underpin the preparation work undertaken by facilitators and clients. Participants need regular drink, loo and stretch breaks. Energies flag just before lunch and after lunch, so facilitators need to be able to incorporate suitable short energizer exercises. Maslow argued that when physiological needs are met, participants can concentrate better on the issues at hand. Critics state that there is little research to prove this and indeed some people isolate themselves on purpose and fast in austere conditions in order to think more clearly. However, for many participants in workshops cooperation improves when their basic physiological needs are met.

Safety needs underpin contracting for ground safe rules, methods for confronting inappropriate behaviour and ethical issues. Indeed the success of workshops frequently depends on the attention paid to building of trust and rapport at the beginning. It is important in outdoor learning not to push discomforts too far. Likewise safety issues at the end of workshops are important, in that a facilitator must prepare participants to re-enter their work and home lives appropriately.

Belonging needs relate to how facilitators manage issues of diversity and exclusivity. Technology enables people to be part of wider groups than ever before (but still does not replace the joy of being face to face with real flesh and blood!).

Issues of self-esteem and recognition are involved in how facilitators treat people with respect at the beginning, during and ending of workshops and how they ensure that others do the same. It also relates to methods to give and receive feedback which needs to be realistic, objective and constructive. In workshops that involve organizational change through 'downsizing', 'right sizing', etc, self-esteem issues need to be handled with care and tact. Likewise in some cultures seniority and years of experience need to be acknowledged. A facilitator needs to be able to 'give face' as well as prevent people from 'losing face'. Checks and balances on how facilitators treat people are kept by evaluating workshops and facilitators.

Self-actualization needs relate self-fulfilment and realizing ones potential. It relates to self-development, career development and lifestyle change workshops.

The model stimulates thinking about participants' needs, but does have some shortcomings. The levels are not necessarily sequential and there is a wide variation in people's needs and expectations. Some highly motivated people pursue their self-actualizing projects (from entrepreneurs to environmentalists) sometimes for years, or even a lifetime, with few physiological needs met. (See Hopson and Scally (1984) for useful card sorts for career and life planning based on Maslow.

Table 8.8 Communication patterns in triads

A to B	B to C	A to B and C
A to C	C to B	B to A and C
B to A	C to A	C to A and B

Size of groups

The larger the group size becomes, the more complex numbers of interactions are possible. This is worth taking into consideration when you are setting up small group work.

For example, in a triad (three people, eg A, B and C) there are nine possible ways of interacting (Table 8.8).

Small groups are advantageous particularly at the beginning of programmes as dyads and triads are less threatening and give maximum participation or 'air space' especially for quieter more reflective participants. Note the increase in complexity of communication patterns as group size increases in Table 8.9.

As group size increases there is more chance of 'social loafing' (laziness) or for some individuals to be left out of discussions. So it is useful to:

- give everyone in a group a task (or invite all members to help in feeding back to the whole group);
- allow people to join group projects of their choice and/or move to other groups if they feel they are not being heard (as in Open Space Technology sessions – see Book 2 Chapter 12);
- ask small-group members to nominate a facilitator whose role is to maximize the participation of all.

Table 8.9 Group size and interactions

Number of people in a group	*Number of possible interactions*
2	2
3	9
4	28
5	75
6	186
7	441
8	1056

Small group discussions

For small group discussions optimum group size has been estimated to be approximately five to seven people. Often, groups focus on re-discussing previously shared information. It is the facilitator's role to help groups feel comfortable to bring out previously unshared information and to ensure that everyone has 'airtime' for giving ideas and opinions. This, it has been assumed, is often achieved more easily in small groups.

Large group interventions

Fred and Merrelyn Emery's ground-breaking, early work with 'Search Conferences' involving up to 100 representatives of a deep slice through hierarchies of organizations and communities (Emery, 1976; Emery and Purser, 1996), the Schnelle brothers' work in Munich Stadium using 'Metaplanning' workshops in Germany (1979) and Owen's work with 'Open Space Technology' (1992, 1995, 1997; Owen and Stadler, 1999) illustrate the benefits of working with whole systems and that large-scale events do have merit.

Bunker and Alban (1997) in the USA analysed these different methods for involving whole organizations for rapid change and decided that success was partly dependent on choosing the right process/es to match the group's purpose. In addition, they suggested that the following principles and values underlie all these methods:

1. **Valuing engagement**. The organization concerned must have a 'bone-deep' belief in participation, as people know when they are being manipulated.
2. **Select the right issue**. The issue needs to be neither too broad nor too narrow and apply to all levels and stakeholders (internal and external). It must be important enough to motivate all and be seen as part of long-term change processes.
3. **Start with a planning committee**. A planning group with representative stakeholders develops ownership and generates suggestions and sometimes raises potential problems. Stakeholders also form a trusted core and the potential backbone of follow-up groups after the event.
4. **Select the right people**. Often groups think too narrowly. The top power-holders need to be involved. Do not omit security people, cleaners, and technicians and selected outsiders.
5. **Structuring for good conversations**. Help people to recognize multiple perspectives, be aware of their own filters and be ready to have their own ideas challenged. A round table of about five-foot diameter maximum allows up to eight people to engage easily with one another. Long rectangles are not as effective.

6. **Allow time for reflection and creative breakthroughs**. Western culture pushes for quick decisive decisions. But we need 'soak time' (according to Marv Weisbord) and 'sleep time' (Hogan) to let our brains process large amounts of information, so we can talk about it and digest it. I attended a one-week, residential 'Human Values in Management Workshop' in Calcutta in 1998. It was 'full on', but in the middle the whole group of about 100 people had one free day where we all went on a boat trip down the Ganges which worked really well. Our brains changed mode from adult to 'free child' on a day off from school and we chatted playfully about our lives and the ideas in the workshop.
7. **Planning turning points: from 'me' to 'we'**. When the whole group becomes aware of the whole picture and takes responsibility for what has happened and needs to happen, there are paradigm shifts from 'me' to 'we' thinking.
8. **Building in an opportunity for the 'if'**. Some people react cynically or are 'turned off' by repeated workshops where they are encouraged to generate bland vision statements, but if they are asked the 'if' question 'If things were working at their best, what would be happening?', ie focusing on results helps people to visualize desirable futures.
9. **Allow opportunities for efficacy and commitment**. People need to feel they have the power to influence and make a difference individually and as a group, ie to feel 'efficacious'.
10. **Attend to logistics**. Large groups move around rather like an elephant; everything is maximized so it is important to attend in detail to issues like room size, break-out spaces, noise and interference, lighting and reliable audio-visual equipment. Good food makes such a difference to people feeling valued.

Developing adult learning skills and knowledge

> Listen to everyone, learn from everyone
> Nobody knows everything, but everyone knows something.
>
> Charlie Hough

People come together in groups to learn from each other and the facilitator. There are five key concepts of adult learning that facilitators can utilize (Burns, 1995):

1. **Purpose**. Adults want to know why they are doing something, ie how it will help them in the performance of their work or quality of work and/or home lives. Where appropriate, it is useful for facilitators to explain the purpose of processes and how they fit into the overall picture of workshop.

Table 8.10 Group size characteristics (adapted from Shaw, 1981)

	Small groups	*Large groups*
Advantages	• Participants usually feel more satisfied because more chance to have a say, ie more 'air time' • More intimate • Finish simple tasks quicker • Individuals feel more important	• More minds, skills and experience to process information • A chance for the whole 'system' to interact • A chance for mixed groups from the whole system to meet to gain appreciation of the whole • Chance to meet others • Shy people can stay anonymous • Emergent leadership or facilitation occurs or needs to be encouraged • Large groups may take higher risks: 'risky shift' which may be useful but may need to be monitored
Disadvantages	• Harder to deal with awkward behaviour • Fewer ideas • Less experience overall • Fewer varieties of discussion groups possible	• Harder to organize • More tension, formality, inhibitions • Sub-groups are likely to form • Group members have 'less airtime' to speak therefore less satisfied • Dominators: possible dominators increase • Less likely to help a person in need because feeling of anonymity • More pressure to conform with a larger group • As groups gets larger there can be more swings of mood/feelings called 'affective contagion' from a few individuals, ie a swing towards joy (eg joyful festivals) or perhaps a swing towards anger (eg a community meeting with a negative minority group)

Table 8.11 Characteristics of pedagogy and andragogy

Pedagogy	*Andragogy*
Teacher and educational authorities responsible for content and process of learning	Learner is responsible, autonomous Knows what he/she wants to learn, enjoys problem-based learning on a 'need-to-know' basis
Learner is passive, dependent	Learner is active, independent
Child's experience not considered useful	Adult's experience honoured and valued
Artificial learning under subject headings	Experiential learning encompassing many areas of knowledge
Assessment by others	Adults involved in setting goals, projects and means of assessment

2. **Mutual enquiry**. Adults want to engage in mutual enquiry rather than be told what to do and how to do it, so facilitators need to be able to 'go with the flow' and adapt when adults seize their autonomy and suggest different ways of achieving the group's goals.
3. **Experiential learning.** Each adult has millions of experiences, so facilitators need to build in time to enable participants to discuss and relate new ideas and new learning to past experiences.
4. **Difference.** Facilitators have to make optimal provision for differences in learning styles, time, place and pace of learning as well as cultural and physical differences. Some adults need frequent stretch breaks because of achy joints. (See Book 2 Chapter 4.)
5. **Andragogy and pedagogy**. The concept and science of teaching adults is called 'andragogy' and is attributed to Malcolm Knowles (1984) and earlier work by John Dewey. 'Pedagogy' is the art and science of teaching children, which is teacher-focused and assumes that children are lacking in skills and knowledge. 'Training' is similar to the world of pedagogy, whilst facilitation is more aligned to andragogy. Facilitators need to understand these concepts as some participants may be alienated from negative experiences at school or college. See Table 8.11.

Experiential learning

> If I hear, I forget
> If I see I remember
> If I do, I understand
>
> Confucius

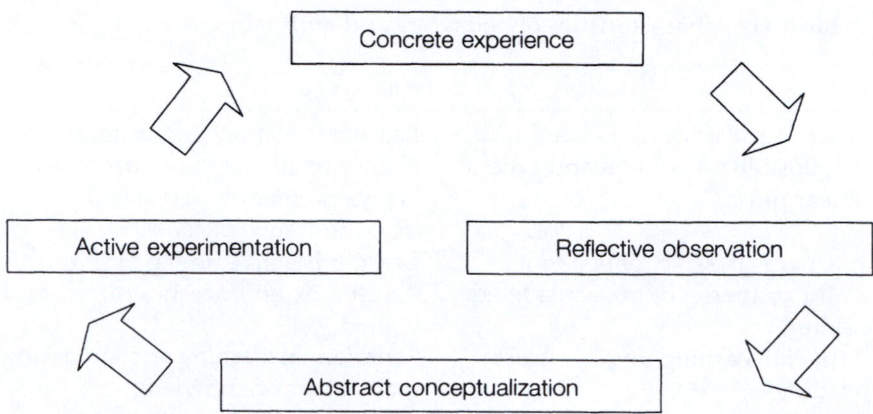

Figure 8.6 Experiential Learning Model

Source: Adapted from Kolb (1984)

From the earliest times when people collaborated to hunt they had to learn from experience or suffer the consequences. But learning from experience is not always automatic, and we often repeat mistakes. We have so many experiences all the time that we often need to take time to stop and reflect in a decisive way.

Learning from experience can be enhanced by knowledge of Kolb's (1984) experiential learning cycle. The model is very simple and you probably followed it at school when conducting science experiments, ie firstly there is an activity, secondly you reflect on what happened, thirdly you draw conclusions and lastly you think about how to try out what you have learnt. See Figure 8.6.

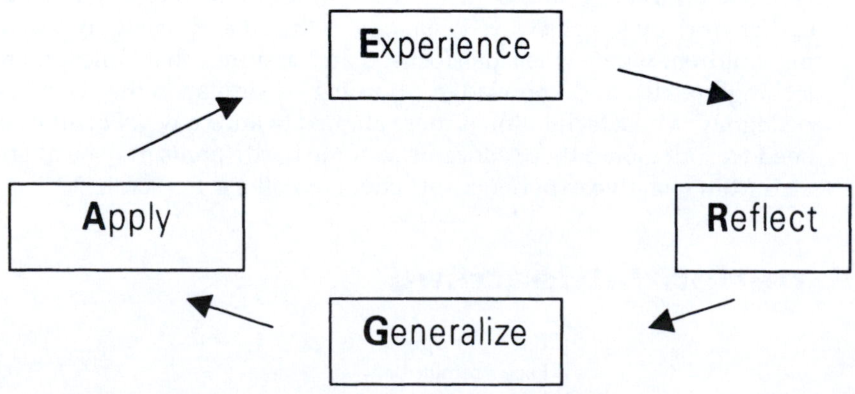

Figure 8.7 Simplified Experiential Learning Model

This process involves an upward spiral of learning and is the basis of action research as developed originally by Kurt Lewin (1951). This spiral of learning is rarely continuous. Frequently learning is intermittent and smooth; fast and slow; sometimes deflating, at other times elevating and multidimensional in time and space.

It is useful to know that the Experiential Learning Theory, Learning styles theory, Barriers to Learning and the ORID process (Spencer, 1989) are all based on the same four learning styles. (See Figures 8.6–8.9.)

I prefer to simplify this model and remember it using the mnemonic 'ERGA' from the first letter of each stage. See Figure 8.7.

We cannot assume that participants learn from all their experiences. We all have so many things happening to us that we often have to make a conscious effort to reflect. Part of the facilitator's job is to help a group to reflect.

Like all models, this is very simplistic. To begin with, learning can start at any stage; you do not necessarily need an experience. Secondly, learning is more like a spiral upwards. Thirdly, all four stages may occur almost simultaneously, as one participant commented: 'When I had to stand in front of the group to make a presentation my mind was working so fast. I talked, watched their eyes and reacted to their body language in a split second of time. It felt amazing.'

Barriers to learning

Both participants and facilitators can prevent learning. For example, participants may say/think:

- 'It won't work, we tried it before', ie clutching to previous experience.
- 'Why change, we've always done it that way.'
- 'Let's stop talking and get on with it; we haven't got time to reflect.'
- 'I won't have a go – I might look foolish.'
- 'Can't see how that relates to my job.'

Some participants have very dominant learning styles in one of the four areas shown above. So I sometimes use the Barriers to Learning Model (Figure 8.8) to encourage people to use all four learning styles in order to complete the experiential learning cycle.

Facilitators too can prevent learning by:

- not building a safe environment;
- packing too much into one session;
- only using teaching/training methods that they feel comfortable with;
- stressing 'no pain no gain', ie learning is always stressful;
- not supporting people through steep learning curves;

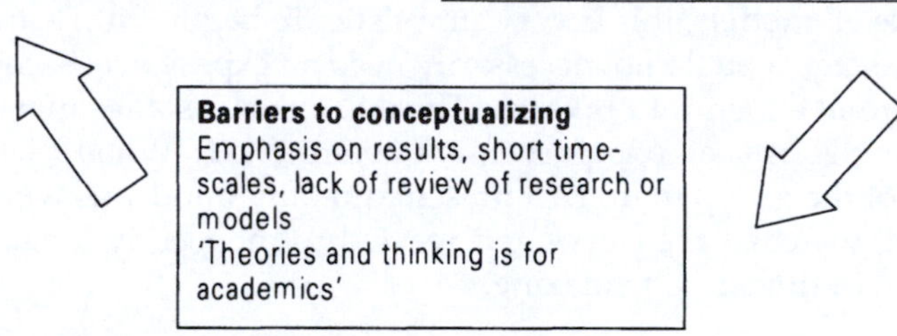

Figure 8.8 Barriers to learning

Source: Adapted from Bennett and Richardson (1984)

- limiting questions in order to finish all the content;
- using technical terms and jargon unnecessarily;
- being impatient or condescending.

Learning styles

> Do not do unto others as you would that they should do unto you.
> Their tastes may not be the same.
>
> George Bernard Shaw

Each of us has preferred ways of learning. Honey and Mumford (1986) called these 'Learning styles' (based on Kolb's earlier work on experiential learning). As facilitators we need to blend in different exercises to massage all four learning styles.

Characteristics of each learning styles are summarized in the boxes in Figure 8.9 whilst a kite-like figure illustrates one person's style, ie a strong

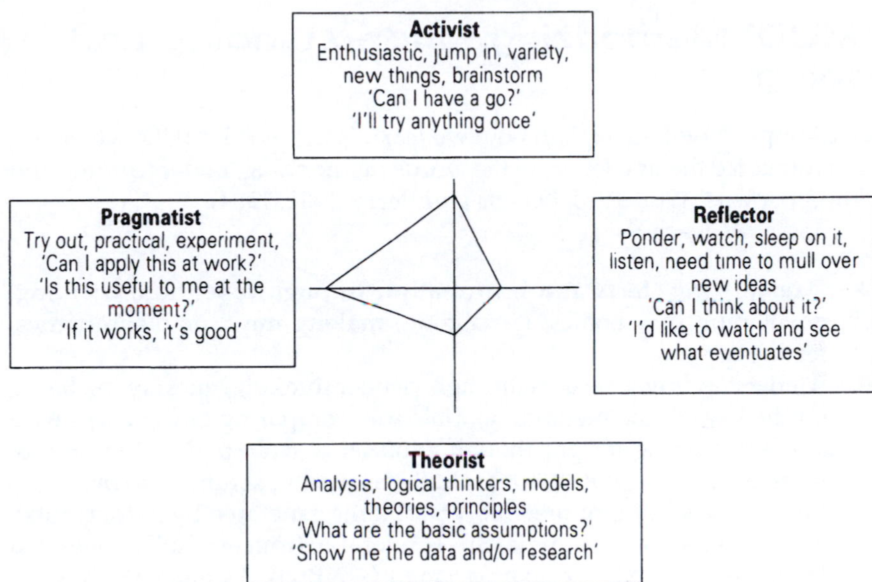

Figure 8.9 Learning styles

Source: Adapted from Honey and Mumford (1992)

preference for activist, pragmatic learning as opposed to reflecting and theorizing. Obviously the ideal is to have a balance of all four types. Learning styles are influenced by our personality, personal and cultural history, career and job roles and allocated tasks. (See also Book 2, Chapter 4 for descriptions of other theories of learning, doing and being.)

How do we learn?

There are many theories about how we learn. I have chosen a few simple constructs that help my facilitation work.

If you ask a group of people 'In how many different ways do you learn something?' answers might include:

I ask for help, I start with the easiest, I start with concrete ideas and work to abstract ideas, I ask for help, I read about it, I have a go and always forget to read instructions, I wait till I need to know something, I write it down, I read instructions, I watch others, I take something apart to see how it works and then put it back together again, I learn best with others.

'MUD' Memorizing, understanding and doing

One simple model to explain how we learn is the word 'MUD' which is a mnemonic for the first letters of the words memorizing, understanding and doing (Downs, 1981, 1995; Downs and Perry, 1982, 1984).

That is, we learn by:

- 'Memorizing' **facts and information** through repetition, chanting, developing mnemonics, visualizing, making mind map summaries, testing recall.
- 'Understanding' **concepts** through: deeper thinking, questioning based on the keys to understanding, dialogue, comparing one concept with another, gaining insight though experience (role plays, simulations, work experience, outdoor learning), discussing solutions to problems (using case studies or preferably problems generated by participants), analysing the causes of problems (preferably from examples generated from the experiences of participants) (see Book 2 Chapter 3, Keys to Understanding).
- 'Doing' new **skills** through practising, trial and error, undoing, observing demonstrations and videos, imagining doing something well.

We learn facts, concepts and skills in different ways, so it is a facilitator's job to choose from and provide a variety of learning experiences suitable to the learning content (see Book 2 Chapter 3, Keys to Understanding).

'KASV': knowledge, attitudes, skills and values

Another useful framework for learning is KASV, which is a mnemonic for Knowledge, Attitudes, Skills and Values. All these areas contribute to a person's 'capacity' to do a job.

Knowledge management (KM)

Knowledge refers to an organized body of information which may be factual or procedural. Intellectual capital/knowledge is heralded as one of the major assets of organizations today (Brewer, 2000; Harman, 2000; Garrick and Rhodes, 2000). De Salvo (2000) cites the first areas of knowledge management. I added the fourth:

- **data**, that is, raw facts, figures;
- **information**, that is, processed data with additional meaning;

- **tacit and explicit knowledge**, that is, wider frames of context and knowledge;
- **wisdom**, that is, applied values, philosophies, knowledge held as relevant and important through time.

How can facilitators help participants to elicit data (from data bases and brains), avoid information overload, analyse it and identify what knowledge is critical to organizational success and turn it into information? Knowledge is power; at a time when many organizations are downsizing, losing corporate knowledge and accumulated wisdom and generating distrust, how can facilitators best regenerate trust so that participants will share their tacit knowledge, make it explicit, evaluate it and disseminate relevant information though organizations? (See Book 2 Chapter 3.)

Participants are often more ready to embrace new behaviour if they understand why a new concept is being brought into the workplace. For example, participants may not take on board issues of 'safety' by being lectured about the new safety regulations, but they may be facilitated to explore the issues of safety by facilitators, for example, using the Keys of Understanding (Downs, 1995) (see Book 2 Chapter 3).

It was Michael Polanyi (a Hungarian physicist and philosopher) in *The Tacit Dimension* (Polanyi, 1966) who promoted the idea of 'personal or tacit' knowledge and skills. As an example, he gave the skill we all have of being able to identify the faces of people we know (this still baffles computer programmers who prefer to use simpler symbols like thumb prints or eyes for identification purposes). Another is the ability to ride a bicycle or the way some cooks know how to make superb cakes without recipes. They know how to do it, but cannot explain exactly how.

Attitudes

> 'Start with a positive intention. Think about why you are doing yoga and what you want to achieve.'
>
> Cheryl Stedman

These are the words of my yoga teacher at the start of every lesson. The teaching is simple yet profound. If we do not approach what we do with a positive attitude then the learning or outcomes may be lessened.

Facilitators may face groups of people who are disheartened, distrustful or angry. They need to be able to vent their feelings. (See Book 2, Chapter 6.)

Changing the attitudes of participants is one of the most difficult roles of a facilitator. Entrenched attitudes can be major obstacles to change. When people reach understanding of new information they might still not change their attitude towards an issue. Attitudes are not only based on knowledge, but also on feelings and on how one used to think. If there is no attitude change towards an issue there will also be no change in responding to the issue. If a desired output of a workshop is a change in attitude then new information and/or skills need to be integrated into the participants' thinking and behaviour.

For example, with safety and/or gender issues, entrenched attitudes are often obstacles to change. For an attitude change to take place appropriate methods need to be chosen. Changes in attitude are based on two-way communication in which the facilitator and participants engage in dialogue (rather than debate). As a result of a workshop new information, new skills and new attitudes should result in changed behaviour. This would need to be monitored on an ongoing basis.

Skills

Skills are the ability to perform tasks correctly with ease and precision. Skills are:

- measurable by observation and testing;
- innate, ie sometimes not observable and even undervalued by people who perform them automatically: 'I always do it this way, it's obvious isn't it?';
- socially constructed and valued, eg in most cultures jobs that are traditionally held to be so-called 'men's work' are more highly valued and paid than jobs that are traditionally held to be so-called 'women's work';
- culturally constructed and valued, eg in Bali painting and musicianship are highly valued;
- being created, eg computer skills;
- dying, eg technical drawing skills, many handicrafts, languages;
- performed by people, animals and now by machines.

However, there is no one accepted definition of what a skill is. It is a contested and subjective concept (Smith, 1998).

Jobs are frequently analysed in terms of competencies required. A 'competency' includes the ability to perform tasks with the necessary skills, knowledge and attitudes. Competencies are small-scale skills broken down into their elements and combined with the required standards or levels of performance criteria and the conditions needed to perform the tasks. (See Chapter 6 for The International Association of Facilitators' list of facilitator competencies.)

Workshops to determine the competencies in a job can be facilitated using the DACUM process, which is an acronym for '**D**eveloping **a** **C**urricul**um**) (Hogan, 1999).

Values

Values are long-term, strongly held beliefs. Cultural, community and organizational values underpin our behaviours, sometimes subconsciously. It is useful to know 'where people are coming from', ie the values that shape the way they perceive the world and interact with it.

Values are often part of mission statements and goal setting. Card sorts are useful for bringing out values. Hopson and Scally (1984) generated a useful card pack of 'Work Values' which are easy to reproduce.

Workshops that impinge on attitudes and values are likely to arouse emotions. (See Book 2 Chapters 3 and 4.)

Unlearning

Conventional wisdom states that the amount of knowledge and skills in the world doubles every year (I wonder who counts?). If this is so, then we need to be able to re-evaluate and challenge, and if necessary unlearn or discard 'things' that were previously held to be true and skills that were previously held to be important. A particularly poignant example of this is during outdoor learning activities when participants abseil for the first time. In order to descend a cliff they have to lean over backwards. Even though participants are well attached to a rope, this contravenes everything they have previously learnt about behaviours on the edge of steep cliffs. (See Book 2 Chapter 13.) Such metaphors are useful to engage participants in evaluating changes in demand for skills and knowledge.

Self-development

Learning is ongoing and we now talk of 'learning organizations' (Senge, 1990). But many managers and workers do not have the time or motivation to attend courses. Some feel uncomfortable to learn or be perceived as ignorant in front of their peers or subordinates (especially in hierarchical cultures). Pedler and Boydell (1988; with Burgoyne, 1986) developed the concept of 'self-development' to enable people to monitor and learn on the job. Facilitators take on the roles of mentors and help participants to conduct needs analyses on themselves, develop learning contracts, devise learning strategies and monitor learning through journals and self-assessment and feedback from others. (See Book 2 Chapter 7.)

Conclusion

In this chapter I have covered a variety of theories that underpin facilitation. Often facilitators have to go with the flow of group process; there are times when theories and models cease to be of use. Indeed this idea is encapsulated in the following quote:

> Learn your theories as well as you can, but put them aside when you touch the miracle of the living soul.
>
> Carl Jung

9

Facilitating culturally diverse groups

> My father in Bangkok would be horrified if he knew I was standing in a circle at a workshop holding hands with a man I had never met before.
>
> Young Thai woman in Australia

Introduction

In this chapter I address the issues faced in facilitating multicultural groups. There are both advantages and disadvantages of groups with high levels of cultural diversity. I explore 'dimensions of cultural' characteristics which help make cultural characteristics more visible. I raise issues regarding some ice-breaker exercises and issues faced by multicultural groups.

In Book 2 Chapter 5, I include a checklist which facilitators can use to enhance workshop design, content and delivery for culturally mixed groups.

Generalizations

> All generalizations are false, including this one.
>
> Source unknown

In this chapter I illustrate ideas with my experiences in Hong Kong, Malaysia, Mongolia, and Lao PDR. For convenience I use the term 'Westerners', realizing that there are many differences between Danes, Australians and English. Likewise terms like 'Nepalese' or 'Mongolian' encompass many different cultures, tribes and ethnic groups. I do not know a way around this problem and hope that no offence is caused.

Humans have 98 per cent genes in common across the world, yet our cultural differences are diverse and need to be understood.

Facilitating groups that contain participants from different cultural backgrounds is becoming the norm in many countries. There are very few groups nowadays that are culturally homogeneous, plus many people have lived and worked in different countries. Similarly, many facilitators are working across cultural and country boundaries. This enables us to draw on a wider array of participants' experiences and perspectives than ever before.

There is now an abundance of research on cultures and behaviours (Hofstede, 1980, 1991; Hall, 1990; Abdullah, 2001). However, it is important to note that within cultural groups there is diversity of behaviours between people of different age groups, genders, city and rural dwellers and regions. It is impossible to generalize about values and behaviours. Hofstede conducted his research in a large international corporation and in some instances his conclusions about a particular culture were drawn from as few as 20 respondents. Also, when people are working on the international scene there may be a veneer and/or deeper adjustment to some western or eastern styles of doing things.

We have to make some generalizations to help us understand different patterns of thinking, presenting and writing ideas. As long as we remember that 'All generalizations are false (including this one)' we can keep an open mind.

I have tried to raise the awareness of the reader to cross-cultural issues in various chapters. This chapter is designed to focus on the issues facing facilitators when working with groups that contain people from mixed cultural and linguistic backgrounds as well as issues when travelling overseas to facilitate groups.

Almost every facilitation workshop now contains people of different cultural and ethnic backgrounds. Yet this area appears to be the poor relation in facilitation texts and research.

Firstly, there is a need to study the role of facilitators as 'cultural translators'. How do facilitators use, adapt or create new analogies, stories and role-plays in cross-cultural settings? How do you get across abstract concepts like facilitation and management in cultures where these concepts do not exist?

Secondly, it is important to recognize and acknowledge existing avenues for analysing and solving problems. What are the similarities and differences between indigenous procedures of facilitation and peaceful conflict resolution?

Globalization, localization and multiculturalism

With the competing forces of globalization, localization and multiculturalism, there is increased need for facilitators to be 'culturally literate'. Indeed, facilitators more than ever before are needed as 'cultural mediators or translators' to enable individuals in multicultural groups to dialogue more effectively.

The impact of film, television and the Internet means that some non-western cultures are exposed to and in some cases are absorbing western values such as individualism, industrialization and materialism at a fast rate:

> The Malays at present, are quite confused. . . Many of the attributes that they are required to adopt for the IT age, such as competitiveness, aggressiveness, egalitarianism and individualism, are at odds with their cultural values of cooperation, humility, hierarchical and community-based oriented thinking.
>
> (Abdullah, 2000: 5)

As a result, facilitators have to be doubly careful not to stereotype people and their cultures.

What is culture?

We are all socialized into many different 'cultures':

- 'national cultures', noting that there are regional, ethnic, language, age and other variations;
- 'organizational or corporate cultures', eg compare fast-moving IT companies with NGOs in developing countries;
- 'professional cultures', eg compare engineering cultures, artistic cultures, academic cultures;
- 'age cultures', eg compare pop cultures, youth cultures, Internet hacker groups, and 'yuppies'.

Concerning the use of the term 'national culture' we refer to:

- beliefs, values customs that are programmed from birth into our minds, thinking, feeling and behaviour;
- something that is shared by a group of people implicitly and explicitly, and is constantly changing;
- something that older members of the group attempt to pass on to younger members;

- something that changes slowly over time;
- something that shapes behaviour, thoughts and perceptions of the world. (Adler, 1997)

Making culture visible

A physical explanation of 'culture' can be given by asking participants to close their eyes and concentrate on one breath. Then generate discussion around the subconscious nature of breathing which is like our cultures. We do not notice culture, 'it is like the air we breathe'. We were born and raised to act in certain ways and to value certain things. We never think about these automatic feelings and reactions until we come into contact with people from different cultures. Then each regards the 'other' as funny, odd, different, peculiar, fascinating and sometimes frustrating, sometimes all at the same time!

STORY: CULTURES ARE CONSTANTLY CHANGING, THERE IS NO ONE CULTURE

At the 4th Annual Facilitators' Conference in Malaysia, November 2001, I chatted to many different participants. One mature, Malay, Moslem, friend chatted to me about her concerns. 'We use western facilitation techniques and people accept them, but underneath we are a collective society, so there is dissonance. I think Malaysian society at the moment has an identity crisis, we are muddled'.

On the other hand, a younger Chinese Malaysian woman said later:

> We are basically living a western life. Both my husband and I work, we chose to send our kids to the International School for a well-rounded education. Something had to give, they cannot speak Malay, well a few words for the maid and we have a Malay language tutor for them on Saturday, but we can get by totally speaking English. We don't really practise our Chinese culture now either: Keeping up with cultural traditions takes time. We don't have the time. Of course, I still believe that we must take care of immediate family, ie our kids, our parents, but beyond that we just don't have time.

An Indian Malaysian woman added, 'We are the same, we do not spend much time with cultural rituals; however, I must admit as I get older I'm now more interested in rediscovering my culture'.

These three short personal anecdotes woven together give an essence of the changing fabric of the cultural life in Malaysia. Cultures are always changing, but a culture is always there, often 'lived' unconsciously. Plus interest in traditions swing back and froth like a pendulum and are re-born in new and emerging forms.

We often introduce western ideas, models, and processes without thinking about their cultural significance or the fact that they are also constantly changing. It may be useful for facilitators to 'offer': 'This model was developed in the West. It may be suitable to apply to some of your local issues or you may need to adapt it to your culture, organization, community. . .'.

Cultural dimensions

Cultures have been classified in order for us to be able to understand them more easily. But in any classification there are problems of over-simplification and generalization.

Significant differences have been identified across (and within) cultures which are sometimes called 'dimensions of difference' of values and attitudes (Laurent, 1983; Trompenaars, 1993; Hofstede, 1980; Hampden-Turner, 1991; Hampden-Turner and Trompenaars, 1995; Abdullah and Shephard, 2000). I will describe the characteristics of each, knowing that on any continuum there is overlap.

The problem in describing differences in bipolar terms is that it triggers dualistic thinking, ie a person is 'this' or 'that' when we are all mixtures, and within any culture some individuals may not exhibit the stereotypical characteristics of that culture. Neither is better or worse than the other, they are just different and each dimension has *consequences*. Sometimes working in cross-cultural groups enables members to seek out some of the preferred traits of the 'other'. However, this sometimes ends in forms of retribution by members of their own group. In Australia, Aboriginal people who have succeeded have sometimes been referred to as 'coconuts', ie brown on the outside and white inside.

More Asian	**More Anglo**
Collectivism	Individualism
High power distance (hierarchy)	Low power distance (equality)
Harmony	Control
Religious/spiritual	Secular
Polychronic time	Monochronic time
Circular high context thinking	Linear low context thinking
Shame	Guilt

Figure 9.0 Generalised cultural dimensions

Individualism and collectivism

In individualistic cultures people have a sense of 'separated self'. They see themselves as unique with defined personal boundaries, space, goals and achievements. People pride themselves in expressing their individuality through their own opinions, dress and idiosyncrasies. But it is wrong to make generalizations. Margaret Thatcher claimed there was no such thing as 'society', only 'individuals'. Yet she expected a rigid conformity in dress, education, behaviour and political stance. Idiosyncrasy during her 'reign' was not acceptable.

People from collective societies have a sense of 'related self'. They value collaboration and group achievement and rewards. Loyalty to the group is placed above achievement of personal goals. They tend to hesitate to state opinions before knowing what others have to say. Individual loyalty to the group offers protection if things go wrong; no individual may be blamed. In China 'guanxi' or connections are highly valued, as a way of gaining access to resources and favours. Often these are through family members, but with the reciprocal gains come many social obligations. People will try to get their family members jobs in their organizations, which is regarded as nepotism by Westerners. (It is practised in the West too, but attempts to get the best person to fit the job are held paramount.)

A facilitator may need to take these dimensions into account when watching levels of participation in discussions relating to goal setting and contentious issues and the ways in which achievements are honoured and valued.

Low power distance (equality) and high power distance (hierarchy)

Power distance relates to how power is received and shared in groups. In low power distance societies, participants value equality; work should be allocated according to competence rather than age or seniority. In high power distance societies managers and CEOs have status, are treated with deference, honorifics and titles are used and team members accept instructions without question. People are given more responsibility according to seniority and age. Interactions between members of different rank are formal, as are dress codes. Empowerment of team workers in high power distance societies such as India, The Philippines, China and Lao PDR could be regarded as a threat, whereas in low power distance societies such as Australia, the USA and Scandinavia empowerment of workers could be regarded more positively.

Consider a western facilitator working with Lao and Australian participants; there is ample scope for misunderstandings. Encouraging all participants to make suggestions on how things should be done and to ask questions at any time may result in very different responses from Australians and Lao people.

Malaysia is a high power distance society. In Kuala Lumpur, one Malaysian woman said to me, 'Harmony in groups comes about because of the unequal distribution of power', ie everyone knows their place. This provoked my thinking: as often as facilitators we are working to minimize the power deferential in order to allow the ideas of people 'lower down the hierarchy' to be heard.

Lao PDR is a high power distance society. I had to adapt to long speeches at the beginning of workshops where the room layout would be very formal (specially prepared banners across a stage citing the name of the workshop, organizations and dates), a large table with flowers for visiting dignitaries, and long tables for participants. Opening welcoming speeches would take over an hour, then there would be a tea/coffee break when the officials would leave and tables would be rearranged to herringbone formation for group discussion or a U-shape in smaller groups.

Career success or Confucian dynamism (tasks and rules) and quality of work life

Societies which value career success (Hong Kong, Singapore, South Korea, Taiwan, USA), will place an emphasis on acquisition of money and things (materialism) and the task at hand, whilst other societies place more focus on 'quality of life' (relationships and balance) involving people, activities, relationships and family (Australia, Scandinavia). These values will lead to different responses to requests for overtime, etc.

Facilitators may need to point this out to multicultural groups. Australians have a reputation for valuing leisure time, long-service leave and vacation time, which may be regarded as lazy by some Americans. Career planning workshop and goals setting may take very different paths according to cultural backgrounds. In some societies there is emphasis on written contracts and agreements whilst in relationship-oriented cultures tasks can only get done when relationships and trust are established and low value is placed on written contracts. In Japan, the younger generation have rebelled against the career drive of parents and many are opting for more quality of life, having seen their parents become ill or even die from overwork.

Harmony and control

People from harmony cultures believe it is more important to be in harmony with others than show initiative or take control of the environment.

Individuals will only take charge when asked. Harmony must be restored and disagreements overcome before work can continue. Indeed notions of politeness, respect and emotional restraint are paramount.

Control cultures value individuals, ie people who challenge and take charge of their environment (within limits). Feelings may be more freely expressed.

In harmony cultures the differences in power are valued as difference maintains harmony, whereas equality upsets harmony. Again these dimensions have implications for facilitators who are trying to get participants to bring hidden agendas out into the open so that they may be resolved. Likewise facilitators themselves working in 'harmony' cultures have to show respect and mute expression of feelings.

Religious/spiritual and secular

In religious/spiritual societies, time must be allocated during work time for prayer even if productivity slows (eg Friday lunchtime prayer time and the fasting weeks of Ramadan in Moslem counties). In Moslem countries workplace ethics, codes of behaviour and dress are guided by Moslem religious teachings. In secular societies ethics are guided by written company codes of conduct. Secular societies do not want work time interrupted by large amounts of time off to conduct religious obligations.

Polychronic and monochronic time

Polychronic cultures tend to regard time as circuitous, non-sequential, and non-linear. Time is regarded as flexible and many tasks may be tackled at once. Less attention is paid to sequencing or ranking tasks in order of importance. Monochronic cultures value turn-taking and queuing, deadlines and punctuality and perceive doing one thing at a time as effective and efficient.

In the West, time management courses espouse monochronic time as the most efficient use of time, plus the need to work in sequence from important to less important, (despite the fact that most parents conduct a multiplicity of tasks whilst managing young children).

Linear (low context) and circular thinking (high context)

In many Anglo cultures, patterns of speech and argument are fairly linear, where an idea is presented and followed with explanation and examples. Directness of speech is well regarded. To deviate too much from this pattern is perceived as 'waffle' or 'off the point'. Oriental patterns of speech tend to circle around the topic, often defining something in terms of what it is not (Kaplan, 1966). Some people from India, for example, proudly use colourful and flowery language to embellish their discourse (as would also be the case for some Brits).

Facilitators need to consider this when inviting people to speak and when interrupting individuals to help the group members move on.

Guilt and shame

In many 'Asian' societies people are governed by 'shame', and 'What will others say?', and external locus of control. There is group pressure to maintain the reputation of the group, for example the family, the team or the organization. If an individual steps out of line, he/she is concerned about what others may say. There may be feelings of shame or 'loss of face' for the individuals and the group to which he/she belongs.

In 'western' societies governed by 'guilt', people are not so concerned about what others will say if they do something wrong. Individuals are raised to answer more to their own conscience and internal sense of right and wrong. Indeed in Judaeo-Catholic societies children are reared with a very strong sense of guilt.

The Restorative Justice movement in NZ, Australia and the USA (described in Book 2 Chapter 12) illustrates a move to bring more reintegrative rather than stigmatic shaming into group pressures on those who harm society.

Related to shame is the concept of 'face'. Dr Asma Abdullah (2001) describes seven different concepts of 'face' in Malaysian society. I have briefly outlined them here as there are many issues which are relevant to facilitators.

Give face

A worker will give face to a manager by being polite and courteous, acting with deference and obedience and never arguing in public. Likewise a manager gives face by smiling and acknowledging everyone in greeting and farewells.

Lose face

A person loses face when publicly challenged or attacked. A person may lose face by his/her own behaviour, for example loss of temper. He/she would lose respect, feel embarrassed, and perhaps be the target of ridicule. To avoid losing face, problems might be settled indirectly in a quiet way or by citing proverbs or stories.

Save face

Face-saving is vital, especially if a manager is giving feedback to a worker. Both parties tend to feel uncomfortable. Sometimes a respected third person would be asked to be the messenger to soften the impact of the message. Abdullah describes an incident where in a meeting a 'western' manager was frustrated because when potential delivery delays were raised, the Malay workers denied that a problem existed. Later delays occurred. The Westerner was frustrated because he saw his job as being to anticipate problems whilst his Malay workers tended to avoid confronting the problem in order to save face.

Gain face

A person gains face when complimented by significant people in front of others. Similarly a Malay person gains face by being linked to people of higher status. Managers and parents gain face if their workers and children do well in their work.

Thick face

A person who has a thick face has no shame, speaks out in an unconventional way and does not care what others think. This sort of person will try to get things done regardless of the impact on others. He/she is not worried about appearance or behaviour and may be regarded as selfish and boastful.

Show face

A person shows face by being present physically or verbally, for example if a manager attends a family function of a subordinate. The relatives will see the face shown and their family member will gain face as a result.

Got face

A person whose speech, behaviour and dress reflect his/her status in a family, business and/or community has got face.

Co-facilitation

In some cross-cultural situations it may be useful to work with a facilitator from another culture. The other facilitator may be a 'cultural interpreter' (ie a person who has had long-term exposure to both cultures and can explain the meaning of each side's communication behaviour. At times this person may explain misunderstandings), as well as be a 'language translator'.

For example, in English the verb 'to reform' means to reorganize and is not pejorative. But in Lao PDR, the direct translation is highly pejorative and dismissive of the past, so verbs like 'to improve' are preferred.

In Lao PDR I had to facilitate groups of Lao and Australian/English nationals. There were few locally trained facilitators. I frequently worked in a team of four people:

- myself as facilitator and scribe in English on flip chart paper (portrait format);
- a bilingual Lao facilitator with interpreting and cultural translator skills who stood beside me;
- a bilingual Lao person who would scribe in Lao on flip chart paper (horizontal format as the Lao language takes up more word space than English);
- a bilingual Lao person who would sit to one side and interpret for me whilst the Lao facilitator spoke Lao to the group for a while. (This saved a lot of time for the group.)

As a result, there were two sets of wall minutes which could be checked by participants (this is important as there is often lack of time and funds to pay for back-translating of workshop data).

The Lao facilitator was also a major factor in cultural translations. He/she would:

- advise me on exercises that needed to be adapted for Lao participants;
- explain why something had been misunderstood by the group;
- sometimes confront Lao participants in different and more culturally sensitive ways than I would.

There appears to be a myth in some Anglo situations that people from non-Anglo cultures do not participate in workshop situations and prefer to be lectured to. My experience is just the opposite, *provided that participants feel safe*. Most people love to talk about issues they are involved with. In very hierarchical societies, like Lao PDR, I arrange the seating at tables in a herringbone formation, facing the front so that I can break up participants for frequent small group discussions. But I carefully orchestrate the seating beforehand so that participants are seated with others from similar levels in the organizational hierarchy. In this way, participation is maximized, as people feel freer to speak out amongst peers. Also, there is usually one person from each table who will undertake to feed back their summary to the whole group. On some occasions a small group would share giving feedback to the whole group.

In societies where status and age are highly respected it is very difficult to confront senior government officials. These people are used to being listened to for long periods of time. Many are used to circuitous dialogue where ideas are repeated and embellished. Some may be very resistant to hearing new ideas, especially from subordinates. Some may be very threatened by younger subordinates who have better qualifications. On the other hand, some younger subordinates will be loath to contradict ideas of their superiors in public. So they may repeat what their bosses have said. 'Western-based' facilitative interventions may be perceived as very bad manners and the participant may 'lose face'. I have used different interventions:

- You have a great deal of experience and learning; please let us make sure we give a chance to younger people to talk and learn.
- Let us round robin the group to hear one idea from everyone.
- What about the others?

Multicultural groups

We cannot assume that multiple groups function using the norms of white, Anglo-Saxon males, and yet much of group and management research emanates from such teams. Multicultural teams contain a wide mix of opinions and ideas, which makes reaching agreement harder. There is more chance for miscommunication and generally stress may increase and the processes to reach agreement may take longer. Facilitators need to spend more time and energy creating cohesion and solidarity.

In Lao PDR, I observed well-meaning individuals from both Lao PDR and Australia working together. Ideas were generated, but at times they reached the 'groan zone'. We used an expression, 'The wheels fell off in the middle of that workshop', meaning that there was a time when chaos prevailed. This was partly because channels of communication and chains of command were at times as obscure for the Lao as well as for the Australians. At the end of workshops I noticed that Lao people went to great lengths to restore face and give face to thank everyone for participating, contributing, etc.

Although more and better ideas are possible in multicultural teams, there is less chance of 'groupthink', but more time is needed to unravel miscommunications that may lead to 'process loss'. Many organizations I observed made no attempt to 'back translate' documents due to lack of time allocated by their aid sponsors. Yet the process of back-translation is vital to prevent miscommunication. There is one tale of a person who was designing a questionnaire and wrote 'Put a cross in the square'. The phrase was translated to 'Put a cross in the piazza'.

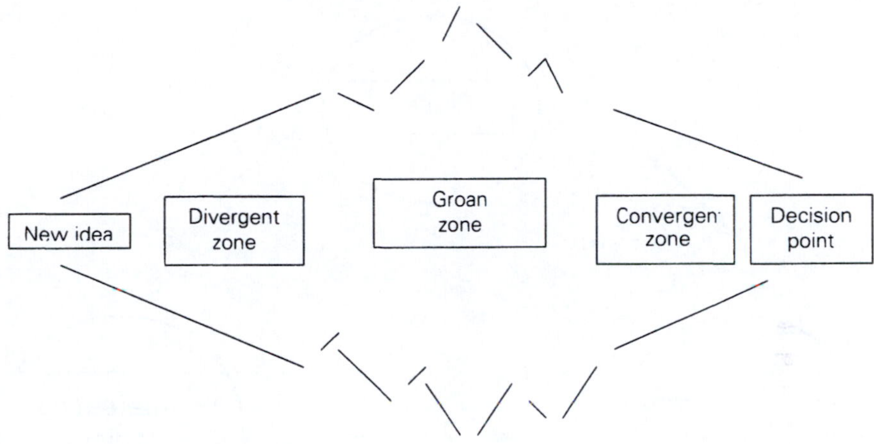

Figure 9.1 Group decision making

Source: After Kaner (1996)

> Actual Productivity = Potential Productivity – Losses due to faulty communication and faulty group process.
>
> (Steiner, 1971)

Advantages and disadvantages of multicultural groups

The aim of this exercise is for participants to share what they had learnt by being part of multicultural groups using the evaluation/comparison process, 'Pluses, Minuses and Interesting points (PMI)' (de Bono, 1987). Participants are divided into three groups each containing a mix of cultures. I used this with a group of Nepalese and Danish development workers from an aid agency workshop that I facilitated in Kathmandu.

One group was asked to discuss pluses, another the minuses and another the interesting points about working in cross-cultural groups. The ground rules were 'describe issues not individuals'. There were three separate work stations equipped with flip chart paper and large pens. Each had instructions and the ground rule on a large sign indicating the focus of each group. After five minutes, each group moved physically to the next workstation until all participants had had a chance to contribute to issues at each of the three work stations. The resulting wall minutes could then be displayed and discussed.

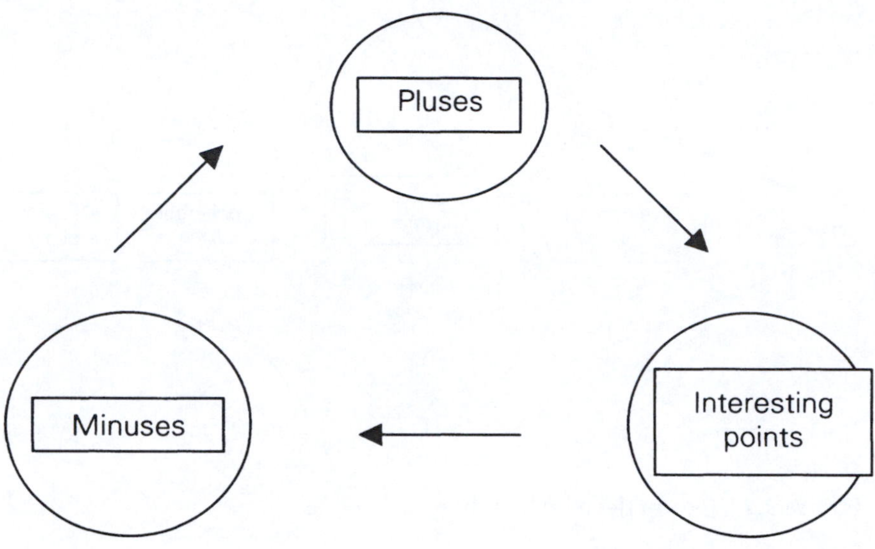

Figure 9.2 Three-stage 'bull ring'

Keeping people moving physically around the room kept them energized. It was also less threatening than generating issues in the whole group. Table 9.1 lists some of the points generated.

It is interesting to compare this list with the one developed by Adler (Table 9.2).

Stages of group development

Group dynamics change all the time and the stages of group development have already been described in Chapter 8. At the 'forming stages' of multicultural groups there is likely to be more mistrust and stereotyping.

People from 'task and time'-oriented cultures (Northern Europe, the USA, Australia) tend to want to get down to business as 'time is money', whilst people from more relationship-oriented cultures, for example Latin America, Aboriginal cultures of Australia and North America, Latin America and Southern Europe, want to take their time finding out about 'the others' and building trust. We tend to build trust and rapport with people who look and/or think like us. We remember faces and names of people from our own culture more quickly. Therefore, with cross-cultural groups, facilitators need to take more time on: 1) meeting participants before a workshop; 2) preparing *suitable* ice-breakers (see Book 2).

Table 9.1 Pluses minuses and interesting points of multicultural groups (Nepalese and Danes)

Pluses	*Minuses*	*Interesting points*
• Sharing of ideas and experiences • Knowledge of culture leads to flexibility, adaptability and unity • Respecting and understanding each other • Friendship • One starts to think about one's own culture • Gain a lot of new information about one another's country and social life • Learn from each other • I learnt that my culture's values do not have to be the right ones • We laugh easily together • We learn new ways of reacting and solving problems	• Language barriers • Different values, eg showing emotions, time, different meaning of what is embarrassing • Understanding gap due to cultural differences • Time consuming to reach understanding • Simplifying the way you speak, communicate, behave • Compromising on your lifestyle and codes of dress (Danes have to dress more modestly) • Tiring because you have to concentrate a great deal • Chance of dominating each other • Feelings of superiority may lead to unexpected/unwanted situations • Trying to hide own faults/weaknesses • Fear of asking questions and showing lack of knowledge and understanding • Difficult/impossible to adopt some new ways/things/behaviours/taste • 'Do it my way' on the part of Europeans indicating lack of trust and ego ('Lindedhipi' in Nepali)	• Exposure to another culture makes you reflect more about your own culture • Questions: Can we understand each other? Can we make friends? Can we cross the barriers in work/communication situations? • You can adopt aspects of different cultures into your own life • You may have to compromise • You may make a wonderful situation • Questions of new energy and motivation from both sides • Different impressions from partners, development workers, villagers, office staff • Coming together of people from different cultural backgrounds gives you a lot, but it is demanding • Develop new ideas

Table 9.2 Advantages and disadvantages of multicultural groups (adapted from Adler, 1997: 132)

Advantages	*Disadvantages*
Increased creativity:	Miscommunication:
• wider perspectives • less chance of groupthink • more ideas • insight how to do things in foreign countries	• slower speech • less accurate • translation problems • back-translation time and costs
Forces concentration to understand others':	Lack of cohesion:
• ideas • meanings • arguments	• mistrust • stereotyping • within-culture conversations • stress/tension • counterproductive behaviour
Increased creativity can lead to:	Lack of cohesion may cause difficulties:
• better problem definition • more alternatives • better and/or more culturally appropriate solutions and decisions • better understanding of the longer ramifications of decisions	• agree when agreement is needed • gain consensus on decisions • take concerted action
Groups may become:	Groups may become:
• more efficient • more effective • more productive	• less efficient • less effective • less productive

Table 9.3 Managing diversity based on stage of group development (adapted from Adler, 1997: 140)

Stage	*Processes*	*Diversity makes the process*	*Processes based on*
Entry: Initial team formation or start of a workshop	Getting to know each other, names, faces, backgrounds, roles Trust building Developing cohesion	More difficult	Using similarities, eg we all feel a bit nervous at the beginning of a workshop
Work: Problem identification and analysis	Generating ideas	Easier if trust is built and people feel comfortable to speak or are given processes to generate ideas anonymously	Using differences of perspectives, using cultural advisers, local experience
Action: Decision making and implementation	Decision making, preferably through consensus building	More difficult	Recognizing and creating similarities. Using different skills of individuals

Once respect and trust are built between participants, and between participants and the facilitator, a group can work on mutual issues and generate new perspectives on ideas.

Conclusion

In this chapter, I have given an overview of definitions of culture and cultural dimensions. I have illustrated the need for co-facilitators and cultural translators and the advantages and disadvantages of multicultural groups.

10

Facilitation and technology

> If the main purpose of good facilitation is to make group work more effectively, then the main purpose of facilitating with technology is to make groups work even more effectively that they could without it.
>
> Olson (1999: 393)

Introduction

For the past half century, facilitators have been increasingly involved with different forms of technology from flip chart paper, black/white boards, card sorts and Post-its, sticky dots (for voting and ranking) and now electronic technologies which are displayed in Table 10.1.

In this chapter I focus on two models, one describing the technologies at the time of writing that are available to facilitators and a second describing the competencies required by e-moderators.

The use of any form of technology will impact in some way for better or worse on a facilitator and the group. It is not a panacea. Adding technology increases the complexity of the facilitation task (Niederman, Beise and Beranek, 1996; Niederman and Volkema, 1999).

In some organizations there is almost a snobbery that the use of technology is 'good'. I have seen PowerPoint used and abused. It is questions like *why* and *how* technology is used to serve facilitators and groups that are important.

Technology to serve facilitators and groups model

During the writing of my thesis on facilitation, my supervisor suggested that in my last chapter I should point to the future uses of technology for

Table 10.1 Technology to serve facilitators and groups

Facilitator/ Group needs	*Technology/ Software*	*Descriptions of uses and issues*	*References/ Resources*
Researching context: organization history	Company Web sites on Internet	Updating of data. Useful to find out difference between 'espoused values' (ie on Web, in mission statements) and 'values in action' (Argyris)	Search engines like Dogpile and Mamma
Researching context: cultural/political/ geographical information about a country		Important for facilitators who submit proposals and/or travel to facilitate overseas in case of political unrest, etc	Wired news, eg www.wired.com Lonely Planet Web site: www.lonelyplanet.com
Training facilitators recording and analysing content, group process participation, facilitator interventions, focus groups, meetings	Video recording of live workshops	Location of cameras and impact on participants' behaviour. Need to delete for confidentiality	
	Purpose-made training videos	Observational learning, debriefing. Critque interventions, values, facilitator styles	*Blue eyes* and *A divided* (1968) with Jane Elliott. Iowa, USA *Collaborative Learning: Working together in small groups* (1996) Murdoch University, Perth, Western Australia *DACUM Developing a Curriculum* (1987) Parmelia Productions, TAFE, Western Australia *Emotional Intelligence* with Daniel Goleman

Table 10.1 *(continued)*

Facilitator/ Group needs	*Technology/ Software*	*Descriptions of uses and issues*	*References/ Resources*
	Commercial film clips	Requires preparation, editing of suitable clips. Copyright issues	*Twelve angry men* (Jury decision making: looks at group pressure, the power of one against the majority, voting, consensus) *Dead Poets Society* (Changing norms, facilitating learning, autonomy) *She'll be wearing pink pyjamas* (All-female outdoor expedition). Gender issues and films with women in lead roles include: *Norma Rae, Steel Magnolias, Broadcast News, Elizabeth, Thelma and Louise, Silkwood, Julia, The Miracle Worker, The Craft.* Descriptions of films on cross-cultural issues (Summerfield, 1993 and Zeigler, 1992)
Contact with all participants before and between workshops	E-mail, GroupWise	Enables facilitator to conduct needs analysis and/or obtain information from individuals and to send out draft workshop for feedback and revision before workshop	
Recording and analysing first impression after talking with prospective clients	Audio recording Tape recorder for personal note taking	Useful, fast way of recording first impressions, hunches that need to be checked out, unasked questions. Can be recorded in car leaving an organization	

Table 10.1 *(continued)*

Facilitator/ Group needs	*Technology/ Software*	*Descriptions of uses and issues*	*References/ Resources*
Recording and analysing content, participation rates, facilitator interventions. Focus groups, meetings	Audio recording Tape recorder	Quality and distribution of microphones. Cannot see body language. Packages like Nudist and Nvivo are useful for sorting and storing data	
Content/discourse analysis	Audio recording Tape recorder	Transcribe from audio (voice-activated computerized transcription still unreliable)	
Synchronous meetings at a distance	Audio teleconferencing Telephone exchange Conference calls by telephone on a single circuit	Cannot read body language. Need to bring in all participants	
	Videoconferencing Point to point. Point to multipoint, eg 1+3 remote sites. Multipoint-to-multipoint. Polycon, PictureTel Vtel + document cameras to display and send visuals + communicating copiers which photocopy and send data via computer + communicating whiteboard records handwriting and transmits via computer	Can see and hear people at a distance. May be recorded and viewed later. Time lapse (N)ETIQUETTE (Desirable electronic group norms)	(Hogan, 1993c, 1993b, 1998;
	Desktop videoconferencing		

Table 10.1 *(continued)*

Facilitator/ Group needs	*Technology/ Software*	*Descriptions of uses and issues*	*References/ Resources*
Synchronous meetings in real time	Groupware: group decision support (GDS), MeetingWorks MyPlaceware Enables brainstorming, prioritizing, ranking, rating, voting comments. Print outs at end of meeting	Requires a dedicated meeting laboratory and computers Laptops create fewer barriers than standard screens. Can be closed for off-the-record discussions Often need a chauffeur. Relationship between facilitator and chauffeur. Enables participants to take home a product, ie minutes	Diamond, 1996) (Whiteley and Garcia, 1996)
Curriculum development in real time	DACUM process using GDS and MeetingWorks software	Need to select participants carefully Threading online complex conversations	(Hogan, 1994)
Curriculum development in asynchronous time	Delphi process + e-mail		
Asynchronous virtual meetings	Groupware: online Lotus Notes Work group Computer-mediated conferencing (CMC)	Tracking and archiving data Integrating lurkers Cannot see people Forget who is and who is not online Easily distracted	(Salmon, 2000, Mittleman, 2000)
Enhancing networking in real time, ice-breakers, monitoring spread of ideas	Electronic name tags, eg 'Lovegety' radio transmitter pendants	Wearers answer five questions. When two people meet badges compare answers with infrared link and flash if answers match. Can monitor spread of ideas	(Choice, 2000:6) ks@shigematsu.co.jp www.interland.co.jp/gety/eigo/index.html
Community participation	Audience response systems (ARS), eg CoNexus, Option Finder System, Xtol handheld radio linked keypads (wired or wireless) linked to a computer. Projection on to screen	Questions posed with a set of response choices. Community decision making Market research surveys using Likert scale or yes/no response. Vote, rank ideas, etc	AmericaSpeaks www.americaspeaks.org/welcome.html

Table 10.1 *(continued)*

Facilitator/ Group needs	*Technology/ Software*	*Descriptions of uses and issues*	*References/ Resources*
Simulated problem-solving activities, system dynamics	The Beer Distribution Game	Simulation used for three decades to introduce systems thinking, dynamics and management	Sterman (2000) Systems dynamics society: system.dynamics@ albany.edu
Planning	Computer modelling Scenario planning Group systems 5		(de Vreede, 1995)
Community/urban planning	Geographic information systems (GIS), ie the plotting of layers of information about resources and environment		(Heckman, 2000)
Recording and displaying group memory	Flip chart paper	Cheap, widely available. Can be used in outdoor learning activities in bush. Lots	
	Electronic whiteboards	of sheets can be viewed at once	
	Computer projection systems: Overhead projector and projection panel or data show	Fast printouts of data Fast printouts of data	
	Digital cameras	Fast, small-size output but can enlarge	
Seeing the whole picture	GDSS cited above Mind mapping, eg Mindman, AMOS software	Ability to plot whole picture plus facility to 'drill-down', ie add hierarchies of levels of meaning. Can incorporate clip art, photos from digital cameras	
Presenting information	Computer + overhead projector and projection panel + PowerPoint software	Useful for facilitators for displaying wall minutes on large screen. Requires a darkened room. Used mainly for presentations rather than facilitation. Presentations may become stilted and lessen audience interaction	

Table 10.1 *(continued)*

Facilitator/ Group needs	*Technology/ Software*	*Descriptions of uses and issues*	*References/ Resources*
Learning names of participants	Digital cameras	Recording participants plus name tags. Can be used to distribute faces and names to group members	
Recording group members before, during, after activities	Digital cameras	Can also be used with online groupware meetings	
Concept exploration	Disposable cameras	Participants given cameras to record idea/symbols representing a concept, eg leadership. Teams pool photos and choose best for display	
Teambuilding, fun stretching limits	Karaoke	Useful for fun, creative activities in cross-cultural groups. Favours certain groups, eg Japanese, Vietnamese, and Lao who use karaoke in their own home for family entertainment	(Whiteley, 1993)
Creating/changing ambiance	Music. CD, tape recorder in workshop room	Background for relaxation or energizing the group. Analysis of meanings of songs. Getting groups to compose and record their own songs.	
	Music files, sent electronically to GDS groups, eg .wav,.mp3	Can change feelings of people at a distance	
Organizing multiple meetings/work groups	Computers + workgroup software Novell: GroupWise Microsoft office: Microsoft Outlook	Group access to synchronize calendars, appointments diary, contact lists, task lists. Does not require a facilitator. Technology supplies facilitation notes, enables group members to take on facilitation role/	

Table 10.1 *(continued)*

Facilitator/ Group needs	*Technology/ Software*	*Descriptions of uses and issues*	*References/ Resources*
Aiding groups to represent their issues to power-holders	Videos Digital cameras	Facilitator enables groups to make own documentaries of issues	
Self-development monitoring of facilitation	Palmtop Observations during a workshop to be transferred to main computer later		
	Computer: Electronic journal	Data collection from needs analyses and evaluations	
Research into facilitation, processes	Informatics: Electronic access to catalogues, library resources, research articles, databases and archives. CD-ROM Digital Versatile disk (DVD)		
Preparation of workshops	Templates: Tables for generating workshop agendas (content, process, time)		
Networking Peer support and exploration of best practice	E-mail discussion groups, eg IAF, AFN (Australian Facilitators' Network)		
	Database of contacts. Addresses printed out on labels	Christmas cards, advertising	
Publicity, networking Credibility	Facilitator's own Web page		
Keep up with changing technology	Web sites: www.polycon.con E-mail: MyPlaceware@browser. netscape.coma		

facilitators. I started to write, and immediately decided that I needed to simplify the uses of technology in a model. I cited all the types of technology useful to facilitators down the vertical axis of a table. However, before long the table had rapidly grown to eight pages, like the fast-growing bean in the fairy tale, *Jack and the Beanstalk*. I was amazed at the number of uses of technology for facilitators, many of which I had inadvertently taken for granted.

After conversations with a colleague, Rod Jarman (Jarman, 2000), I revised the model from a focus on the technologies themselves on the vertical axis to a focus on the needs of a facilitator and groups. I also found it hard to categorize some media which perform multifunctions with different hardware and software and was relieved to find that IT specialists like Jarman, and Martin (2000), made the same observations.

Needless to say, this is merely a snapshot in time. The cliché of technological change is perhaps over-used, but as facilitators we are on a steep learning curve and need to be able to talk with programmers (or become programmers) to develop technology that serves our needs and, where necessary, protects the anonymity or privacy of individuals.

Choosing the most appropriate technology

All communications technologies are media and facilitators may wish to consider the key qualities of different media, eg the degree to which a medium is personal, warm/cold, urgent, novel, fast/slow, easy/hard to use, cheap/expensive, accessible to all or a few ('technological divide') and, last but not least, what media are most suitable for teams that are 'co-located', ie in the same location or 'distributed teams' (Kimball, 2002).

In community development in developing countries facilitators improvise using the ground instead of a whiteboard (to focus participants on issues rather than personalities) and local materials: sticks, stones, coloured powder to enable participants to plot their ideas. The technologies of such workshops may appear deceptively simple, but in some ways they are more robust in that they do not break down and are not susceptible to power cuts and the vagaries of viruses.

The development of more sophisticated technology does not mean that the simpler technologies are redundant. The questions that facilitators must ask are 'What am I trying to do'? and 'What is most appropriate technology?' (Martin, 2000) and 'How do people adopt, use and adapt these technologies?' (Jarman, 2000). Indeed in development work in countries in the 'South', local resources, for example sticks, stones and sand, are the most appropriate technologies for community mapping in participatory rural appraisal workshops. When electrical power supplies are unreliable it is less stressful to use flip chart paper rather than electronic recording devices. Facilitators need to ask why, when, where and which technologies are most suitable *and always* to have backup paper technologies for use in case of equipment and/or electronic failures.

'If the main purpose of good facilitation is to make group work more effectively, then the main purpose of facilitating with technology is to make groups work even more effectively that they could without it' (Olson, 1999: 393). Unfortunately it is not as simple and straightforward as Olson advises. People have used technology to aid communication for centuries, from carrier pigeons to smoke signals to jungle drums (Jarman, 2000). But the use of technology for facilitation purposes is still in its infancy, that is, since 1985 for face-to-face meetings; however, the potential uses of technology are endless, but are limited at any time in history by the developmental stage of the technology, software cost *and* its reliability and the human creativity in its use. All technologies need some level of facilitation to a degree; for example, communal folders of materials networked on a server require the facilitation of a shared understanding of ground rules for overwriting the current version of a document. A facilitator is not needed as there are different levels of access and privileges written into the system; others eliminate the facilitator or change the role/s of the facilitator. Other systems, for example MeetingWorks (used for synchronous meetings in one location), require the addition of technological chauffeurs and the support of technocrats behind the scenes. Some software, for example MeetingWorks, is programmed to enhance confidentiality whilst others, for example Grouputer, are programmed so that the generator of ideas may be traced.

Some participants and facilitators may be nervous and need time to experiment with new 'toys'. There will be mistakes, so it is better, at first, to take a playful approach to help people overcome initial reticence. 'Luddites', that is, people who are anti-technology, those who are scared of new technology and people who are keyboard illiterate may be at a disadvantage. A facilitator needs to meet with management and participants beforehand in order to find out experience levels, answer questions and prepare agendas with them.

Technologies and software packages are tools and should be regarded as a means to an end rather than an end in themselves. Facilitators therefore now require not only a knowledge of processes and interventions, but also a working knowledge and understanding of a number of technologies. They need to be able to offer clients a choice of appropriate processes and strategies based on needs and economies of time and scale rather than a promotion of a particular favourite technology or 'toy'. It is the human aspect in the use of technology that will cause people to want or not want to use it (Martin, 2000). Technology may trap inexperienced facilitators into communicating and/or teaching in a certain way and as a result the tool often shapes the facilitator/teacher. However, it should be the other way around, that is, the goal of the meeting or the teaching goal should be paramount when choosing a particular technology. Technology does not make up for poor facilitation or poor teaching: it exacerbates it (Olson, 1999).

Facilitators have always had to focus on the needs of the group first (nothing has changed there), but now facilitators have to be able to offer far wider choices of interventions, processes and technology and make informed choices of their uses. See Table 10.2.

Table 10.2 Choosing media for group communication (adapted from Kimball, 2002)

Media	*Questions for facilitators on the effect on team dynamics*
Electronic discussion group	What norms need to be established for: response time, whether or not e-mail can be forwarded to others, whether or not an e-mail may be quoted without the author's permission? What kind of information is acceptable to 'go public' to a wider audience outside the organization? Should the discussion list be moderated or not? If 'yes', who moderates and makes the ground rules? What happens if these ground rules are broken?
Decision support systems in synchronous time	How does the ability to contribute anonymously affect the group norms? How can you test whether 'consensus' and/or rankings generated through computer processing are valid?
Decision support systems in asynchronous time	What time limits should be placed on conversations? How can you maintain links in strings of conversations? How can you archive information?
Audio (telephone) conferencing	How can you help participants have a sense of who is 'present' at a meeting? How can you equalize participation? How can you sense when people have something to say when you cannot observe body language? How can you maintain concentration and interest?
Videoconferencing	How can you manage the attention span of participants? When is it best to use videoconferencing instead of audioconferencing? (eg job interviews and meetings where you need to be able to see body language). How can you sense what is going on 'off camera' whilst someone is speaking and shown in close-up? How can you make videoconferencing interactive for teaching at a distance? Who has control of the camera?
Document sharing	How can you balance the need to access and process large amounts of information with the goal of developing relationship and trust? Who has the right to change data?

For more information on the uses of technology for 'distributed teams' look at the following Web sites: http://www.caucus.com/whitepapers.html and http://www.caucus.com/published.html.

The human dimension

The success or failure of technology is based on whether it effectively and efficiently performs its intended functions. Overlaid on this is the vital human aspect that the facilitator brings to the equipment. It should be the facilitator who shapes the use of the technology, not vice versa.

The use to technology has also led to development of a new vocabulary, for instance netiquette, virtual reality, lurkers, chat room, moderator (instead of facilitator), cyberspace, to name a few. As a result, on a macro level facilitators need to:

- keep themselves updated with new technologies, and learn that different tools cover various time and space dimensions;
- understand that different kinds of tools may be appropriate to different kinds of groups and different stages of group development;
- develop some degree of technical awareness of the design and use of tools they wish to use;
- be prepared to learn from and/or co-facilitate with an IT person because many of them understand what is necessary to make the most of implementing technology (Whiteley and Garcia, 1996);
- be actively involved with programmers in the design of new software to match participatory processes;
- ensure that certain ground rules are designed into programs, for example the need for anonymity in some packages.

Evaluation of the facilitation and technology model

The technology model was designed to help facilitators make choices of the variety of technologies available, depending on client needs, workshop goals and context. At times, it appears as if technologies may be used for effect or novelty value rather than what is most appropriate. Hence, the range of technologies available for particular functions has been listed together. For example, in order to record and display the participants' ideas a facilitator may choose from flip chart paper to electronic whiteboards to computer projection systems.

The model makes no attempt, however, to evaluate the different outcomes by using different technologies. Mittleman, Briggs and Naunamaker (2000) cite Woolley (1999) who lists 146 products for conferencing on the World Wide Web and his list is growing continuously. Whilst on the surface flip chart paper may be quick to prepare, the typing and distribution of material may be quite time consuming. Superficially, the use of computer projection systems and group decision support equipment may appear quicker. However, at this stage of technological development, breakdown of equipment, maintenance time and costs may make flip chart paper both quicker and more economic.

E-moderating learning groups competencies model

Developments in technology, eg audioconferencing, videoconferencing, group support systems (GSS), computer conferencing and e-mail discussion groups, have led to the development of 'e-moderators': people who preside over an electronic online meetings or conferences. E-moderating involves new ways of teaching and learning, particularly in higher education (Salmon, 2000). Indeed educationalists and learners are experimenting with new and varied ways of 'networked learning'.

Gilly Salmon at the Open University in the UK developed a table of competencies for facilitators using online technologies for computer-mediated conferencing (CMC). She calls these facilitators 'e-moderators'. In these meetings participants are geographically separate (distributed groups) and communicate usually, though not always, in asynchronous time. The e-moderator table is a classificatory model. It focuses on facilitators' competencies with communication technologies, including the protocols and conventions associated with their use.

Attention is paid to facilitators' desirable personal characteristics and skills, along with their abilities to facilitate and participate in networking, conferences, and in online learning communication. In the model the technological emphasis is integrated with the more usual facilitation skills, such as building trust, classifying issues, fostering and pacing discussion, and so on. Flexibility, creativity and ongoing learning are noted as desirable, so too is sensitivity to and value of cultural diversity and the needs of 'lurkers' (people who watch but do not participate for a variety of reasons). The appropriate use of time when online and the evaluation of conferences are two noteworthy inclusions. This is a useful model for drawing together the socio-technical aspects of facilitation, and provides a basis for assessing competence in this area of the discipline. It could also be used to design a course of instruction perhaps co-facilitated by an IT and facilitation specialist.

Table 10.3 E-moderator online competencies (from Salmon, 2000:40). CMC = Computer moderated conferencing

Quality Characteristic	*1. Confident*	*2. Constructive*	*3. Developmental*	*4. Facilitating*	*5. Knowledge*	*6. Creative*
Understanding of online process	Confident in providing a focus for conferences, intervening, judging participants' interest, experimenting with different approaches	Able to build online trust and purpose; to know who should be online and what they should be doing	Ability to develop and enable others, act as catalyst, foster discussion, summarize, restate, challenge, monitor understanding and misunderstanding, take feedback	Know when to control groups, when to let go, how to bring in non-participants, know how to pace discussion and use time online	Able to explore ideas, develop arguments. Promote valuable threads, close off unproductive threads, choose when to archive. Build a learning community	Able to use a range of CMC conferencing approaches, from structured activities to freewheeling discussions, and to evaluate and success of conferences
Technical skills	Confident in operational understanding of software in use by a user; reasonable keyboard skills; good access	Able to appreciate the basic structures of CMC, and WWW and Intent's potential for learning	Know how to use special features of software for e-moderation, eg controlling, archiving	Able to use special features of software to explore learners' use, eg message history	Able to create links between CMC and other features of learning programmes	Able to use software facilities to create and manipulate conferences and to generate an online learning environment

Quality Characteristic	*1. Confident*	*2. Constructive*	*3. Developmental*	*4. Facilitating*	*5. Knowledge*	*6. Creative*
Online communication skills	Confident in being courteous, polite, and respectful in online (written) communication	Able to write concise, energizing, personable online messages	Able to engage with people online (not the machine or the software)	Able to interact through e-mail and conferencing and achieve interaction between others	Able to value diversity with cultural sensitivity	Able to communicate comfortably without visual cues
Content expertise	Confident in having knowledge and experience to share, and willing and able to add own contributions	Able to encourage sound contributions from others	Able to trigger debates by posing intriguing questions	Carry authority by awarding marks fairly to students for their CMC participation and contributions	Know about valuable resources (eg on the WWW) and refer participants to them	Able to enliven conference through use of multimedia and electronic resources
Personal characteristics	Confident in being determined and motivated as an e-moderator	Able to establish an online identity as e-moderator	Able to adapt to new teaching contexts, methods, audiences and roles	Show sensitivity to online relationships and communication	Show a positive attitude, commitment and enthusiasm for online learning	Know how to create a useful, relevant online learning community

In many ways Salmon's table complements and is similar in style to the IAF model in that it is competency based. She focuses on e-moderator qualities and characteristics on the horizontal and vertical axes respectively. She cites the impact of technology on teachers who rely on their personal charisma in the classroom to motivate students and describes the need to transform this to written dialogue. Her model illustrates the wide variety of technical, communication and interpersonal skills required by e-moderators. Her model is the first to bring together the many interpersonal skills needed by an e-moderator in that technological skills are not enough to guarantee the success of an online meeting. The success or failure of a workshop or teaching programme often depends on the skills of the facilitator or moderator (Clawson, Bostrom and Anson, 1993; Niederman and Volkema, 1999; Whiteley and Garcia, 1996). Salmon's model (shown in Table 10.3) may be used for training, recruiting, assessing and evaluating e-moderators. It is interesting to note that the technical skills form only a fifth of the model. She also includes a table of techniques for different CMC structures, for example online tutorials, debating, and even some fun, for example online wine tasting!

Evaluation of the e-moderator online competencies model

The e-moderator online competencies model provided a much-needed contribution to the fast-changing field of facilitating in a virtual world. Salmon's model (2000) is illuminated with extracts from e-moderators' diaries, case studies and down-to-earth information as well as research-based data on learner needs and outcomes. Salmon also addresses the difficulty of costing time and money inputs into CMC and the training of e-moderators and raises the issue of whether or not learning institutions will survive and prosper if they do not offer flexible learning via the growing number of electronic communication means available. Salmon omits the issue of high licensing costs and high demands on lecturers' time which is sometimes neither acknowledged nor rewarded. There are also issues of bureaucratic red tape and gatekeepers, which e-tech innovators have to deal with, regarding the adoption and diffusion of new technology by organizations and consumers.

Although focussed on e-learning, the information is of relevance to facilitators of computer-mediated conferencing. However, there is a gap in the area of uses of technology for facilitators which I tried to fill in the 'Uses of technology' model (Table 10.1).

Table 10.4 Table of facilitation and technology models

Model	*Author/s date/place*	*Type of model*	*What does the model summarize?*	*What are its main emphases?*	*What are its main uses?*
1. E-moderator online competencies model	Salmon (2000) UK	Classificatory grid	Desirable knowledge skills and attitudes of e-moderators	● Competent use of communication technologies ● Development and/or modification of interpersonal skills for electronic communication	● Competencies as a basis for selecting and developing e-moderators ● Course design
2. Facilitation and technology model	Hogan (2001) Australia	Classificatory grid	Varieties of technologies directly useful for facilitation with individuals, groups and/or networks	● Technological diversity and multiple functions ● Selection of appropriate technologies for particular needs and context	● Alerting facilitators to technologies available and possible advantages, issues and problems ● Could be used as a basis for the design of a specialized course co-taught by facilitation and IT specialists

Web sites

Gilly Salmon's Web site: www.oubs.open.ac.uk/e-moderating
Zane Berge and Mauri Collins' Web site: www.emoderators.com/moderators.shtml

Comparison of models

The models described above enable us to understand the phenomenon of facilitation more easily, but none 'map the territory' completely. Nor with technology is it possible to be and/or stay up to date. Table 10.4 gives a summary and comparison of each.

Conclusion

In this chapter I have described and evaluated two models relating to the uses of technology for facilitators and how facilitators may best use technologies in helping people to learn and communicate online. This chapter is a small snapshot in time in a very fast-evolving field. (See also Book 2 Chapter 14.)

11

Professionalism and ethics

> If business comes with no moral sympathy,
> or honorable code of behavior
> God help us all.
>
> Anita Roddick (2001: 15)

Introduction

In this chapter I describe current changes in the facilitation movement and analyse two recent case studies which highlight issues regarding the ethics of facilitation. I then trace the current movement towards the professionalization of facilitation, and examine the development of codes of ethics and systems of accreditation, both from an examination of the literature and from my own standpoint and experiences and that of the International Association of Facilitators.

The facilitation movement

Throughout history, there has been a wide range of human developments. In some cases these developments involved enthusiastic experimentation (Bunker and Alban, 1997), in others, they have been subject to the dictates of fascist or totalitarian leaders (Chang, 1991). There are claims that facilitation, as an evolving 'movement', has led to some major achievements in the fields of human communication, group learning, management, community support, health, therapy and developments towards creating a 'civil society' (Andrews, 1995; Burbidge, 1977; Ross, 1989; Bunker and Alban, 1997).

The facilitation movement has produced some well-meaning amateurs who decide to facilitate groups with the best of intentions, but without any background or experience in group dynamics. Sometimes these amateurish efforts have been successful, sometimes disastrous. There have been some individuals who have set out with ethical intentions, but without feedback and/or some kind of monitoring or supervision have become dangerous and left emotional casualties in their wake (Rowe and Winborn, 1973; De George, 1995; Corey, Corey and Callanan, 1993).

Many authors describe some of the issues raised during the human potential movement of the 1960s and 1970s (Rowe and Winborn, 1973; Andrews, 1995; Corey, Corey and Callanan, 1993). There were 'Encounter Groups' where blacks and whites attempted to resolve racial biases on a face-to-face level. There were 'T or Training Groups' of all types where people were encouraged to say exactly what they wanted to each other; some groups involved intimate touching or even nudity to increase intimacy or aggressive techniques to break down resistance (Corey *et al*, 1988). For example, there were 12–48-hour marathon group meetings conducted by George Bach and the so-called 'Synanon game' that consisted of participants conducting extreme verbal attacks on an individual, based on the belief: 'That which does not kill me makes me stronger' (Nietzsche).

In the sixties and seventies many group sessions were perceived by the general public as being associated with direct confrontation, brutal honesty, and a 'let it all hang out' philosophy. Rowe and Winborn (1973) analysed 36 journal articles in their attempt to analyse 'What people fear about group work'. Their findings indicate that the primary reservation of participants was a lack of confidence in people who lead groups followed by lack of standards in leadership training. At that time, that is, 1973, there were no adequate performance criteria or guidelines. There were also concerns regarding 'post-group adjustment problems' and 're-entry difficulties'. As a result of these negative incidents the American Psychological Association (1973, 1992) developed a code of ethics for conducting growth groups. However, there is doubt about whether these codes have been enforced. Do clients know how and where they can complain? How are complaints handled? In the more general facilitation field, a quarter of a century later, there are now accredited and formalized courses on facilitation, but there is still little in the way of consumer protection in the facilitation 'industry'.

Two case studies

I will now illustrate the dilemmas described above with two case studies: one from the UK and the other from Holland.

Case study 1: Ouch: getting toes burnt

In July 1998, the *Daily Mail* in the UK published an article describing a facilitation event undertaken by Eagle Star Life, an insurance company that employs over 1,000 people (Woodward, 1998: 5). The company paid a private consulting group to facilitate a one-day motivational programme for their 10 new marketing managers at a hotel near the insurance's giant headquarters in Cheltenham, Gloucestershire. Apparently to test resolve, in a 'culmination' exercise, the new managers were asked to walk on a bed of hot coals. Seven quickly suffered very badly burnt feet and were sent to hospital; two of these were so seriously burnt that they had to be transferred to the regional major burns unit in Bristol, 40 miles away.

The consultants had failed to do their usual preparation; the coals had not had enough time to cool down *and* they were placed on a four-foot metal tray. But that is not the point. The frightening aspects are: firstly, Eagle Star Life had not done their ground work in assessing risk; secondly, seven participants ended up in hospital with extreme burns to their feet; and thirdly, no one dared either to challenge the validity of the activity or to say 'No'. It was a classic case of 'groupthink' (Janis, 1972) where a group was cohesive, but still at the 'norming' stage of group development.

I spoke to a member of the Human Resources Department of Eagle Star by phone in February 1999. She informed me that all participants knew of the proposed fire-walking exercise 'they all signed consent forms and... they were all back at work within two months' (her tone implied that this was nothing). Mr Jeff Wagland, a spokesperson for Eagle Star Life, reportedly commented that the participants had expected some sort of 'challenge event' at the end. 'It has to be said that on those types of motivational courses, which might include a rock climb at the end, there is scarcely any chance of getting hurt, if it's carried out correctly' (Woodward, 1998: 5). If this was reported accurately, it could be an example of gross negligence. Even a rock climb can be potentially hazardous to people with a sedentary lifestyle unless proper health checks are made. Yet in today's competitive environment, some people may not wish to divulge to their employers that they have a health problem.

Discussion

Before we make judgements about these course participants, for example 'How could they have been so stupid?' or 'I wouldn't have done that', we should consider the context of their actions. These managers were new, having been employed only nine months previously. They were being groomed to 'perform'. I imagine the majority was motivated to do well in their new positions. Marketing is a 'go-getting' type of profession, and no doubt the managers were selected for this characteristic in their psyche. There is also the paradox that they would probably consider themselves as rugged individuals who were tough and could out-compete their colleagues; in addition, the influences of the group norms on managers may mean that they do as they are told and certainly do not organize collective opposition to instructions. (Some organizations actually use selection processes which are designed to exclude people who ask too many questions, whilst others actually seek free-thinking individuals.)

We should consider also the increasing pressures on people at work. Organizations are becoming bigger and more powerful. Employees can no longer be sure of permanence. Job seekers can no longer assume there are vacancies or choices of vacancies in a particular field in the employment market. With workplace agreements, employees now have far less bargaining power (that is, when negotiating renewal of contracts). Most workers have families of all ages to support, mortgages and bills, and many of them view the future with uncertainty. As a result, in many organizations the forces for conformity are stronger than ever before. Consider the following overt and covert messages in many organizations in western society:

- Compete with each other and the outside world. . . or else (Hamel and Prahalad, 1996).
- Produce more. . . or else.
- Do more with less. . . or else.
- Growth is everything. . . or else.
- Make more profit. . . or else.

I recall an anecdote about Margaret Thatcher who during her 'reign' as Prime Minister visited a gathering of some of the best research scientists in the UK at Imperial College in London. Her opening statement basically said, 'Gentlemen, I have one thing to say to you. . . profit.' These messages are increasing just at a time when organizations need people to generate creative ideas, some of which may be diametrically opposed to the status quo. There is the myth of 'growth for growth's sake'. This is like the genetic programming of a cancer cell. Humans, plants and animals all stop growing at a certain point (Suzuki, 1999). Cancer is the only life structure which doesn't stop growing, yet the 'groupthink' (Janis, 1972) in many organizations (and indeed many political parties) is 'growth for growth's sake'.

With such a prevailing message, is it possible that facilitators like myself may be co-opted? For example, if we undertake a contract to facilitate strategic planning workshops without asking the organizers beforehand about the fundamental values base of their organization, are we not colluding with this economic–rationalist imperative? Or some other set of values and objectives which may conflict with our own value bases? We need to ask ourselves, 'Do we or do we not agree with such and such a values stance?' Facilitators for whom the organizational values are congruent with their own would not feel co-opted or compromised. However, where there is a marked dissonance in outlook between the facilitator and the prevailing philosophical stance of the contracting organization, this could present ethical and professional dilemmas. On the one hand, facilitators may see their services in encouraging participants to plan or make decisions as being what they are enabled to do by their training and experience. As the aim is for participants to go where they will, is it legitimate for facilitators to determine where they want the planning to go? There is the difference here between scenario building and manipulation. On the other hand, if there is sufficient value incongruence, is it more ethical for the facilitators to refuse the contract? In this respect, facilitators and consultants share some ethical dilemmas with other professionals, for example doctors who will or will not support terminations or euthanasia.

A further consideration is the issue of outsourcing human resource development activities. 'Outsourcing' is the catchword for perceived greater efficiency in monetary terms by contracting out 'non-core' functions and thus saving on insurance, leave and other entitlements. Outsourcing may appear superficially cheaper (in the short term), but has not necessarily been proved more efficient. There are times when it is useful to bring in specialist expertise. But there must be prior assessment of consultants and careful evaluation of a company's activities, potential for and support of change. For stressed HRD managers and consultant-facilitators it is understandable, though not excusable, that corners are cut. There are at least two issues here: 1) Does the facilitator approve of what this organization does? 2) Can the facilitator have a beneficial influence on the processes of interaction (however defined)?

Often the ideal situation for effective facilitation is a mix of facilitators working together from 'inside' and 'outside' the organization. The insiders have the informal knowledge of who does what and how. The outsiders can pinpoint things that are not obvious to the insiders. They can often see patterns of fixed behaviour, groupthink and barriers to change which are not so obvious to those entrenched in a culture where these things become part of everyday culture or 'ways we do things around here'. They can also confront power-holders more easily as they are not part of the permanent power structure and they can take an apparently 'naive observer' role and ask apparently 'innocent' questions to generate a rethink of issues. Such a mix, however, does bring up additional requirements for coordinating these different orientations effectively, both conceptually and organizationally. If this is not done, the result can be confusion for participants and facilitators alike.

Case Study 2: Is this the path to perfection?

Consider a second case reported in *The Australian Financial Review* (Rubin, 1999b) entitled 'No prisoners on the path to perfection'. The author, Harriet

Rubin, describes workshops facilitated by Fernando Flores, the ex-Chilean Minister of Finance, who maintains that three years of imprisonment during Pinochet's fascist regime transformed his outlook. He now espouses the view that 'communication, truth and trust are at the heart of power' (1999b: 28). These appear to be reasonable, though rather simplistic sentiments. It is *how* he puts them into action in his workshops that is of concern.

The article recounts a workshop in which Flores has flown from California to Holland to 'transform' two executive teams of a global construction giant which is losing market share. What follows is a quote directly from Rubin's article:

> One executive says to Flores: 'You're our last hope'.
>
> 'Hope is the raw material of losers, Flores shoots back.
>
> Flores lifts his 180cm, 100kg frame from his chair. Imagine a bear rising up on its hind legs: the men are simply not prepared for how big Flores is when he stands – or how fierce. He turns on Tomas, a relative newcomer to Flores's sessions.
>
> 'Tomas', Flores begins, 'tell me: why is change taking so long here?' Tomas responds: 'The group is resisting Flores's approach'. To Flores, Tomas's answer sounds like projection. It is Tomas who is resisting change. Flores invites Tomas's colleagues to 'assess' Tomas. One executive leaps to the challenge.
>
> 'Tomas, you are blind, egotistical, and inwardly focused', he says. 'I cannot challenge you without you getting defensive'.
>
> The words leave Tomas stunned.
>
> 'Tomas', Flores says, 'say "Thank you" for that assessment'.
>
> The words are part of a script written on an easel next to Flores. Tomas tries to repeat them, but he stutters when he gets to the word 'sincerity'. Flores prompts Tomas, 'Follow the script exactly as it is, ie "Assessor: (Name), negative assessment. I appreciate your sincerity. I would like to have further conversations with you about the topic. Thank you.
>
> Person assessed: You're welcome."'
>
> Another colleague begins, 'Tomas you are a bureaucrat. You are married to rules, not listening' (Rubin, 1999b: 28).

But that it not where it ends. Flores provokes Tomas, saying:

> 'Tomas stand up and tell me honestly what you think of me. This is how you develop trust. I know you have been saying things behind my back. I promise that no matter what you say to my face, I will reply with, "Thank you for the assessment"'.

Tomas measures out his words as if each were a drop of poison: 'I. . . don't. . . like. . . your. . . style.'

Flores corrects him: 'You hate my style.'

'I hate your style', Tomas says.

'Thank you very much for your assessment, Tomas. I appreciate your sincerity. Now here is my assessment of you. You are an arsehole, but less of an arsehole than you were two minutes ago. You have opinions on things that you know nothing about. If you give me permission, I will train you. If you agree to be trained and don't follow my lead, I will kill you. And that's worse than my style' (Rubin, 1999b).

Discussion

This kind of behaviour is reminiscent of descriptions of meetings run in some totalitarian regimes. Some therapists in the past used the confrontational method with the idea of breaking down the 'old' so as to build the 'new'. This technique was also used at one time in the armed services. According to Rubin, the reporter, Flores charges fees of over US$1 million (A$1.6 million) and, according to the article, he gets results in changes to company profits.

The first frightening thing was that the article was reported without any comment on the strategies Flores uses. Certainly open and honest feedback can be useful, provided it is carefully thought through; but does it have to be public? There was no questioning by the journalist of the ethics of facilitation or people's rights at workshops. To me this is a story similar to the 'Emperor's New Clothes' (see Book 2 Chapter 4) except that in this instance we do not have an example of 'no clothes' but 'false clothes'. No doubt the company CEOs had a great deal invested in Flores. Would anyone dare, like the little boy in the Hans Christian Anderson story, to stand up and say the equivalent of 'Flores, you are wearing false clothes'? Indeed Flores was wearing false clothes, espousing, but not using, authentic facilitative behaviour. After all, what message are the CEOs giving their workers here? And what about the human casualties? Adams and Balfour (1998) address similar issues in *Unmasking Administrative Evil* where they assert the need to name some behaviours in which there are destructive assaults on human dignity as 'evil' rather than 'dysfunctional' behaviour and comment:

> The modern age, with its scientific-analytic mind-set and technical-rational approach to social and political problems enables a new and frightening form of evil – administrative evil. It is frightening because it wears many masks, making it easy for ordinary people to do evil, even when they do not intend it to do so.
>
> (1998: 4)

They go on to discuss the difficulty of unmasking administrative evil as the invitation to behave in an evil way often comes from an expert or technical role 'couched in appropriate language, or it may even come packaged as a good and worthy project, representing what we call a *moral inversion*, in which something evil or destructive has been redefined as good and worthy' (Adams and Balfour, 1998: 4).

Flores uses language that is potentially dehumanizing depending on the tone of the delivery: 'Everyone believes that you Europeans are impeccable. But I know you are jerks.' When one executive says 'You're our last hope', Flores shoots back 'Hope is the raw material of losers'. Adams and Balfour point how our everyday language is taken for granted or tacit (Polanyi, 1966) and that this makes us susceptible to participation in evil. 'Follow the script exactly as it is', barks Flores (that is, 'You have no choice'). This has remarkable overtones of perpetrators in the Holocaust who claimed 'I had no choice; I just followed orders.'

You might argue that the article states that Flores gets results, in monetary terms at least. Now I want to examine why. Firstly, one could attribute this in part to the 'Hawthorne effect', that is, the workers were so pleased that their managers spent one million dollars on them that they worked harder and more effectively. Secondly, the 'Emperor's New Clothes' syndrome – as they had a large sum invested, presumably they wanted to believe they got value for money. But I think the third and main reason lies in the underlying impact of sheer *fear*. If the CEOs were backing the confronting techniques used by Flores, who would dare to stand up against this approach for fear of getting more psychological abuse or even the sack?

Flores, I believe, is making the following assumptions:

- all people want to be changed by someone else;
- all people want to change and grow;
- all people want to change and grow fast;
- he has the right and the power to make this change come about;
- he has the mandate to use any coercive strategies without censorship.

Most people fear speaking in public. Some, I hear, fear it more than death itself. Giving negative feedback to another in public is even more fear-inspiring and it could be considered unethical and demeaning. It would also be culturally inappropriate. People who have trouble giving open feedback cannot be forced into it. If people fear speaking out in front of a group because of previous embarrassment, the depth of their hurt does not change overnight. Some processes will help people move on, but a facilitator cannot make the assumption that one strategy will help all, nor that the rate of change will be the same for all individuals. One of the implicit messages which could have been drawn from the behaviour of Flores is that openness and dissent are dangerous and punishable (similar to the symptoms of groupthink).

Facilitators can hide behind the pretence of 'openness' and this can be a subtle form of manipulation:

> They can camouflage their incompetence, fearfulness, or insecurity by seeking to create the impression that they are all-knowing and all-powerful. They can keep their real feelings hidden and project only what is consistent with the impression they wish to create; and they can choose techniques that perpetuate this illusion.
>
> (Corey *et al*, 1988: 18)

Participants at workshops often attribute exaggerated power and wisdom to facilitators and leaders. There is a temptation for facilitators who are motivated by a need for power to reinforce this misconception unethically. Robson and Beary (1995) uses the term 'facipulation' to describe the case when a facilitator 'jumps into' the content by suggesting openly or covertly some solution or future action to a group. Facipulation should be handled with great care as a facilitator's main job is concerned with process. There is an ethical problem here. Yes, facilitation involves process and the facilitator should not predetermine or influence outcomes. But if 'process' leads to 'evil conclusions' (as perceived by the facilitator) what happens then?

It is very easy, therefore, for facilitators to slip into what Smart (1994: 1) calls 'expertosis'. She comments that we all suffer from this disease at times: 'Expertosis develops when we believe our knowledge is the only knowledge or the best knowledge and impose it on others. It is particularly common among professionals. . . none of us is immune.' In my judgement Flores has fallen into the seduction of being the 'expert'.

So there are a number of different ethical aspects here:

- The facilitator 'manipulates' participants because he/she wants them to move in a certain direction which he/she feels/thinks is 'good', but participants do not.
- The facilitator is led to be complicit with the ideals of the employing body in a way he/she feels/thinks is not right, but does nothing to withdraw or support the participants against the organization (eg Eagle Insurance).
- So ideally a facilitator needs to:
  - be aware of his/her own values;
  - be aware of participants' values (this is a huge area);
  - consider employing agency values. Where there is dissonance, can/should he/she do something, and if so, what?

The more I read about facilitation and groups, the more I realize how much there is to learn and that in some ways we are still in the dark ages in terms of understanding how people interrelate. I now see why I hesitate when I receive phone calls along the lines of, 'Oh, Chris, I rang you because I heard you were the expert in facilitation...' I reply something on the lines of 'I have expertise in some areas of facilitation...'

Groupthink

Both case studies include symptoms of groupthink. Facilitators need to be sure that groups reach the 'performing' stage, ie where disagreement is an accepted and welcomed norm of behaviour (Tuckman and Jensen, 1977) (see Chapter 8).

Is facilitation one of the current management fads?

There is a wealth of current literature on the shallowness of some current management fads (Pratt, 1997; Kleiner, 1996; Hilmer and Donaldson, 1998). Micklethwait and Wooldridge (1997) go as far as calling some management gurus 'witch doctors' (which is the title of their book). This seems to coincide with the growing concern regarding some HRD fads (Hogan, 1992; Sims, 1999; Pratt, 1997). Any evolving profession has the exciting tingle of spontaneity and inventiveness. But creativity and experimentation have to be balanced with caution. Some processes are powerful and may lead to unexpected results. Some facilitators may not abuse facilitation techniques purposefully, but there has to be a balance. I believe that facilitation is *not* just a passing fad, though the skills and processes of facilitation may at times be used unethically to mask and/or implement fads in management. This leads me to a discussion on the process of professionalizing facilitation.

Professionalizing facilitation

What is meant by a profession? According to the *Shorter Oxford Dictionary* it refers to an 'occupation which one professes to be skilled in and to follow; a vocation in which a professed knowledge of some department of learning is used in its application to the affairs of others' (1980: 1680). In some ways, professions are similar to the crafts-people, engineers, and priests of the Middle Ages. Since then, automation has taken over unskilled work and people now require more and more training to perform tasks. The complexity of modern society has led to greater specialization and specialized knowledge. This in turn has resulted in a growth in specialized teaching and accreditation systems in many fields. Groups have formed to identify themselves as professions, for example doctors, nurses, lawyers, social workers, teachers, psychologists, surveyors, engineers, anthropologists, accountants, librarians. In the UK professions have a long history; the Institute of Civil Engineers was formed in 1818 and the Law Society in 1825 (Larson, 1977). Professionals earn their living by practising some skills for which they have been accredited. This accreditation is often part of the professionalization process. The degree to which this accreditation is taken seriously by society may be from self-promotion to legal sanctions. For instance, non-accredited people may not portray themselves as a lawyer or doctor. However, there are a number of fields where professionalization is less strict, and/or more recent, and amateurs may hold themselves out to 'practise' a number of skills. Facilitators do not have full legal accreditation and protection, and the reasons for this are many and varied, including the vast range of areas in which facilitation is used.

The reasons for this professionalism are many: to exchange knowledge and skills, to develop a code of ethics, to gain prestige, respect, social status, autonomy, and in recent times, wealth (De George, 1995). Having rigid accreditation may inhibit the practice of and entry to the discipline. Larson (1977) attributes the rise of professionalism in the USA and the UK to the 'great transformation' and reorganization of economy and society around the market and heavily shaped by competitive capitalism. She argues that professionalization is an attempt to translate scarce resources (that is, knowledge and skills) into other resources: social and economic rewards. The resulting system is then worked as a monopoly of expertise in the markets (that is, 'market power'). She notes that professions are either typical occupations of the middle class or typical aspirations of the socially mobile children of industrial or clerical workers. I abhor the thought that access to the facilitation profession is limited by the chances of one's economic birthright or birthplace.

Many futurists (Cox, 1995; Macy and Brown, 1998; Max-Neef, 1991; Ferguson, 1982) argue that there is now a need to break down the barriers between disciplines and fields of learning in order to solve the interconnected, complex problems we face. Perhaps it is a key role of facilitators as 'translators' to help people from different professions, callings, cultures and creeds to engage in dialogue and discourse. Likewise Harris (2000) describes why economists have problems with professions. Firstly, they sometimes give consumers a false sense of security by suggesting that because a person is licensed, belongs to a profession, or belongs to a professional body, they are competent. Secondly, some professions try to limit the number of competitors so that their own profits are maintained. Thirdly, sometimes regulations stifle the ways in which consumers' needs can be met.

Larsen concludes that the professionalization phenomenon does not have clear boundaries. For example, the call is that professional training must be 'prolonged', 'specialized' and have a 'theoretical base', but no one has stated 'how long?', 'how theoretical?' or 'how specialized?' training needs to be in order to 'qualify' as a so-called 'professional facilitator'. Partly, 'professionalism' is a matter of being 'good enough' at whatever (however this is defined), and partly a matter of distinguishing one profession from another, for example doctors and nurses, facilitators and therapists. It is necessary to define 'boundaries', and reconcile this with the need for cooperation and prevent demarcation disputes between professionals. At times it may be necessary for a facilitator to branch into therapy if a person in a group is overly distressed, that is, it would not be ethical to say, 'It is more than my job's worth to listen to your problems.' However, in such an instance it would be necessary to listen and then suggest that a participant seek further help if appropriate, that is, 'I've overstepped the boundaries of my skills and knowledge, I recommend you seek expert help, but of course, the choice is yours.'

Indeed the different definitions and qualifications of professionals from different countries reflect the differing structures and resources of those countries. This poses very real problems for professional migrants to Australia, the USA and the UK to this day. The fact that the current movement to form the facilitation profession is happening more openly via the Internet may to some extent overcome this problem.

Management as a profession

Mary Parker Follett (1868–1933) wrote about the development of management as a profession in the 1920s. Her comments, written over 70 years ago, have stood the 'test of time':

> The word 'profession' connotes for most people a foundation of *science* and a motive of *service*. That is, a profession is said to rest on the basis of a proven body of knowledge, and such knowledge is supposed to be used in the service of others rather than merely for one's own purposes. (Follett, 1989: 7)

In her writing Follett calls for the need to study the science of cooperation: 'It is my plea above everything else that we learn *how* to cooperate' (Follett, 1989: 7). Axelrod (1990) studied cooperation in depth using the issue of the 'prisoner's dilemma' and computerized decision making. Hunter, Bailey and Taylor (1997) went further to coin a new term, 'co-operacy', meaning 'the technology of collective or consensus decision making as distinct from democracy and autocracy'. Indeed, facilitation as a profession has advanced enormously, partly because of concurrent advances in electronic communication to help support and debate ideas.

As a result of casualties caused in some personal development group work in the sixties and seventies, the American Psychologists Association developed 'Codes of Practice' in 1973 and revised them in 1992. With a code of ethics, individuals may be barred from practising a profession for some time, or forever for major misdemeanours. However, a code has to be actively enforced. A client or participant needs to be able to raise a complaint and be heard by a professional body. Unfortunately, this is not always the case and frequently little action is taken (Andrews, 1999). Currently, anyone can say, 'I'm a facilitator.' If an unqualified person said 'I'm a lawyer or a doctor', he/she could face severe punishment in the community, as professions like law and medicine have a legislative base.

What are the issues raised with ethical codes of conduct?

There are many pros and cons to the professionalization of a new field of human endeavour. Mary Palmer argues that facilitation does not yet fit into the same professional mould as doctors, nurses, accountants, lawyers and architects (Palmer, 1999). But there is a growing need to protect both clients and participants and help them to be careful consumers of facilitator services.

Most professions are self-governing, but codes of ethics need to be achievable and policeable because human beings do not always act rationally or consistently. A code cannot cover every eventuality, merely the key essences of desirable behaviours. Facilitators not only have to model ethical behaviour but try to establish ethical codes by contracting for desirable group norms/codes of behaviour with participants. This will involve 'educating' participants as to what the codes are and giving the codes to them before a workshop.

Professional cooperation

At the time of writing there is a very strong community spirit amongst facilitators in Western Australia, even amongst people who are potential competitors in the marketplace (despite the current government's policy to increase competitiveness). Perhaps this is inherent in the 'pioneering mode' of any new field? I hope this esprit de corps is not lost as the profession develops.

Another issue is: Is one code of ethics suitable for all facilitators? What about facilitators who are working in the community development field? Facilitators in developing countries are innovating in the fields of literacy, numeracy and community development; however, it would be a costly business to 'accredit' facilitators in these countries. It is not appropriate to discuss this issue further here, but the question 'Will one code suit all?' needs to be raised.

Ethical consistency

Facilitation is not like the popular perception of science, which assumes that it is guided by simple rules of cause and effect. It is more like a dance, and at times a facilitator can step on toes and egos. Typically, facilitation deals with emerging situations not clearly predicted or foreseen, but with which the facilitator has to deal. The facilitator faces constant challenges, dilemmas and choices. In making operational choices in such situations, rapid value checks are necessary. Paulo Freire noted some of these dilemmas, in a conversation published two months before his death in 1997 (see Hunter, Bailey and Taylor, 1999):

> One of the major struggles in every individual is to diminish the difference between what one says and does, between the discourse and the practice. Ethics really is fighting to decrease the distance. I think that in politicians one will encounter the maximum distance between the two. You listen to the speech of a candidate for mayor, but after being elected his or her actions do not look at all like the discourse. Like the educator and like, the people, I think that one of the values that we should search for is exactly this – the value of consistence.
>
> I remember when I started being a father. With my first wife what was important was the exercise to diminish the distance between what we did and what we dreamed. *This is a fight, a daily fight, but a beautiful fight, a delicious fight. I remember that sometimes I asked forgiveness of one of my sons or daughters for the contradiction in what I taught. It is important that the child knows that the father is also incomplete, that he can make mistakes. We should be satisfied with the knowledge that we are daily fighting for this consistency.* (My emphasis in italics)

Many issues are raised here. The argument is reminiscent of the concepts raised by Argyris and Schön (1994) who puzzle as to why even after training, managers who were under stress would go back to their previous undesirable modes of behaviour. They called these conflicting modes of behaviour 'espoused theory' (that is, how we wish to behave, namely, our stated values) versus 'theory in use' (that is, how we behave when under pressure). There appear to be issues of consistency with one's espoused values, not only in the behaviour of a facilitator with groups, but also when a facilitator decides whether to accept a request to facilitate a group (as my story from consulting days illustrated). I liked the way Freire framed the battle for consistency in such a positive way: 'it's a challenge not a heavy burden'. This concept of consistency has been built into my 'facilitation frame' and expressed as 'espoused values' versus 'values-in-use'. The ideas of ethics and consistency raise another issue regarding the ethical accreditation processes of facilitators: should some realistic, but potentially 'stressful' role-play situations be developed to see how facilitators behave under pressure?

What are the purposes of ethical codes of conduct?

Codes of conduct serve many purposes (De George, 1995). Basically, I believe, they need to include not only principles and practice, but also methods for ensuring these are adhered to; otherwise they have 'no teeth'. According to De George, codes of conduct indicate that a particular group is a profession; codes of conduct are often read out at ceremonies to induct new members; they are ideals to guide practice and benchmarks to measure success; they spell out etiquette and procedures. He describes the following required characteristics. They should: be regulative, protect the public interest, not be self-serving, be specific and honest, and be policeable and policed. Policing ensures that codes are not just a wish list of ideals. However, codes should not be a 'restrictive trade practice' or a means of stifling innovation.

Education of facilitators

In addition to a code of practice, accreditation and practical examinations, there have to be agreed competencies and education. And if so, should whole courses in facilitation (rather than just units) be offered at university level? And if so, of what should they comprise? This issue was discussed on the International Association of Facilitators (IAF) e-mail discussion group and published in 2000 (Pierce, Chesebrow and Braun, 2000), and is discussed in Chapter 6. Edward Ruete (1999) agrees with the need for a common set of core of facilitator competencies, but argues for freedom to decide how each of us reaches those competencies. He uses a guitar analogy, in that he calls himself a 'guitarist' and could use cotton-roll finger picking really well, but could not use flat picking, jazz chords or blues licks, and asks which of these competencies would he need to call himself a guitar player? A similar question may be asked of facilitators.

At what age should people start to learn facilitation skills?

But is facilitation ready to be a profession with sanctions? As an educator, I believe facilitation is a set of skills and beliefs, some of which can be easily taught to children at an early age. Some appear to have a natural talent. Facilitative interventions may be made by anyone in group situations. Two examples of this have had a profound effect on me. The first was in Melbourne in 1986 when I met with primary children of seven years of age who were learning to run their own meetings. The other was in 1995 when

I attended a meeting of the Gandhi Foundation in the Houses of Parliament in London and saw four 10-year-old children from Northern Ireland demonstrate their co-mediation skills to settle playground disputes. In Perth, Western Australia, Bellevue Primary School has trained its year-seven students for the past five years in mediation of playground disputes (Ashworth, 1999: 1). The principal and another teacher train students in conflict resolution, problem-solving skills and negotiation skills. Students are trained to be impartial. During each recess break, two mediators, identified by their bright red T-shirts, are rostered to step in to help if there are incidents of bullying or argumentative behaviour in the playground. As a result there has been a big reduction (75 per cent) in the school's suspension rates. But let us look at the issues behind this. Firstly, teachers, as in Northern Ireland, had to invest large amounts of time and energy into mediation training. Secondly, and perhaps most importantly, they had to be both willing and able to delegate and share power with students. They were not abdicating responsibility, and indeed still monitor the process and manage more complex and/or violent cases of conflict. Thirdly, secondary schools have to continue this work to ensure that skills are internalized (which may have helped to avoid violence as seen in the killing in a Denver High school in the USA in April 1999).

I have asserted above, and the primary school cases discussed earlier illustrate, that children can learn basic facilitative skills at an early age. Teachers are called in to use high-level facilitation and mediation skills in cases of complex conflict. This is similar to the current trend for professional secretaries who are now required to construct highly complicated diagrams as opposed to mere touch-typing, which is fast becoming a ubiquitous life skill. Surely the facilitation profession will develop to a new level and hopefully basic 'group and process literacy' will become life skills?

It was my experiences and the case studies described above that made me realize that for all of us to maximize our full potential as citizens working towards a 'civil society', we need to learn the skills of putting democracy into practice from a young age so that these skills are internalized by adulthood. Goleman (1996, 1998) advocates the need for the development of 'emotional intelligence' and Postle (1989) and Heron (1993) advocate the development of 'emotional intelligence/competence'; Doyle (in Kaner, 1996: viii) advocates the development of 'group literacy', an awareness of and strong skills in group dynamics, meeting facilitation and consensus-building tools. According to Hunter, Bailey and Taylor (1993), the problem is that democracy is a confrontation-style philosophy which assumes people are on different sides. Democracy is based on the premise that majority decision is the best way of making decisions. At times it is; as mentioned in a previous chapter, however, 'When things go wrong, democracy is an orphan' (source unknown). At other times, autocracy may be required.

Hunter *et al* (1993) compare the shift from democracy to co-operacy as being of the same magnitude as the historical shift from feudalism (autocracy) to democracy and will require as big a paradigm shift. They also compare it to personal development in terms of the shift from dependence (autocracy) through independence (democracy) to interdependence (co-operacy). See Figure 11.1.

The changing role of educators

So how will these changes impact on educators? For the first 1,500 years of Christianity, the clergy regarded themselves as gatekeepers: enabling or barring people's entrance to heaven. As clerics were some of the few who could read and write, they were also the guardians and gatekeepers of books and learning. The Renaissance and the advent of the printing press increased demand for relatively cheap printed material and led to a new paradigm: mass access to learning via the printed word. The universities and their associated libraries still retained their power as seats of knowledge and wisdom until the second half of the 20th century. The advent of the computer has and is having an increasing impact. Teachers, lecturers, universities no longer hold (if they ever did) the 'keys to wisdom' through which a learner must learn. Computer-based literature searches have enabled student-centred learning to develop to a previously unheard of depth and detail. As Freire (1972, 1974) and Heron (1989, 1993) point out, the roles of educators and developers are changing to those of facilitator, supervisor, guide and provocateur. As a result of these changes teachers, community developers and universities, willingly or otherwise, have lost some of their traditional status and power based on knowledge. They now have to increase their facilitative and process skills and knowledge (Gibbs, 1982, 1992; Ramsden, 1992).

The education of facilitators

The International Association of Facilitators, in conjunction with the Institute of Cultural Affairs in the USA, has already produced (via a number of workshops and Internet discussions) a set of 'Facilitator Competencies'

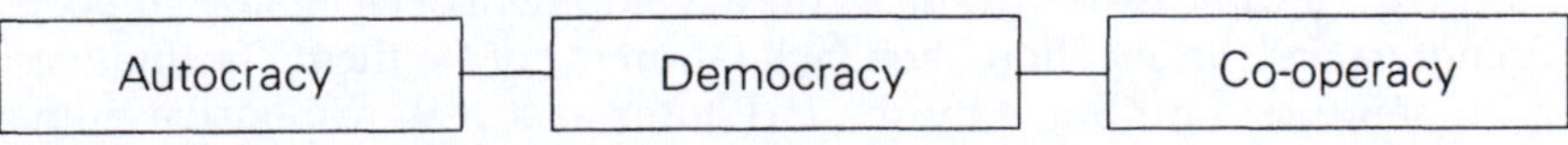

Figure 11.1 Changing shifts in decision making

Source: Hunter, Bailey and Taylor (1993: 6)

(Pierce, Cheesebrow and Braun, 2000), as discussed in Chapter 6. It includes sections commending that facilitators should 'Engage in professional growth' and 'Commit to a life of integrity'. Facilitators can go to great lengths to generate lists of desirable behaviours and ethical codes that are useful for themselves and their clients. However, these are motherhood statements; what of the operational details? How can an organization police each member? One answer is to educate the client to be able to recognize what constitutes professional practice, but this is a long process. An alternative approach is to accredit facilitators and this process is under way. But there are ethical as well as competency issues here. Flores may be knowledgeable; but, as I have implied above, his 'values-in-practice' may need to be monitored closely. But who will monitor facilitators like Flores? And with what authority? And with what sanctions? And will people like Flores 'recognize' such an authority?

Robson and Beary (1995) claim that it is important for people who train facilitators to ensure that trainees understand the true origins and purposes of the job. They need to be monitored as they begin to practise their newly developed skills, that is, the teaching–learning process must reflect the content. I recall an early course I attended in the 1980s entitled 'Working with groups', which, though interesting, was limited as it was totally lecture-based. According to Cross (1976, cited in Heron, 1989), training programmes should include facilitators who model professional facilitative behaviours. Cross goes further and proposes that facilitators who train others should:

- include methods for discriminating between and evaluating a variety of processes and strategies and their uses;
- show videos of other professional facilitators in action;
- enable participants to practise in role-plays and small groups;
- ensure there is constructive feedback through peer, self and teacher's assessment (Cross in Heron, 1989).

Some of the trainee facilitators in my classes indicate that they model their facilitation style/s on group facilitators they admire. This gives them a repertoire of strategies that they can then build on as they develop their own facilitator styles. Much may be learnt regarding useful and non-useful facilitative strategies through attentive observational learning.

There is a value issue, I argue, in the development of facilitators. If people do not value 'participation' then facilitation is not for them: 'facilitation is a human role contributed by the facilitator as a real, responsive human being. No technique, procedure or methodology will be sufficient to substitute for genuine involvement of the facilitator with the people and subject at hand' (Jago, in press: 31).

At the beginning of my courses on facilitation, I notice that students or would-be facilitators often appear egocentric, saying 'I want tricks to "wow" em' or 'I want to find ways of dealing with difficult participants' (that is, I want to be able to stay in control and protect myself), which is understandable. Without wanting to stifle initial motivation, I work on opening up the 'box of tricks' mindset. After all, the most expensive set of tools does not necessarily make a good carpenter. As the course progresses I hope participants have a clearer idea about the responsibilities and spirit of professional facilitation, that every tool or technique must have a purpose and a 'considered purpose' at that: to make a point, to increase interest or awareness of different viewpoints and so on. Techniques should never be used to get one's own needs met for approval, status or to achieve high rating on evaluation sheets. However, they are useful for gaining and keeping attention, increasing enjoyment, aiding learning, enhancing participation and understanding. What is important here is the *intention of the facilitator*. At the end of semester, participants indicate in their evaluations that they realize there is far more to facilitation than they previously thought and they are far more aware of the complexities of human behaviour and the responsibilities of their facilitation roles. There is a realization of the many dilemmas and the issues they may face if outcomes are anti-democratic or subject to the disapproval of the facilitator on moral grounds.

In the development field there has been an interesting reaction against the development of 'how to do it' manuals for facilitators of the 'REFLECT' adult literacy process. (The REFLECT method is based on the philosophy espoused by Paulo Freire (1972, 1974, 1997) in that illiterate villagers are facilitated in their language programmes to develop their own textbooks and stories based on their world and experiences.) David Archer in Phnuyal (1998) describes outcomes from a workshop of 15 leading facilitators from 11 countries: 'We have already learnt that the most effective approach at the facilitator level is not to "train" facilitators as if they are delivery instruments; rather facilitators have to be actively engaged in constructing their own texts, taking ownership of the approach and internalizing it' (1998: 31).

Speaking with my teacher-facilitator hat on, I endeavour to show students that there are three ways they can shape their practice with facilitation processes:

- use processes as documented in the literature (and evaluate them);
- adapt documented processes (and evaluate them);
- create their own processes (and evaluate them).

Above all, I stress the importance of explaining the purpose of processes or why they have been adapted. Wherever possible, I assert the need to keep processes open and 'transparent', partly so that participants do not feel manipulated, but also to help people in the community at large also become more 'process aware'. Transparency would seem to be a critical success factor.

How can facilitators gain credibility and experience?

There appear to be many strategies which professional facilitators can use to establish their credibility with groups, and which clients can use to evaluate the worth of a facilitator:

- a description of the facilitator's values and ways of working with groups;
- educational achievements in that field (at community, college and/or university levels);
- experience in facilitation;
- diversity of life experiences;
- evidence of past evaluation by groups (the least developed part of the art of facilitation in my opinion);
- accreditation by a recognized body.

The accreditation process is under way in the UK, USA and Europe (www.facilitator-accreditation.com). The issue of evaluation by past clients appears to me to be the poor relation at the moment in the development of the facilitation field and indeed other professions (compared to planning and implementation). Experience is another factor. As with the other professions, facilitators need practical experience and supervision through on-the-job mentoring and/or working with a co-facilitator.

Developing own code of ethics

Apart from having a common code of ethics, facilitators need to write their own codes. In any working relationship, for example between facilitator and clients, it is useful to develop a 'strategic alignment', that is, an agreed written, common purpose, expressed through a mission statement and specific goals and/or objectives (Hunter, Bailey and Taylor, 1997). This can be achieved if facilitators themselves are clear about their purpose in facilitation. Hunter *et al* (1997) also suggest an 'alignment check' every three months if the facilitator is engaged on a long project where personnel and/or company strategy may change.

I have developed my own code of ethics, which I started in 1994 to distribute to clients to make my values explicit. At first I hoped to advise clients what to expect of me. I now realize this document has a dual purpose: it also gives clients and participants benchmarks with which to evaluate my behaviour. As a result of linking the code to my evaluation, I hope to be more 'accountable' in my work as a facilitator. (See Book 2, Chapter 1).

Developing an international professional code of ethics

The International Association of Facilitators (IAF) has made three important contributions to the field of facilitation: firstly, the development of a set of competencies (described in Chapter 6), secondly, the Certification Programme, and at the time of writing, a draft 'Code of ethics' (Figure 11.2), all designed to strengthen the credibility of group facilitation as a profession. The latter was developed during 2000–2001 by the International Association of Facilitators' Ethics and Values Think Tank (EVTT), a virtual group using electronic communications technology, specifically e-mail and Web-based technologies.

1. **Client Service**
   We are in service to the clients, using our group facilitation to add value to their work.
2. **Conflict of Interest**
   We openly acknowledge any potential conflict of interest.
3. **Group Autonomy**
   We respect the culture, rights, and autonomy of the group .
4. **Processes, Methods, and Tools**
   We use processes, methods and tools responsibly.
5. **Respect, Safety, Equity, and Trust**
   We strive to engender an environment of respect and safety where all participants trust that they can speak freely and where individual boundaries are honoured. We use our skills, knowledge, tools, and wisdom to elicit and honour the perspectives of all.
6. **Stewardship of Process**
   We practice stewardship of process and impartiality toward content.
7. **Confidentiality**
   We maintain confidentiality of information.
8. **Professional Development**
   We are responsible for continuous improvement of our facilitation skills and knowledge.

Figure 11.2 The draft IAF Code of Ethics (draft downloaded January 2002).

For details see www.iaf-world.org/iafethics.htm

As with all professions, the questions need to be asked, 'Who monitors the keeping of these codes?' and 'What happens to those who break these codes?'

Professional accreditation

In 1998, a Task Force called 'The Facilitation Accreditation Board' (FAB) was formed (based in the UK, but under the auspices of the IAF) to develop and pilot an accreditation scheme for professional facilitators. It was agreed that the International Association of Facilitators Europe/Africa would develop the scheme, although it would be designed for worldwide application. The Task Force was briefed to identify the core facilitation competencies required for meetings and workshops within a business environment and to develop a strategy to assess individuals against those competencies (Godwin, 1999: 16).

According to Godwin, arguments have understandably raged, not only concerning competencies, but also regarding assessment, including questions like, 'How can you assess an art?' and 'Who assesses the assessors'? I would add to this discussion, is facilitation an art, a craft, a set of competencies, or all of the above? I have observed occasional acts of facilitative artistry, but how can you assess these? According to Godwin, a suitable assessment process 'was born' and evaluated by the FAB team itself in July 1998 in Edinburgh, and later in London and Belgium. It is designed to enable assessors to observe, record, classify and grade the competencies displayed by candidates. The process begins with candidates applying to the FAB and submitting a synopsis and career résumé covering facilitation experience, qualifications and training. Once this is accepted, two accredited assessors are then assigned to each candidate. They review the résumé against the competencies. Next, successful candidates have to submit a report on workshops they have facilitated. Competencies such as pre-workshop preparation, assessment of client needs, workshop design and client feedback are assessed. If they are successful they are then invited to an assessment centre for a full-day practical review of their skills against the competencies. The assessment day comprises three sections. Firstly, there is an initial interview by assessors to confirm their synopsis and explore the candidate's experience further. Secondly, there is a practical workshop on a pre-selected issue led by the candidate. Thirdly, there is a final interview and feedback session. Successful candidates have the option of being included on an 'Accredited Facilitators List' held by the IAF that is made available to clients seeking the services of a facilitator. There are now assessment centres in Edinburgh, London and Brussels and across the USA. Details of the scheme can be obtained from www.iaf-world.org/iafcertinfo.htm

Accommodating various styles of facilitation

One problem of having a blanket accreditation is that there are different contexts for and different styles of facilitation. As a result, it may be necessary to develop different standards for different styles. However, there are limits to this diversity. Fernando Flores, cited above, clearly believes in '*confrontational facilitation*'. Confrontation, I agree, is an acceptable tool in facilitation providing it is done compassionately and competently. But how it is done, where and for what purpose and with what results are crucial questions that have to be asked. Sometimes direct confrontation may be necessary, but I prefer a more subtle approach like Dick espouses (1984: 272). For example, the shape of a minor intervention might consist of 'Inform. . . suggest. . . invite' (that is, inform an individual and/or group of a problem, suggest a suitable procedure, and invite a response). For example:

Inform: Since the beginning of this session Jane appeared to be staring out of the window and Alan and George kept having private conversations.
Suggest: It appears that listening could be better. Why don't we try. . .?
Invite: What do you think?

The suggestion is offered tentatively because it is based on the facilitator's assumptions of the nature of the problem, which may or may not be accurate.

Some facilitators encourage group members to go to deep levels of feeling using '*cathartic facilitation*' strategies. Again, I contend, catharsis has its place; however, I agree with Corey *et al* (1988: 5–6) who propose:

> Catharsis can be exciting, and yet it can feed a false sense of productivity. The leader who is too hungry to produce a heavy emotional session may use techniques to generate the appearance of movement without being sensitive to the need to work the material through and to gain some comprehension of its meaning and implications.

One of Flores's critics calls him 'dangerous' and compares him to the Magician in Thomas Mann's haunting story 'Mario the Magician' (Rubin, 1999a: 151). In that story the magician transforms people on stage; he gets men to bray like donkeys and women to embrace him in front of the audience. (Ironically, at the end of the story one of the participants walks on to the stage and shoots the magician.)

Corey *et al* (1988: 89) state: 'Too often those who lead groups look for techniques for every possible occurrence... in doing so they become mechanical facilitators.' There are skills that can be learnt, but occasionally the intuitive and/or creative response may be the most appropriate. In these instances facilitation becomes an art. Students need to know about skills and processes as well as the 'essence' of facilitation (Hunter, Bailey and Taylor, 1999).

None of the learnt skills or accreditation or codes of ethics will work unless a facilitator can handle pain and conflict with compassion (Frost, 1999). Hunter *et al* (1999) even call for 'ruthless compassion'; that is, bringing compassion to the purpose of the group, avoiding 'clobbering' or 'pussy footing' when making a group intervention (Heron, 1989). Clearly the two case studies (taken from events in the UK with Eagle Star Life and Holland with Fernando Flores) illustrate the lack of basic compassion and self-awareness, and the need to keep excesses in check.

What are the future developments for facilitation?

I now turn to future trends in facilitation and will deal with the uses of technology, the thoughts of some prominent 'future seekers', facilitator maintenance and management of 'toxic waste', finishing with some development of facilitating healing.

Facilitation and the future seekers

The rise of facilitation in the past 25 years has coincided with the emergence of 'future seekers' across the world. These people have united in what Marilyn Ferguson called 'The Aquarian Conspiracy':

> A leaderless but powerful network is working to bring about radical change... it is a conspiracy without a political doctrine. Without a manifesto. With conspirators who seek power only to disperse it... Activists asking different kinds of questions, challenging the establishment from within.
>
> (Ferguson, 1982: 23)

Manfred Max-Neef, a Chilean economist, has called for an awakening to the complexity of the combined effects of the economic, social and political crises in many so-called 'Third World' countries where existing systems can no longer cope. He called it a 'crisis of utopia' in that:

> we are losing, if we have not lost it already, our capacity to dream. We are struggling in an exhausting insomnia which impairs the lucidity so desperately needed to cope with our problems forcefully and imaginatively. Instead, we have become drowsy managers of a crisis which we feel is impossible to solve by our own means.
>
> (1991: 3)

He calls for the aid of 'facilitators' rather than 'development tourists' to enable communities at the grassroots level to discover their 'human needs' (both material and non-material) and 'satisfiers' so that people become protagonists of their own future and sustainable development. This process needs to be conducted on a human scale through active participation of people rather than in gigantic systems where decisions flow from top to bottom. Max-Neef calls, most importantly, for the development and training of indigenous professional facilitators. (See also discussion of bottom-up Participatory Rural Appraisal (PRA) techniques in Chapter 3.)

Another future seeker, Eva Cox, in *A Truly Civil Society* (1995) identifies four types of 'wealth'. Firstly, 'financial capital', which is the focus of most governments; secondly, 'physical capital', which is now on the agenda because of environmental catastrophes; thirdly, 'human capital', our accumulated skills and knowledge (which is offset by the many losses of unemployment); and finally 'social capital', 'the processes between people which establish networks, norms and social trust and facilitate coordination and cooperation for mutual benefit. . . social capital should be the pre-eminent and most valued form of capital as it provides the basis on which we build a truly civil society' (Cox, 1995: 15–16). Clearly one way in which human and social capital may be maximized is with effective facilitation.

In the West, there now appears to be a paradigm shift occurring. The interconnectedness between people, and between people and the animal and plant world, is at last sinking in to the western psyche, partly because pollution and its related effects can no longer be ignored. Macy (1996) adopts the term 'deep ecology', coined by the Norwegian philosopher, Arne Naess, in contrast to 'shallow environmentalism'. 'Deep ecology' implies that we are not individuals in charge of ourselves and the universe, but are embedded in a living matrix based on reciprocity.

In some ways there is nothing new in this approach. Some, though not all Amerindians, Maoris and Australian Aborigines and other indigenous peoples have practised this lifestyle for centuries. Not, I might add, always with complete success and minimal impact (Flannery, 1995). Adventurers and administrators from colonial powers, in the main unfortunately, did not even attempt to find out different perspectives on life or if they did they regarded these ideas as quaint, illogical or unrealistic. It is pathetic that it has taken the West so long to honour some of the traditions and philosophies of indigenous peoples. Indeed it is only when we suffer from the seeds of our own destruction: social breakdown, wars, nuclear proliferation and the destruction of the biosphere, that we start to take a more holistic look at the world and our roles in it. We all belong to so many groups throughout our lives. The more people who develop facilitation skills, arguably the more group effectiveness may be achieved (Hunter, Bailey and Taylor, 1993). However, this may be rather idealistic and places too much responsibility on facilitation since group effectiveness is also about valuing and supporting participative planning, conflict resolution, evaluation and provision of adequate basic resources.

The Shambhala warriors: a prophesy from Tibetan Buddhism

In 1995, I visited Tibet and was struck by the number of ancient stories in the Tibetan tradition which related to the current dilemmas in the human condition. Macy (1991) describes the ancient Tibetan prophesy of the Shambhala warriors who emerge during a time of great danger of apocalypse and the coming of the kingdom of Shambhala which may be a metaphor for an internal spiritual event, or an external event. She describes the prophesy of a time when the earth is in great danger. There are two great powers with great wealth, which each uses to prepare to annihilate the other with weapons of unfathomable destructive power, and technologies that lay waste our world. Then the kingdom of Shambhala begins to emerge. It is not a place, but exists in the hearts and minds of Shambhala warriors. These warriors have no uniform, nor come from one particular area, but tread amongst the barbarians themselves, to dismantle the man-made weapons. In order to do this, they go into training to use two weapons: *compassion and insight*. The former gives the juice to move, to act, but can lead to burnout. The latter: insight into the radical interdependence of all phenomena and the wisdom that it is not a battle between the good guys and the bad guys, but a battle that runs through the landscape of every human heart. Compassion and insight sustain each Shambhala warrior as agents of wholesome change. 'They are gifts for us to claim now in the healing of our world' Macy (1991: 180).

Margaret Wheatley, another future seeker, in *Leadership and the New Science* (1992) cites the physicist, John Archibald Wheeler, who proposes that we live in a participative universe: 'a place where the act of looking for certain information evokes the information we go looking for... the whole universe is a participatory process, where we create not only the present with our observations, but the past as well' (1992: 63).

Wheatley draws on quantum physics, chaos theory and molecular biology and proposes that the more participants we engage in this participative universe, the more ownership will result. If we gain more viewpoints and make better sense of the world we will become wiser in the process.

Spiritual and emotional dimensions of facilitation

The hours that those with employment spend at work appear to be increasing (as opposed to the literature in the 1970s which foretold a shortening of the working week). At the same time there appears to be a shift in thinking in the West in that there is a plethora of books currently being published on bringing back some kind of spiritual sense into the workplace (Bolman and Deal, 1995; Kornfield, 1994; Muller, 1997; Hillman, 1996). This is not spirit in the religious sense, but individual spirit, team spirit and organizational spirit.

There's a spiritual dimension to it (that is facilitation). We're all spiritual beings operating in this world and we have certain ways of behaving, some of which are productive and some counter-productive. The facilitator works with these behaviours, but is always honouring the whole person or the spiritual beings in the group. That might sound a bit esoteric but that's really what it's all about (Hunter, 1993: 199).

In conventional thinking the rational and instrumental side of learning, along with a preference for linear logic and reasoning, was regarded as antithetical to emotion. However, there is recently a re-awakening to wider considerations such as evident in studies of creativity, lateral thinking, the intuitive insights in scientific hypothesis formation, and in cathartic learning during psychotherapy, just to name a few. The significance of emotions is also receiving increased attention in sociological theory (Barbalet, 1998; Goleman, 1996, 1998; Heron, 1999). Goleman coined the phrases 'emotional intelligence' and 'emotional literacy' and writes of five domains of emotional intelligence: knowing one's emotions, managing emotions, motivating oneself, recognizing emotion in others and handling relationships.

Suffice here to say that in my own facilitation practice a monitoring and management of emotional components is important, for instance:

- need to see that participants in group situations do not get emotionally 'monstered';
- my provision of a relaxing and informal atmosphere using 'props', physical exercises, music;
- visual stimuli, for example art work and cards to help participants describe emotions (Deal and Veeken, 1997, Cooney, 1986: 280);
- the relevance of debriefing, mentoring, and emotional support in order to handle facilitator stress engendered by 'toxic' situations;
- the possibility of cathartic learning, as is illustrated from some of the more traumatic case material.

Ongoing maintenance of facilitators: managing toxicity

The discussion so far indicates the variety of roles and responsibilities that facilitators take. There appear to be at least three issues that full-time practising facilitators need to take into account. For a facilitator to be effective there needs to be ways of dealing with fatigue, with negative or aggressive feedback whilst maintaining one's equanimity. One student asked, 'What do you do if you did your very best and still things went wrong and you feel terrible?' Dick (1984) describes some of the processes in his book, for example the 'Acts of god' process (for working with angry groups), as 'robust processes'. Certainly I have had success using these processes. However, I assert that anyone working with issues to do with human endeavour has to deal with degrees of uncertainties; facilitators always have to be on the lookout for unexpected happenings in groups: both serendipitous and disastrous.

Secondly, there is the issue of learning to handle the toxicity of angry and/or negative groups (or individuals) without being destroyed inside (ie stress-related illnesses) (Frost and Robinson, 1999, White, 1997: 468). I know I work through issues in dreams and sleepless nights before and after workshops. For the past eight years, I have benefited from being a member of informal groups of facilitators who meet regularly to debrief problems and traumas and celebrate joys and successes. In summary, then, intensive interpersonal activities which require constant monitoring can be stressful. Questions that need to be answered are: How is this stress managed? How can provision made in courses for facilitators and HRD practitioners to prepare them for a career in facilitation? These issues will be discussed further in Book 2.

Conclusion

In this chapter I analysed two case studies regarding the ethics of facilitation. I then traced the current movement towards the professionalization of facilitation: the development of a code of ethics and accreditation systems and future trends.

Book 2 complements the theoretical approach of this book and elaborates on the breadth, depth and diversity of a facilitator's tool kit.

Appendix 1: Journals, e-mail discussion groups and Web sites

As I said in the introduction, theory in the area of facilitation is dense and we are on a steep learning curve about human behaviour and group development.

Group work

Useful journals

There are a wide variety of journals available on group work. Examples include:

Group Facilitation: A Research and Applications Journal
The Facilitator
Small Group Behaviour
Small Group Research
Group Decision and Negotiation
Empowerment in Organizations
Participation & Empowerment
The Learning Organization
Training and Management Development Methods
The Conflict Resolution Network News
Organizational Dynamics
Management Development Review
Leadership and Organization Development Journal

MCB University Press

MCB University Press, based in the UK, publishes many different journals (paper and electronic) on management, training and development. Practitioner journals like *Training and Management Development Methods* welcome articles from facilitators. Journal titles include:

Training and Management Development Methods
Empowerment in Organizations
The Learning Organization
Management Development Review
Education and Training

Web site: www.mcb.co.uk
E-mail: HELP@EMERALDINSIGHT.COM

Full text electronic databases

There are a number of electronic databases available via university libraries where you can type in key words and download the full text of articles, including diagrams and pictures. Some examples include:

ABI/Inform Global Proquest Direct (includes a list of latest books)
Science Direct
Social Science Plus
SwetsNet.

Internet sites and discussion groups

There are a number of discussion groups on the Internet where you can:

- post facilitation issues/problems
- look at previous discussion of issues
- find out about short courses and resources.

There are many electronic discussion groups. Here is a selection:

International Association of Facilitators
Web site: www.iaf-world.org/
7630 West 145th Street
#202, St Paul, MN 55124

Membership US~$125.00 per year.
E-mail: office@iafworld.org
Journal: *Group Facilitation: A Research and Applications Journal*
The site includes the IAF mission and core values, IAF task forces and think tanks, Facilitation certification, upcoming conferences and past conference proceedings, find a facilitator, lists of resources.

IAF site of facilitation Web sites
A huge site that makes searching easier by having so many sites on one page:
http://search.atomz.com/search/?sp-q=web+sites&sp-a=sp1000f9ce

IAF Manuals for disaster intervention
www.iaf-world.org/mandis.htm

Directory of regional facilitation networks
http://iaf-world.org/iafnetworks.htm

Southeast Asia Facilitators' Network
This organization holds quarterly forums in Kuala Lumpur and hosted the fourth Asia Facilitators' Conference in 2002 in Penang.
Ann Epps: jlepps@pc.jaring.my

Australian Facilitators' Network: E-mail discussion groups
Australian Facilitators' Network (afn-l@scu.edu.au).
If you want to subscribe, send mail to listproc@scu.edu.au with the following request:
subscribe AFN-L Your Name

International Association of Facilitators (IAF) Europe
www.circleindigo.com/IAFEurope2001/forms.html

Coordinación Latinoamericana
Apartado Aéreo 50717, Santafé de Bogotá, Colombia
E-mail: mbr@amauta.org

Central and Eastern Europe (Zhaba Facilitators Collective)
Contact: Jan Haverkamp
E-mail: jan.haverkamp@ecn.cz

Facilitation articles in Spanish
www.iaf-world.org/bibvirt.html

International Facilitators' Networking group
How to subscribe to the electronic mailing list for group facilitators:

Send an e-mail message to: LISTSERV@CNSIBM.ALBANY.EDU
You may leave the SUBJECT field blank. In the body of the message type:
SUBSCRIBE GRP-FACL Your Real Name
Do not include any other information or signature in the message.

'The Facilitator' Professional Newsletter
The Facilitator is a quarterly publication available through subscription.
US subscribers US$35
Non-US subscribers – US$40
www.thefacilitator.com/

The Master Facilitator Journal
www.masterfacilitatorjournal.com/
E-mail: steve@masterfacilitatorjournal.com

The Conflict Resolution Network
The Conflict Resolution Network, Box 1016, Chatswood, NSW 2067. This network has a newsletter, workshops and books. The site contains 12 skills for conflict resolution (elaborated in Hollier, F *et al* (1993) *Conflict Resolution Trainers Manual*, Conflict Resolution Network, New South Wales), dialogue and debate, the gentle revolution: gender issues, reconciliaton, conflict-resolving game,dialogue and debate.

Web site: www.crnhq.org
E-mail: crn@crnhq.org

Institute of Cultural Affairs
ICA Australia is a network of individuals who are committed to creative change in a diverse range of communities, organizations and networks. It is a private, non-profit organization concerned with the human factor in community and organizational development.

'ICA stands for the Institute of Cultural Affairs. For us, the word 'culture' is about human perspectives. Like most people, we want to make a difference. For us, that means looking at more than just money or politics. We believe that anybody who wants to make a serious difference has to look at underlying perspectives which influence the patterns of the world around us'.

ICA Worldwide www.icaworld.org
ICA (Canada) www.icacan.ca
ICA (Australia) http://members.ozemail.com.au/~jago/ica_oz.htm

Cooperative learning

'A fellow learner is the best teacher you can have'
www.clcrc.com/pages/overviewpaper.html
www.clcrc.com/pages/peace-meta.html
www.clcrc.com/pages/CLandD.html

Dialogue

See Conflict Resolution Network
www.crnhq.org/govt2.html

David Bohm's concept of dialogue
http://world.std.com/~lo/bohm/0000.html
http://world.std.com/~lo/bohm/0001.html

Workforce – HR Trends and Tools for Business Results

Web site: www.workforce.com.
E-mail: mailroom@workforce.com

University Associates Incorporated

Consulting, training and resources
Web site: www.universityassociates.com

Open Space Technology

www.openspacetechnology.com
www.openspaceworld.org
www.ourfuture.com
www.openspaceworld.com/brief_history.htm

The Learning Organization

The Web site is a good example of the application of P Senge's Fifth Discipline principles in an e-mail discussion group.
http://world.std.com/~lo.

The Society for Organizational Learning

www.sol-ne.org/

3M Meeting Network Web site
www.3m.com/meetingnetwork

Facilitation and technology

Useful journals

International Journal of Information Management
Journal of Computer Assisted Learning
Information Systems Research
Management Information Systems Quarterly

Web references

There are many Web sites; a small sample are given here.

Resources for moderators and facilitators of online discussion

For moderators

www.emoderators.com/moderators.shtml
Site devoted to how to moderate online groups – this page in the site is a list of resources that cover a lot of areas but there are some specific articles for moderators on how to and what to do.

The Moderator's Home Page

http://jan.ucc.nau.edu/~mpc3/moderators.html
A growing set of resources, mostly scholarly, for moderators of online discussions, including chats, listservs and newsgroups. This is an extensive bibliography of netiquette guides, sample editorial policies, using online discussion groups in classrooms, tips for moderating, and information on teaching online.

How to host online discussion

www.serviceleader.org/vv/vhosts.html

www.fullcirc.com/community/cardcatalog.htm
This page contains an interesting range of articles about online facilitation

(as well as other forms of facilitation). Lisa Kimball writes prolifically about the area of online groups so her articles are worth a look.

Using technology to help facilitation

Paper on group systems support technologies
http://iaf-world.org/iaf99/Thread4/macdonald.html

www.deepwoods.com/transform/pubs/DDB.htm
Article about the difficulties of building a community using online means – the time and effort involved in doing this.

Berge, Zane L (1992)
The Roles of the Moderator in Scholarly Discussion Groups (SDGs)
This is a presentation by Zane L Berge made on the IPCT-L discussion list and the ensuing discussion taken from the following IPCT-L logs, archived at LISTSERV@LISTSERV.georgetown.edu: IPCT LOG9210D, IPCT LOG9210E, IPCT LOG9212B

Using technology with large groups

America Speaks: engaging citizen voices in governance
www.americaspeaks.org/asmodel.htm
www.listeningtothecity.org

Appendix 2: IAF Statement of Values and Code of Ethics

Downloaded July 2002 from: http://iaf-world.org/iafethicsTT.htm

The IAF Ethics and Values Think Tank (EVTT) has concluded its work in developing a Statement of Values and Ethics for Group Facilitators (the Code).

The work of EVTT has taken place over two years (June 2000 – May 2002) and has involved an estimated 150 people. An online group of 85 people exchanging more than 900 emails and engaged in thousands of thinking and discussion hours on the EVTT e-group. In addition two forums involving 40 people were held at IAF Conference 2001 at Minnesota. Workshops and discussions were also held at regional conferences and on regional e-groups.

The development of the Code has involved a wide diversity of views and the working through of different perspectives to achieve a consensus across regional and cultural boundaries. This has taken a considerable effort and is a major achievement.

The following Draft Statement of Values and Code of Ethics (the Code) was adopted by ACT and will be formally reviewed in two years. During the two years the Ethics and Values Think Tank will solicit feedback from IAF members and other stakeholders, and continue to provide a forum for discussion of pertinent issues and potential revisions. The Code should be made widely available and copies distributed to all IAF members.

Adopted by ACT 21/5/02

The International Association of Facilitators

Draft statement of values and code of ethics for group facilitators

Preamble

Facilitators are called upon to fill an impartial role in helping groups become more effective. We act as process guides to create a balance between participation and results.

We, the members of the International Association of Facilitators (IAF), believe that our profession gives us a unique opportunity to make a positive contribution to individuals, organizations, and society. Our effectiveness is based on our personal integrity and the trust developed between ourselves and those with whom we work. Therefore, we recognize the importance of defining and making known the values and ethical principles that guide our actions.

This Statement of Values and Code of Ethics recognizes the complexity of our roles, including the full spectrum of personal, professional and cultural diversity in the IAF membership and in the field of facilitation. Members of the International Association of Facilitators are committed to using these values and ethics to guide their professional practice. These principles are expressed in broad statements to guide ethical practice; they provide a framework and are not intended to dictate conduct for particular situations. Questions or advice about the application of these values and ethics may be addressed to the International Association of Facilitators.

Statement of values

As group facilitators, we believe in the inherent value of the individual and the collective wisdom of the group. We strive to help the group make the best use of the contributions of each of its members. We set aside our personal opinions and support the group's right to make its own choices. We believe that collaborative and cooperative interaction builds consensus and produces meaningful outcomes. We value professional collaboration to improve our profession.

Code of ethics

1. Client service

   We are in service to our clients, using our group facilitation competencies to add value to their work.

Our clients include the groups we facilitate and those who contract with us on their behalf. We work closely with our clients to understand their expectations so that we provide the appropriate service, and that the group produces the desired outcomes. It is our responsibility to ensure that we are competent to handle the intervention.

If the group decides it needs to go in a direction other than that originally intended by either the group or its representatives, our role is to help the group move forward, reconciling the original intent with the emergent direction.

2. Conflict of interest

   We openly acknowledge any potential conflict of interest.

   Prior to agreeing to work with our clients, we discuss openly and honestly any possible conflict of interest, personal bias, prior knowledge of the organization or any other matter which may be perceived as preventing us from working effectively with the interests of all group members. We do this so that, together, we may make an informed decision about proceeding and to prevent misunderstanding that could detract from the success or credibility of the clients or ourselves. We refrain from using our position to secure unfair or inappropriate privilege, gain, or benefit.

3. Group autonomy

   We respect the culture, rights, and autonomy of the group.

   We seek the group's conscious agreement to the process and their commitment to participate. We do not impose anything that risks the welfare and dignity of the participants, the freedom of choice of the group, or the credibility of its work.

4. Processes, methods and tools

   We use processes, methods and tools responsibly.

   In dialogue with the group or its representatives we design processes that will achieve the group's goals, and select and adapt the most appropriate methods and tools. We avoid using processes, methods or tools with which we are insufficiently skilled, or which are poorly matched to the needs of the group.

5. Respect, safety, equity and trust

   We strive to engender an environment of respect and safety where all participants trust that they can speak freely and where individual boundaries are honoured. We use our skills, knowledge, tools, and wisdom to elicit and honour the perspectives of all.

   We seek to have all relevant stakeholders represented and involved. We promote equitable relationships among the participants and facilitator and ensure that all participants have an opportunity to examine and share their thoughts and feelings. We use a variety of methods to enable the group to access the natural gifts, talents and life experiences of each member. We work in ways that honour the wholeness and self-expression of others, designing sessions that respect different styles of interaction. We understand that any action we take is an intervention that may affect the process.

6. Stewardship of process
   We practice stewardship of process and impartiality toward content.
   While participants bring knowledge and expertise concerning the substance of their situation, we bring knowledge and expertise concerning the group interaction process. We are vigilant to minimize our influence on group outcomes.
   When we have content knowledge not otherwise available to the group, and that the group must have to be effective, we offer it after explaining our change in role.
7. Confidentiality
   We maintain confidentiality of information.
   We observe confidentiality of all client information. Therefore, we do not share information about a client within or outside of the client's organization, nor do we report on group content, or the individual opinions or behaviour of members of the group without consent.
8. Professional development
   We are responsible for continuous improvement of our facilitation skills and knowledge.
   We continuously learn and grow. We seek opportunities to improve our knowledge and facilitation skills to better assist groups in their work. We remain current in the field of facilitation through our practical group experiences and ongoing personal development. We offer our skills within a spirit of collaboration to develop our professional work practices.

References

Aasch, S (1958) *Social psychology*, Prentice Hall, Englewood Cliffs, USA

Abdullah, A (2000) *Interview with Asma Abdullah*, Interviewed by: Zuraudah Omar, Radio AM, Kuala Lumpur, Malaysia, 15 November

Abdullah, A (2001) *The Influence of Values on Management in Malaysia*, PhD thesis, Universiti Kebangsaan, Bangi, Malaysia

Abdullah, A and Shephard, P (2000) *The Cross Cultural Game*, Braindominance Technologies, Kuala Lumpur, Malaysia

Adams, G B and Balfour, D L (1998) *Unmasking Administrative Evil*, Sage, Thousand Oaks, USA

Adler, N (1997) *International Dimensions of Organizational Behaviour*, 3rd edn, International Thomson Publishing, Cincinnati, USA

Allen, R E (1995) *Winnie the Pooh on Management*, Doubleday, London, England

American Psychological Association (1973) Guidelines for psychologists conducting growth groups, *American Psychologist*, **28**, p 933

American Psychological Association (1992) Ethical principles of psychologists, *American Psychologist*, **45** (3), pp 390–395

Andrews, H B (1995) *Group Design and Leadership: Strategies for Creating Successful Common Theme Groups*, Allwyn and Bacon, Needham Heights, USA

Andrews, H B L, School of Psychology, Curtin University of Technology (1999) Problems of psychology profession, *Personal Communication with the author*, ed Hogan, C F

Argyris, C (1990) *Overcoming Organizational Defences: Facilitating organizational learning*, Prentice Hall, Englewood Cliffs, USA

Argyris, C and Schön, D (1994) *Theory in Practice: Increasing Organizational Effectiveness*, Jossey-Bass, San Francisco, USA

Arnstein, SR (1969) 'A ladder of citizen participation in the USA', *Journal of the American Planning Association,* vol. 35, no. 4, July, pp 216–24

Ashworth, K (1999) Peer power is a class act, in *The West Australian*, Perth, p 1

Axelrod, R (1990) *The Evolution of Co-operation*, Penguin, London, England

Bank, J (1994) *Outdoor Development for Managers*, 2nd edn, Gower Publishing, Aldershot, England

Barbalet, J M (1998) *Emotion, Social Theory and Social Structure*, Cambridge University Press, Cambridge, England

Barbour, R S and Kitzinger, J (1999) *Developing Focus Group Research: Politics, Theory and Practice*, Sage, London, England

Barnhart, R B (ed) (1988) *The Barnhart Dictionary of Etymology*, HW Wilson and Co, New York, USA

Baxter, G (2000) *The difference between facilitation and therapy*, e-mail, 20 September

Beckett, A (2000) Is Coke still it?, in *Guardian Weekly*, 12–18 October, p 25

Benne, K D and Sheats, P (1948) Functional roles of group members, *Journal of Social Issues*, **4**, pp 41–49

Bennett, B and Richardson, J (1984) Applying learning techniques to on-the-job development, *Journal of European and Industrial Training*, **8** (1)

Bennett, B, Rolheiser, C and Stevahn, L (1991) *Co-operative Learning: Where Heart Meets Mind*, Educational Connections, Toronto, Ontario, Canada

Bentley, T (1994) *Facilitation: Providing Opportunities for Learning*, McGraw Book Company, Maidenhead, England

Berge, Zane L (1996) The Role of the Online Instructor/Facilitator. This article lists the roles and functions of the online instructor/facilitator in computer conferencing.

Berge, Zane L and Collins, Mauri P (2000) Perceptions of e-moderators about their roles and functions in moderating electronic mailing lists. *Distance Education: An International Journal*, **21**(1), pp 81–100.

Berne, E (1961) *Transactional Analysis in Psychotherapy*, Grove Press, New York, USA

Boal, A (1992) *Games for Actors and Non-actors*, Routledge, London, England

Bolman, L G and Deal, T E (1995) *Leading with Soul: An Uncommon Journey of Spirit*, Jossey-Bass, San Francisco, USA

Boud, D (1995) *Enhancing Learning through Self Assessment*, Kogan Page, London, England

Boud, D, Keogh, R and Walker, D (eds) (1985) *Reflection: Turning Experience into Learning*, Kogan Page, London, England

Brewer, G (2000) Creating knowledge: Knowledge productivity through experiential learning, *Training Journal*, May, pp 24–25

Brody, C M E (1987) *Women's Therapy Groups – Paradigms of Feminist Treatment*, Springer Publishing Company, New York, USA

Bronfenbrenner, U (1979) *The Ecology of Human Development: Experiments by Nature and Design*, Harvard University Press, Cambridge, USA

Bruffee, KA (1993) *Collaborative Learning*, The Johns Hopkins University Press, London

Bunker, B B and Alban, B T (1997) *Large Group Interventions: Engaging the Whole System for Rapid Change*, Jossey-Bass, San Francisco, USA

Burbidge, J (ed) (1977) *Beyond Prince and Merchant – Citizen Participation and the Rise of Civil Society*, Pact Publications, New York, USA

Burns, R (1995) *The Adult Learner at Work*, Business and Professional Publishing, Sydney, Australia

Burton, J (1990) *Conflict: Resolution and Prevention*, Macmillan Press, Basingstoke, England

Campbell, J (1973) *The Hero with a Thousand Faces*, Princeton University Press, Princeton, New Jersey, USA

Chakraborty, S K (1998) *Values and Ethics for Organizations*, Oxford University Press, Delhi, India

Chambers, R (1983) *Rural development: Putting the last first*, Longman Scientific and Technical, Harlow, England

Chambers, R (1994) 'The origins of participatory rural appraisal', *World Development*, vol. 22, no. 7, pp 953–69

Chang, J (1991) *Wild Swans: Three Daughters of China*, Flamingo, London, England

Clawson, V K, Bostrom, R P and Anson, R (1993) The role of the facilitator in computer-supported meetings, *Small Group Research*, **24** (4), pp 547–65

Cooper, S & Heenan, C (1980) *Preparing, designing and leading workshops*, CBI, Mass. USA

Corey, G, Corey, M S and Callanan, P (1993) *Issues and Ethics in the Helping Professions*, 4th edn, Brooks/Cole, Pacific Grove, USA

Corey, G, Corey, M S, Callanan, P J and Russell, J M (1988) *Group Techniques*, 2nd edn, Brooks/Cole, Pacific Grove, USA

Cox, E (1995) *A Truly Civil Society*, Australian Broadcasting Corporation, Sydney, Australia

Crapo, R F (1986) It's time to stop training and start facilitating, *Public Personnel Management*, **15**, (4), pp 443–9

Cross, K P and Angelo, T (1988) *Classroom Assessment Techniques*, University of Michigan, Michigan, USA

Cunningham, I (1994) *The Wisdom of Strategic Learning: The Self Managed Learning Solution*, McGraw-Hill, London, England

de Bono, E (1987) *The CoRT Thinking Process*, Pergamon Press, London, England

De George, R T (1995) *Business Ethics*, 4th edn, Prentice Hall, Englewood Cliffs, USA

de Salvo, C (2000) Time out for trainers, *Training Journal*, May, pp 18–20

de Vreede, G J (1995) *Facilitating Organizational Change: The Participative Application of Dynamic Modelling*, PhD thesis, School of Systems Engineering, Policy Analysis and Management, Delft University of Technology, Delft, The Netherlands

Deal, R and Veeken, J (1997) *The Bears*, St Luke's Innovative Resources, Bendigo, Australia

Dewey, J (1916) *Democracy and Education*, Free Press, New York, USA

Dewey, J (1938) *Experience in Education*, Collier Macmillan Publishers, London, England

Diamond, L (1996) *Effective videoconferencing: Techniques for better business meetings*, Crisp Publications Inc, Menlo Park, California

Dick, B (1991) *Helping Groups to be Effective*, Chapel Hill, QLD, Australia

Dick, B (1991) *Helping Groups to be Effective: Skills, Processes and Concepts for Group Facilitation*, 2 edn, Interchange, Chapel Hill, Australia

Dick, B (1997) Process invention, In *Conversation with author*, ed C F Hogan, Senior Lecturer, U o Q

Dictionary, T S O E (1980), Clarendon Press, Oxford, England

Dorner, D (1996) *The Logic of Failure: Recognizing and Avoiding Error in Complex Situations*, Perseus Press, Cambridge, USA

Downs, S (1981) *How Do I Learn?*, Further Education and Curriculum Review and Development Unit, London, England

Downs, S (1995) *Learning at Work – Effective Strategies for Making Learning Happen*, Kogan Page, London, England

Downs, S and Perry, P (1982) Research report: How do I learn?, *Journal of European and Industrial Training*, **6** (6), pp 27–32

Downs, S and Perry, P (1984) *Developing Skilled Learners – Learning to Learn in YTS*, Manpower Services Commission and Occupational Research Unit, University of Wales Institute of Science and Technology, Research and Development: No 22

Doyle, M and Straus, D (1976) *How to Make Meetings Work: The New Interaction Method*, Jove Publications, New York, USA

Eck, D L and Jain, D E (1987) *Speaking of Faith: Global Perspectives on Women, Religion and Social Change*, New Society Publishers, Philadelphia, USA

Egri, C P and Frost, P J (1991) Shamanism and change: Bringing back the magic in organizational transformation, *Organizational Change and Development*, **5**, pp 175–221

Emery, F (1974) *Futures We're In*, Centre for Continuing Education, Australian National University, Canberra, Australia

Emery, M (1976) *Searching: for New Directions, in New Ways, for New Times*, The Australian National University, Canberra, Australia

Emery, M and Purser, R E (1996) *The Search Conference: A Powerful Method for Planning Organizational Change and Community Action*, Jossey-Bass, San Francisco, USA

Emory, C W and Cooper, D R (1991) *Business Research Methods*, Irwin, Boston, USA

Epps, J (2001) Facilitation from the inside out, in *Facilitation News*, International Association of Facilitators, St Paul, USA

Ferguson, M (1982) *The Aquarian Conspiracy – Personal and Social Transformation in the 1980's*, Paladin, London, England

Fisher and Ury (1988) *Getting to Yes: Negotiating Agreement Without Giving In* 'Business Books' London

Flannery, T (1995) *The Future Eaters*, Reed Books, Chatswood, Australia

Follett, M P (1989) Management as a profession, *Management and Organizational Behavior Classics*, eds M T Matteson and J M Ivancevich, BPI Irwin, Homewood, USA, pp 7–18

Freire, P (1972) *Pedagogy of the Oppressed*, Penguin, Harmondsworth, England

Freire, P (1974) *Education: The Practice of Freedom*, Writers and Readers Publishing Cooperative, London, England

Freire, P (1997) *Pedagogy of Hope: Reliving Pedagogy of the Oppressed*, Continuum, New York, USA

Frost, P J (1999) Why compassion counts!, *Journal of Management Inquiry*, 8 (2), June, pp 127–33

Frost, P J and Robinson, S L (1999) The toxic handler: Organizational hero and casualty, *Harvard Business Review*, July–August, pp 96–106

Gallegher, J, Kraut, R E and Egiolo, C (1990) *Intellectual Teamwork*, Lawrence Erlbaum Associates, New Jersey, USA

Gardner, H (1982) *Art, Mind and Brain: A Cognitive Approach to Creativity*, Basic Books, New York, USA

Garrick, J & Rhodes, C (2000) *Research and knowledge at work*, Routledge, London

Gibbs, G (1982) Twenty terrible reasons for lecturing, *SCED*, Occasional Paper, 8, pp 1–30

Gibbs, G (1992) *Improving the Quality of Student Learning*, Technical and Educational Services, Bristol, England

Godwin, J (1999) Facilitator accreditation, *The Facilitator*, Spring, pp 16–18

Goleman, D (1996) *Emotional Intelligence*, Bloomsbury, London, England

Goleman, D (1998) *Working with Emotional Intelligence*, Bloomsbury, London, England

Green, T, Woodrow, P and Peavey, F (1994) *Insight and Action: How to Discover and Support a Life of Integrity and Commitment to Change*, New Society Publishers, Philadelphia, USA

Hall, E T (1990) *Understanding Cultural Differences*, Intercultural Press, Yarmouth, Maine, USA

Hamel, G and Prahalad, C K (1996) *Competing for the Future*, Harvard Business School, Boston, USA

Hampden-Turner, C (1991) *Charting The Corporate Mind*, Blackwell, Oxford, England

Hampden-Turner, C and Trompenaars, F (1995) *The Seven Cultures of Capitalism*, Doubleday, New York, USA

Hancock, G (1991) *Lords of Poverty*, Mandarin Paperback, London, England

Harman, C & Brelade, S (2000) *Knowledge management and the role of HR*, Financial Times, Prentice Hall, London

Harris, T (2000) Opening closed shops, *The Australian Financial Review*, p 33

Heckman, L A (2000) *Methodology Matters: Devising a Research Program for Investigating PPGIS in Collaborative Neighbourhood Planning* (14 October)

Heider, J (1986) *The Tao of Leadership*, Gower, Aldershot, England

Heron, J (1975) *Six Category Intervention Analysis*, Human Potential Research Project University of Surrey, Guildford, England

Heron, J (1977) *Dimensions of Facilitator Style*, Human Potential Research Project University of Surrey, Guildford, England

Heron, J (1989) *The Facilitator's Handbook*, Kogan Page, London, England

Heron, J (1993) *The Facilitator's Handbook*, Kogan Page, London, England

Heron, J (1993) *Group Facilitation: Theories and Models for Practice*, Kogan Page, London, England

Heron, J (1996) *Cooperative inquiry: Research into the Human Condition*, Kogan Page, London, England

Heron, J (1997) *My Model*, Available: [jheron@sirtpisait], 28 June

Heron, J (1999) *The complete facilitator's handbook*, Kogan Page, London, England

Hill, S and Hill, T (1990) *The Collaborative Classroom*, Eleanor Curtin Publishing, Armidale, Australia

Hillman, J (1996) *The Soul's Code: In Search of Character and Calling*, Random House, Milsom's Point, NSW, Australia

Hilmer, F G and Donaldson, L (1998) *Management Redeemed: Debunking the Fads that Undermine Corporate Performance*, The Free Press, East Roseville, Australia

Hofstede, G (1980, *Culture's Consequences: International Differences in World-Related Values*, Sage, Beverly Hills, USA

Hofstede, G (1991) *Cultures and Organizations: Software of the Mind*, McGraw Hill, Maidenhead, England

Hogan, C F (1992) Strategies for enhancing empowerment, *Training and Management Development Methods*, **6** (3), pp 325–41

Hogan, C F (1993) Simultaneously teaching facilitation skills to students at separate locations using interactive videoconferencing, *Training and Management Development Methods*, **7**, pp 517–32

Hogan, C F (1993a) 'Dances with patients', in *Annual Conference of the Association for Quality in Health Care: Quality Service the People Factor*, Observation City, Perth, Western Australia

Hogan, C F (1993b) 'How to get more out of video conference meetings', *Training and Management Development Methods*, vol 7

Hogan, C F (1993c) 'Let's explode some myths about power and empowerment', in *Women, Communication and Power*, National Conference Proceedings

Hogan, C F (1994) Course design in half the time: How to generate ideas using a network of computers, *Training and Management Development Methods*, **8** (2), pp 501–14

Hogan, C F (1998) 'If you are going to stick to talking heads, why not send them a video?', *Training and Management Development Methods*, vol 12

Hogan, C F (1999) *Facilitating Learning: Practical Strategies for College and University*, Eruditions, Melbourne, Australia

Hogan, C F (2000) *Facilitating Empowerment: A Handbook for Facilitators, Trainers and Individuals*, Kogan Page, London, England

Hogan, C F (2001) *The makings of myself as a facilitator: An autoethnography of professional practice*, PhD thesis, Curtin University of Technology, Perth, Western Australia

Honey, P (2000) Learned compliance, *Training Journal*, May, p 9

Honey, P and Mumford, A (1986) *Using your Learning Styles*, Peter Honey, Maidenhead, England

Honey, P and Mumford, A (1992) *The Manual of Learning Styles*, 3rd edn, Peter Honey, Maidenhead, England

Hopson, B and Scally, M (1981) *Lifeskills Teaching*, McGraw Hill, Maidenhead, England

Hopson, B and Scally, M (1984) *Build your Own Rainbow: A Workbook for Career and Life Management*, Lifeskills Associates, Leeds, England

Horn, R E (1998) *Visual Language*, MacroVU Press, Washington, USA

Hunter, D, Bailey, A and Taylor, B (1992) *The Zen of Groups: A Handbook for People Meeting with a Purpose*, Tandem Press, Auckland, New Zealand

Hunter, D, Bailey, A and Taylor, B (1993) *The Art of Facilitation*, Tandem Press, Auckland, New Zealand

Hunter, D, Bailey, A and Taylor, B (1997) *Co-operacy: A New Way of Being at Work*, Tandem Press, Birkenhead, New Zealand

Hunter, D, Bailey, A and Taylor, B (1999) *The Essence of Facilitation: Being in Action in Groups*, Tandem Press, Auckland, New Zealand

Illich, I (1971) *Deschooling Society*, Harper and Rowe, New York, USA

Illich, I (1977) *The Disabling Professions*, Marion Boyars, London, England

Jackins, H (1994) *The Human Side of Human Beings – The Theory of Re-evaluation Counselling* (rev edn), Rational Island Publishers, Seattle, USA

Jago, C, in press, *The Foundations of Facilitation*

Janis, I (1972) *Victims of Groupthink: A Psychological Study of Foreign-Policy Decisions and Fiascos*, Houghton Mifflin, Boston, USA

Jarman, R (2000) Uses of technology, in *Conversation with the Author*, ed C F Hogan, C F, Lecturer, School of Information Systems, Curtin University of Technology, Perth, Australia

Justice, T and Jamieson, D W (1999) *The Facilitator's Fieldbook*, American Management Association, New York, USA

Kaner, S (1996) *Facilitator's Guide to Participatory Decision-Making*, New Society Publishers, Gabriola Island, Canada

Kaplan, R B (1966) Cultural thought patterns in inter-cultural education, *Language Learning*, **16**, pp 1–20
Keltner, J S (1989) Facilitation: Catalyst for group problem solving, *Management Communication Quarterly*, **3** (1), pp 8–32
Kimball, L (2002) *Choosing Media Strategically for Team Communications:* http://wwwcaucuscom/pw-choosemediahtmlMarch 31
Kirkpatrick, D L (1975) *Evaluating Training Programmes*, American Society for Training and Development Inc, Washington, USA
Kiser, A G (1998) *Masterful Facilitation: Becoming a Catalyst for Meaningful Change*, American Management Association, New York, USA
Kleiner, A (1996) *The Age of Heretics: Heroes, Outlaws, and the Forerunners of Corporate Change*, Nicholas Breasley, London, England
Klinck, P (1992) Women in leadership: Collegial support groups – A facilitator's perspective, in *Women, Communication and Power*, Unpublished proceedings, Edith Cowan University, Perth, Australia
Knight, J and Scott, W (1997) *Co-facilitation: A Practical Guide to Using Partnerships in Facilitation*, Kogan Page, London, England
Knowles, M S (1984) *The Adult Learner: The Neglected Species*, Gulf Publishing, Houston, USA
Knowles, M S (1986) *Using Learning Contracts*, Jossey Bass, San Francisco, USA
Kolb, D A (1984) *Experiential Learning: Experience as the Source of Learning and Development*, Prentice-Hall, Englewood Cliffs, USA
Kornfield, J (1994) *A Path with Heart: A Guide through the Perils and Promises of Spiritual Life*, Random House, Sydney, Australia
Kubler-Ross, E (1970) *On Death and Dying*, Tavistock Publications, London, England
Larson, M S (1977) *The Rise of Professionalism: A Sociological Analysis*, University of California Press, Berkeley, USA
Laurent, A (1983) The cultural diversity of western conceptions of management, *International Studies of Management and Organization*, **13** (1–2), pp 75–96
Lewin, K (1951) *Field Theory in Social Science*, Harper and Rowe, New York, USA
Lewin, K (1958) Group decisions and social change, in *Readings in Social Psychology*, eds G E Swanson, T M Newcomb and E L Hartley, Holt, Rhinehart and Winston, New York, USA
Lorenze, E (1964) The problem of deducing the climate from the governing equations, *Tellus*, **16**, pp 1–11
Luft, J (1969) *Of Human Interaction*, Natural Press, Palo Alto, USA
Macy, J (1991) *World as Lover, World as Self*, Parallax Press, Berkeley, USA
Macy, J and Brown, M Y (1998) *Coming Back to Life: Practices to Reconnect our Lives, our World*, New Society Publishers, Gabriola Island, Canada
Mansfield, S (1995) *Laos*, Elsworth Books, Hong Kong, China

Margulies, N (1992) *Mapping Inner Space: Learning and Teaching Mind Mapping*, Hawker Brownlow Education, Cheltenham, Australia

Martin, K (2000) Facilitation and technology, in *Personal Comunication with the Author*, ed C F Hogan, P O C f S D U o W, Australia

Martin, M (work in progress), *Understanding Co-facilitation Experiences*, PhD, School of Management, Curtin University of Technology, Perth, Australia

Maslow, A (1943) A theory of human motivation, *Psychological Review*, **50**, pp 370–96

Maslow, A (1954) *Motivation and Personality*, Harper and Rowe, New York, USA

Max-Neef, M A (1991) *Human Scale Development – Conception, Application and Further Reflections*, The Apex Press, New York, USA

McClure, B A (1998) *Putting a New Spin on Groups: The Science of Chaos*, Lawrence Erlbaum Associates, Mahwah, USA

McConnell, M (1988) *Challenger: A Major Malfunction*, Unwin Hyman, London

Micklethwait, J and Wooldridge, A (1997) *The Witch doctors: What the Management Gurus Are Saying, Why It Matters and How to Make Sense of it*, Mandarin, London, England

Mittleman, D, Briggs, R O and Naunamaker, J F (2000) Best practice in facilitating virtual meetings: Some notes from initial experience, *Group Facilitation: A Research and Applications Journal*, **2** (2), Winter, pp 5–14

Mongeau, P A and Morr, M C (1999) Reconsidering brainstorming, *Group Facilitation: A Research and Applications Journal*, **1** (1), Winter, pp 14–21

Montessori, M (1974) *The Discovery of the Child*, Ballantine Books, New York, USA

Muller, W (1997) *How, Then, Shall We Live? Four Simple Questions that Reveal the Beauty and Meaning of our Lives*, Bantam, New York, USA

Mumford, A and Honey, P (1992) *The Learning Styles Handbook*, London: Peter Honey

Neill, A S (1978) *Summerhill: For and Against*, Pocket Books, New York, USA

Niederman, F, Beise, C M and Beranek, P M (1996) *Issues and Concerns about Computer-Supported Meetings: The Facilitator's Perspective*, 17 December

Niederman, F and Volkema, R (1999) The effects of facilitator characteristics on meeting preparation, set up and implementation, *Small Group Research*, **30** (3), pp 330–60

Olson, E (1999) Facilitating with technology: An overview, in *The Facilitator's Fieldbook*, eds T Justice and D W Jamieson, AMACOM, New York, USA

Owen, H (1992) *Open Space Technology: A User's Guide*, Abbott Publishing, Potomac, USA

Owen, H (ed) (1995) *Tales from Open Space*, Abbott Publishing, Cabin John, Maryland, USA

Owen, H (1997) *Expanding our Now: The Story of Open Space Technology*, Berrett-Koehler, San Francisco, USA

Owen, H and Stadler, A (1999) *Open Space Technology*, Berrett-Koehler Communications Inc, San Francisco, USA

Palmer, M (1999) *Facilitation as a Profession* (2/10/99)

Paulson, I, Burroughs, J C, and Gelb, C B (1976) Cotherapy: what is the crux of the relationship?, *The International Journal of Group Psychotherapy*, **26**

Pedler, M and Burgoyne, T (1988) *Applying Self Development in Organizations*, Prentice Hall, Hertfordshire, England

Pedler, M, Burgoyne, T and Boydell, T A (1986) *Manager's Guide to Self Development*, 2nd edn, McGraw-Hill, Maidenhead, England

Pfeiffer, J W and Jones, J E (1975) Cofacilitating, *The 1975 Annual for Group Facilitators*, University Associates, San Diego

Phnuyal, B (1998) The organic process of participation and empowerment in REFLECT, *Participatory Learning and Action (PLA Notes)*, **32**, June, pp 36–9

Phnuyal, B, Archer, D and Cottingham, S (1997) Participation, literacy and empowerment: reflections on reflect, *Education Action*, **8**, October, pp 27–35

Pierce, V, Chesebrow, D and Braun, L M (2000) Facilitator competencies, *Group Facilitation: A Research and Applications Journal*, **2** (2), pp 24–31

Polanyi, M (1966) *The Tacit Dimension*, Routledge and Kegan Paul, London, England

Postle, D (1989) *The Mind Gymnasium: How to Use Your Mind for Personal Growth*, Simon and Schuster, Brookvale, Australia

Pratt, D (1997) *How Shiny Is Your Goldfish? And Other Cautionary Tales*, Fast Books, Sydney, Australia

Quinn, R E, Faerman, S R, Thompson, M P and R, M M (1990) *Becoming a Master Manager: A Competency Framework*, John Wiley and Sons, New York, USA

Ramsden, P (1992) *Learning to Teach in Higher Education*, Routledge, London, England

Reason, P (1988) *Human Inquiry in Action: Developments in New Paradigm Research*, Sage, London, England

Reich, R (1987) Entrepreneurship reconsidered: The team as hero, *Harvard Business Review*, May–June, pp 77–83

Richardson, G P and Anderson, D F (1995) Teamwork in group model building, *Systems Dynamic Review*, **11** (2), Summer, John Wiley and Sons, New York

Robert, H M (1979) *Robert's Rules of Order Revised*, William Morrow and Co, New York, USA

Robert, H M (R b P, D) (1989) *Robert's Rules of Order*, Berkley Publishing Group, New York, USA

Robson, M and Beary, C (1995) *Facilitating*, Gower, Aldershot, England

Rocha, E M (1997) A ladder of empowerment, *Journal of Planning, Education and Research*, **17**, pp 31–44

Roddick, A (2001) *Take It Personally: How Globalization Affects You and Powerful Ways to Challenge It*, Thorsons (Harper Collins), London, England

Rogers, C A (1967) *On Becoming a Person: A Therapist's View of Psychotherapy*, Constable, London, England

Rogers, C A (1978) *Carl Rogers on Personal Power*, Constable and Company, London, England

Rogers, C R (1951) *Client-Centred Therapy: Its Current Practice, Implications and Theory*, Houghton Mifflin, Boston, USA

Rogers, C R (1969) *Freedom to Learn – A View of What Education Might Become*, Charles E Merrill, Columbus, USA

Ross, R S (1989) *Small Groups in Organizational Settings*, Prentice Hall, Englewood Cliffs, USA

Rowe, W and Winborn, B B (1973) What people fear about group work: An analysis of 36 selected critical articles, *Educational Technology*, **13** (1)

Rubin, H (1999a) The power of words, *Fast Company*, pp 142–151

Rubin, H (1999b) No prisoners on the path to perfection, *The Australian Financial Review*, pp 28–29

Ruete, E (1999) Facilitation as a profession, *GRP-FACL@CNSIBMALBANYEDU* [Electronic]

Sachs, W (ed) (1995) *The Development Dictionary: A Guide to Knowledge as Power*, Zed Books, London, England

Salmon, G (2000) *E-Moderating: The Key to Teaching and Learning Online*, Kogan Page, London, England

Schein, E (1988) *Process Consultation Vol 1: Its Role in Organization Development*, Addison Wesley, Reading, USA

Schnelle, E (1979) *The Metaplan-Method – Communication Tools for Planning and Learning Groups*, Quickborn, West Germany

Schrage, M (1995) *No More Teams*, Doubleday, New York

Schutz, W C (1972) *Here Comes Everybody*, Harrow Books, New York, USA

Schwarz, R M (1994) *The Skilled Facilitator: Practical Wisdom for Developing Effective Groups*, Jossey Bass, San Francisco, USA

Schwarz, R M (2000) Comments on facilitator competencies, *Group facilitation: A Research and Applications Journal*, **2** (2), Winter, pp 33–4

Scoones, I and Thompson, J (1994) *Beyond Farmer First: Rural People's Knowledge, Agricultural Research and Extension Practice*, Intermediate Technology Publications, London, England

Scriven, M (ed) (1967) *The Methodology of Evaluation*, McNally, Chicago, USA

Senge, P M (1990) *The Fifth Discipline: The Art and Practice of the Learning Organization*, Doubleday, New York, USA

Sharp, G (1974) The politics of nonviolent action, in *Methods of Nonviolent Action*, ed M Finklestein, Porter-Sargent Publications, Boston, USA

Shaw, M E (1981) *Group Dynamics: The Psychology of Small Group Behaviour*, 3rd edn, McGraw-Hill, New York, USA

Sims, R R (1999) *Reinventing Training and Development*, Quorum Books, Westport, USA

Sirolli, E (1995) *Ripples in the Zambezi: Passion, Unpredictability and Economic Development*, Murdoch University, Murdoch, Australia

Smith, A (1998) *Training and Development in Australia*, 2nd edn, Butterworths, Chatswood, Australia

Smith, G (2001) Group development: a review of the literature and a commentary on future research directions, *Group Facilitation: A Research and Applications Journal*, **3**, Spring, International Association of Facilitators, St Paul, MN, pp 14–45

Spencer, L (1989) *Winning through Participation*, Kendall Hunt Publishing Co, Iowa, USA

Spinks, T and Clements, P (1993) *A Practical Guide to Facilitation Skills*, Kogan Page, London, England

Stanfield, B (2001) Magic of the facilitator, in *Facilitation News*, International Association of Facilitators, St Paul, USA

Steiner, I D (1971) *Group Process and Productivity*, Academic Press, New York, USA

Summerfield, E (1993) *Crossing Cultures through Film*, Intercultural Press, Yarmouth USA

Suzuki, D (1999) Growth obsession 'suicidal', University of Western Australia, Perth, Australia, p 38

Tarnas, R (1991) *The Passion of the Western Mind: Understanding the Ideas that have Shaped our World View*, Ballantine Books, New York, USA

Tashlik, P (1995) What's Zen got to do with business writing?, *Communication World*, **12** (10), pp 12–13

Tennant, M (1986) An evaluation of Malcolm Knowles' theory of adult learning, *International Journal of Lifelong Education*, **2**, pp 113–22

Trompenaars, F (1993) *Riding the Waves of Culture: Understanding Cultural Diversity in Business*, Economist Books, London, England

Tuckman, B W and Jensen, M A (1977) Stages of small group development revisited, *Group and Organizational Studies*, **2** (4), pp 419–27

Vogler, C (1992) *The Writer's Journey: Mythic Structure for Storytellers and Screenwriters*, Michael Wiese Productions, Studio City, USA

Ward, J (1993) *Facilitative and Effective Management Skills for Local Government: Ideals, Principles and Practices for the Productive 90s*, Partnership Press, Oakleigh

Warihay, F (1992) Are good facilitators born or can they be developed?, *Journal of Quality and Participation*, Jan/Feb, pp 60–3

Webne-Behrman, H (1998) *The Practice Of Facilitation: Managing Group Process and Solving Problems*, Quorum books, Westport, USA

Wellins, RS, Byham, WC & Dixon, GR (1994) *Inside teams: How twenty world-class organizations are winning though teamwork*, Jossey-Bass, San Francisco, USA

Wheatley, M J (1992) *Leadership and the New Science: Learning about Organization from an Orderly Universe*, Berrett-Koehler Publishers, San Francisco, USA

White, W L (1997) *The Incestuous workplace: Stress and distress in the organizational family*, 2 edn, Hazelden, Center City, Minn, USA

Whiteley, A (1993) The use of metaphor in organizational transformation: Karaoke as the mediator, *Organizational Behaviour Teaching Conference*, Bucknell University, Pennsylvania, USA

Whiteley, A M and Garcia, J E (1996) The facilitator and the chauffeur in GSS: Explorations in the forging of a relationship, *Group Decision and Negotiation*, **5**, pp 31–50

Whiting, S (1999) History of Quakerism, in *Conversation with the Author*, ed Project Officer, T t T P, personal communication

Wilkinson, M (2000) Comments on facilitator competencies, *Group facilitation: A Research and Applications Journal*, **2** (2), Winter, pp 36–7

Wilson, J B (1979) *The Story Experience*, The Scarecrow Press Inc, London, England

Wilson, K and Wilson, J (2000) Models of facilitation, in *Conversations with the Author*, ed consultants, M

Woodward, T (1998) The baptism of fire, *Daily Mail*, London, p 5

Woolley, D R (1999) *Conferencing software on the web* (September 1st http://thinkofitcom/webconf/)

Zimmerman, A L and Evans, C J (1993) *Facilitation: From Discussion to Decision*, Nichols Publishing, New Jersey, USA

Index

Abdullah, A 154, 155, 161
Action Aid 44, 45
acts of God process 48, 216
Adams, GB 195–96
Adler, N 165, 168, 169
adult literacy 10, 41, 44–45
  see also education and training
aid agencies 44, 45
  see also developing countries
Alban, BT 18, 19, 139–41
Alcoholics Anonymous 8, 9
American Psychological Association 190, 200–01
Anderson, DF 95
andragogy 27, 31, 32, 141, 143
Archer, D 207
Argyris, C 202
Arnstein, Sherry 37–40
Arnstein's ladder *see* Arnstein, Sherry
Australia 46–47, 158–59, 204
Axelrod, R 200

Bach, George 190
Bailey, A 75–76, 117, 127, 200, 202, 208
Balfour, DL 195–96
Bangladesh 44–45
Bank, J 26
Bank of America 23
Barbour RS 9
Barford Conference 21
barriers to learning 143, 145–46
Baxter, G 55, 117, 123
Barnhart, RB 11
Beary, C 30, 50, 206
Benne, KD 131, 132–33
Bentley, Trevor 50
Berge, ZL 223
Berne, Eric 30
Blanchard, Ken 21
BMW 23
Boal, Augusto 45–46
Bohm, David 121, 221
Boud, David 30
Boydell, TA 151
Braun, LM 8, 67–69, 203
Brazil 41, 45
Bristol aero-engine company 21
Brody, CME 9
Bronfenbrenner, Urie 114, 115
Bunker, BB 18, 19, 139–41
Burns, R 141

chairpersons 22
Chakraborty, SK 12
Chambers, Dr Robert 43
Cheesebrow, D 8, 67–69, 203
China 158
circular thinking 160–61
Clements, P 89
co-facilitation 85, 112
  aspects to consider 92–93
  choosing 87, 93–94
  definitions 85–86
  easier or harder? (Tab) 91
  framework – questions to ask (Fig) 103
  guidelines (Tab) 106–11

models 94–99
multicultural groups 162–64
outcomes 88–92
relationship development 99–101
requirements 86–87
resolving differences 105, 112
working relationships 101–05
codes of conduct *see* professionalism and ethics
collegial support groups 33–34
community development 8–9, 10, 13, 35, 48, 179
adult literacy 44–45
approaches to learning (Tab) 42
developing countries 42–44
influential writers 40–42
participation 37–40
Quaker movement 36–37
small rural businesses 46–47
street theatre 45–46
see also developing countries
competency model 66–70
computer-mediated conferencing *see* technology
cooperative learning web sites 221
Corey, G&MS 197, 211–12
Cox, E 213
Crapo, Robert 31, 32, 33
Cross, KP 206
cultural diversity *see* multicultural groups
Cunningham, Ian 33, 34

DACUM 150
De George, RT 203
definitions of facilitation *see* facilitation
Deschooling Society 40
developing countries 8–9, 10, 44–45, 179, 212–14
evolution of facilitation 42–44
see also community development
Dewey, John 8, 9, 25, 141
Dick, Bob 29, 48, 216
disabled persons 119
Dorner, D 114
Downs, S 41, 147–48
Doyle, M 8, 9, 22–23, 51–52, 204
e-moderating 14, 183–86
online competencies (Tab) 184–85
resources 222, 223
see also technology
Eagle Star Life case study 190–93
Eck, DL 10
education and training 8, 9, 25
adult learners 27–30, 141–43
advantages of facilitating 33
approaches to learning (Tab) 42
educational reform 30–31
experiential learning model (Fig) 29
hidden curriculum 30
influential writers 40–42
innovators 25–26
peer support groups 33–34
teaching models/learning relationship (Fig) 28
training in preference to facilitating 32–33
versus facilitation 31–32
see also adult literacy
educators 205
Egri, CP 11
El Salvador 44–45
electronic databases 218
see also Internet; web sites
electronic discussion groups 8, 9, 218–22
Emery, F&M 19, 20–21, 113–14, 134, 139
encounter groups 190
English Civil War 36
equal co-facilitation 95–96
Essence of Facilitation 54–55
ethics *see* professionalism and ethics
Evans, CJ 11
experiential learning 28–29, 143–46

FAB (Facilitation Accreditation Board) 210
'face' 161–62
Facilitating Empowerment 50
facilitation 7–8, 55, 57–58
as parts of speech (Tab) 11
context 53–55

definitions/metaphors 49–53, 57
external/internal facilitators, comparison (Tab) 54
fields using 8–10
future trends 212–16
levels of 55–57
passing fad? 198
rise of 11–14
roles of manager/facilitator (Fig) 51–52
sources and meaning 10–11
see also co-facilitation; models of facilitation; professionalism and ethics
Facilitation Accreditation Board (FAB) 210
facilitators *see* facilitation; professionalism and ethics
feminist movement 9, 10
Ferguson, M 212
Fifth Dimension 33
Flores, Fernando 81, 193–96, 206, 211–12
Follett, Mary Parker 17–18, 200–01
Ford, Henry 13, 16–17
Forum Theatre 46
Fox, George 36
Freedom to Learn 26
Freire, Paulo 40, 41, 202, 205, 207
Frost, PJ 11, 21, 212

Garcia, JE 14
General Motors 20
gender issues 119–20
Godwin, J 210
Goleman, D 204, 215
Gordonstoun School 26
Group Facilitation: theories and models for practice 63
group work 33–34, 113, 151, 190
adult learning 141–43
pedagogy/andragogy characteristics (Tab) 143
behaviours and needs 131–38
defensive behaviours (Fig) 135
examples of behaviours (Tab) 134
Maslow's hierarchy (Tab) 136–37
roles played (Tab) 132–33
communication 120–21
dialogue or argument? (Tab) 122
web sites 121
contexts and systems 113–17
behaviour fluctuation (Fig) 116
macro model (Fig) 116
model of human behaviour (Fig) 115
web sites 114
diversity 117–20
group members (Fig) 118
dynamics 18–20
experiential learning 143–46
barriers to learning (Fig) 145
learning styles (Fig) 147
models (Figs) 144
how we learn 146–50
journals 217
self-development 151
size of groups 138–41
characteristics (Tab) 142
interaction numbers (Tabs) 138, 139
stages of development 121–31
group/car comparison (Tab) 131
groupthink symptoms/examples (Tab) 129–30
unlearning 150–51
see also multicultural groups
groupthink 129–30, 191, 198
Grouputer 180
guilt 161

Hahn, Kurt 26
Hancock, Graham 43
Handy, Charles 21
Harris, T 199
Heron, J 9, 12, 29, 34, 50, 52, 121, 204, 205
defensive behaviours (Fig) 135
dimensions of facilitation (Fig) 60

group development stages (Tab) 123, 124–25
model of facilitation styles 60–66
web site 66
Hofstede, G 154
Hogan, CF 150, 187
living frame of facilitation 76–84
Honey, P 31, 146
Hopson, B 74, 138, 150
human relations model 18–20
human rights 12
Hunter, D 50–51, 54–56, 117, 127, 200, 202, 204–05, 208
model of facilitation 75–76

Iacocca, Lee 13
IAF (International Association of Facilitators) 203, 205–06
contact details 218–19
draft code of ethics (Fig) 209
model of facilitation 66–70
IBM 23
ICA (Institute of Cultural Affairs) 29, 49, 66–67, 205–06, 220
Illich, Ivan 40–41
Image Theatre 45
In Search of Excellence 21
Institute of Cultural Affairs *see* ICA
interactive meetings 8, 9
internal process model 15–18
International Association of Facilitators *see* IAF
International Institute for Environment and Development 43, 44
Internet 8, 9, 10, 218–22
see also web sites
intervenor/recorder co-facilitation 96, 97
Invisible Theatre 45
Italian Agency of Technical Cooperation 46

Jackins, H 9
Jago, C 12–13, 23, 206
Jain, DE 10
Janis, Irving 126, 129–30, 191, 192
Jarman, R 179, 180
Johari window 31
Jones, JE 89, 101
journals 217–18, 222

Kaner, S 13, 165
KASV (Knowledge, Attitudes, Skills, Values) 148–50
Keltner, JS 56–57
Keys of Understanding 148
Kimball, L 222
Kiser masterful model of facilitation 70–74
Kitzinger, J 9
Klinck, P 33–34
Knight, J 85, 100, 101
Knowledge, Attitudes, Skills, Values (KASV) 148–50
knowledge workers 12–13
Knowles, Malcolm 27–28, 31, 41–42, 141
Kolb, David 28–29, 143, 144
Kubler-Ross, Elizabeth 130

Lao PDR 158–59, 162–63, 164
Larson, MS 199
Leadership and the New Science 214
learning sets 33
learning styles 143, 146, 147
legal system 9, 10
LENS process 30
Lewin, Kurt 9, 18–19, 74, 116, 143
linear thinking 160–61
Lippitt, Ronald 19
local government 9, 14
Locke 12
Luft, J 31

Macy, J 213, 214
Malaysian society 156, 159, 161–62
management 15, 24
1900–25 15–18
1926–50 18–20
1951–75 20–21
1976–present 21–24
as a profession 200–01
managerial competency framework (Fig) 16
meeting agenda (Tab) 23

roles of manager/facilitator (Fig) 51–52
Mansfield, S 154
Martin, K 179, 180
Martin, Marie 53
see also co-facilitation
Maslow, Abraham 134–38
Maslow's hierarchy of needs *see* Maslow, Abraham
mature co-facilitation 96, 97–98
Max-Neef, Manfred 212–13
MCB University Press 218
McClure, BA 115, 116, 123–26
mediation practices 9, 10
meetings 22–24
sample agenda (Tab) 23
MeetingWorks 180
Memorizing, Understanding, Doing (MUD) 147–48
Metaplan 23–24, 139
Micklethwait, J 21
models of facilitation 59–60, 84
dimensions of facilitation (Fig) 60
Heron 60–66, 84
Hogan 76–81, 84
Hunter 75–76, 84
IAF 66–70, 84
Kiser 70–74, 84
summary of models (Tab) 82–83
moderators 23, 222
Mongeau, PA 70
monochronic cultures 160
Montessori, Maria 25, 26
Moslem societies 160
MUD (Memorizing, Understanding, Doing) 147–48
multicultural groups 153–55, 164
advantages/disadvantages 165, 168
co-facilitation 162–64
cultural dimensions 157–62
group decision making (Fig) 165
managing diversity (Tab) 169
pluses, minuses and interesting points (PMI) (Tab) 167
stages of development 166
what is culture? 155–57
see also group work

National Training Laboratory in Group Development (NTL) 19
Neill, Alexander Sutherland 26
Neighbourhood Learning Centres 8, 9
New Society Publishers 37
Niederman, F 13
NTL (National Training Laboratory in Group Development) 19

Olson, E 180, 181
open space technology 52–53, 139, 221
open systems model 20–21
organizations 8, 9
ORID process 30, 143
outsourcing 193
Outward Bound 26
Owen, Harrison 52–53, 139

Palmer, Mary 201
PAR (participatory action research) 8–9, 10
Parker Follett, Mary *see* Follett, Mary Parker
participation 37–40
Arnstein's ladder (Fig) 38
participatory action research *see* PAR
participatory learning and action *see* PLA
Participatory Learning and Action 44
participatory rapid/rural appraisal *see* PRA
peace movements 9, 10
peer support groups 33–34
pedagogy 27, 141, 143
Pedler, M 151
Pfeiffer, JW 89, 101
Philips 20, 23
Phnuyal, B 10, 44, 45, 207
Pierce, V 8, 67–69, 203
PLA (participatory learning and action) 44
Pluses, Minuses and Interesting points *see* PMI
PMI (Pluses, Minuses and Interesting points) 165, 167
Polanyi, M 148–49, 196

polychronic cultures 160
PRA (participatory rapid/rural appraisal) 9, 10, 43–44
process consultant 26
professionalism and ethics 189–90
accreditation 210–12
case study: Eagle Star Life 190–93
case study: Fernando Flores 193–97
codes of conduct 201, 203, 208–09
draft code of ethics (Fig) 209
definitions and qualifications 198–200
education of facilitators 203–09
ethical consistency 202
management as a profession 200–01
professional competition 201
web sites 208, 209

Quaker movement 36–37, 119
quality of work life (QWL) 20–21
Quinn, RE 15–16, 19–20
QWL (quality of work life) 20–21

rational goal model 15–18
Reason, P 9
reflect method 10, 44–45, 207
Reich, Robert 13, 21
Reimer, Harold 22
Religious Society of Friends *see* Quaker movement
research 9
Research Centre for Group Dynamics 18
Restorative Justice Movement 161
Richardson, GP 95
Robert, Major HM 9, 17, 22
Robert's Rules of Order *see* Robert, Major HM
Robinson, SL 21
Robson, M 30, 50, 197, 206
Rocha, EM 40, 114
Rogers, Carl 26
Rowe, W 190
Rubin, Harriet 193–95
Ruete, E 203
rural development 9, 10, 43, 46–47

Sachs, Wolfgang 43
Salmon, G 14, 183–86, 187
Scally, M 74, 138, 150
Schein, Edgar 26
Schnelle, E&W 23, 139
Schön, D 202
schools 204
Schutz, WC 123
Schwarz, RM 53, 67, 70, 95–96, 97
Scott, W 85, 100, 101
seamless co-facilitation 95, 96
Search Conference Process 21, 139
self-development 151
self-facilitation 55–57
Senge, Peter 33, 114, 151, 221
Shambhala warriors 214
Sharp, G 36
Shaw, ME 142
Sheats, P 131, 132–33
Siddeley aero-engine company 21
Siemens 23
Sirolli, E 23, 46–47
Skinner, BF 26
small businesses 46–47
Smith, A 150
Smith, G 99, 100
social work 8, 9
Society for Organizational Learning 222
sociotechnical approach to management 20
Spencer, Laura 49–50
Spencer, Marilyn 29–30
Spinks, T 89
Straus, D 8, 9, 22–23, 51–52
student representation 30–31
style model 60–66
Summerhill 26
Synanon game 190

T Groups (Training Groups) 19, 190
TA (Transactional Analysis) 30
Tacit Dimension, The 148
tandem co-facilitation 96, 97
Tarnas, R 12
Tashlik, P 12
Tavistock Institute of Human Relations 19, 20

Taylor, B 75–76, 117, 127, 200, 202, 208
Taylor, Frederick 16–17, 21
team co-facilitation 96, 97
technology 14, 171
  choosing appropriate 179–82
    for group communication (Tab) 181
  comparison of models (Tab) 187
  e-moderators 183–86
  human aspect 182
  journals 222
  resources 223
  serving facilitator/group needs (Tab) 171–79, 182–83
  web sites 182, 186, 222–23
Tennant, M 27
Thatcher, Margaret 127, 158, 192
Theatre of the Oppressed 45, 46
therapeutic work 8, 9
Third World *see* developing countries
Tibet 214
training *see* education and training
Training Groups (T Groups) 19, 190
Transactional Analysis (TA) 30
Trist, Eric 19, 20–21
Truly Civil Society 213
Truman, President 42
Tuckman, BW 123, 124–25, 126, 130
Turning the Tide 37

Uganda 44–45
unequal co-facilitation 96, 97
University Associates Incorporated 221
University of London 30
unlearning 150–51
Unmasking Administrative Evil 195–96

visualization techniques 23–24
Vogler, C 47
Volkema, R 13
Volkswagen 23
Volvo 20

Warihay, F 51
web sites 114, 121, 182, 186, 208, 209, 218–22
  see also Internet; World Wide Web
Weber, Max 17
Webne-Behrman, H 25
Western Australia 46–47
Wheatley, M 214
Wheeler, John Archibald 214
Whiteley, AM 14
Whiting, S 36
Wilkinson, M 67
Wilson, K&J 116
Winborn, BB 190
women's groups 9, 10
Woodward, T 191
Wooldridge, A 21
Woolman, John 36
World Wide Web 40–41
  see also web sites

Xerox 23

Zimmerman, AL 11